ADVANCED PRAISE FO
99 PROBLEMS FINDING T

AF621095

"In this social media present, where we find ourselves increasingly subject to the ephemeral whims and weaponized polarity of The Discourse™, *99 Problems Finding the 1* serves up a nutritional nuance our internet-heavy idea diets so desperately lack. It's no wonder that Asim's punk-rock sensibilities render so colorfully on the page; these essay-notes clang with abandon against the brick walls of identity spaces that seem Black-and-white, making room instead for inquisitive expansion, seemingly oxymoronic human truths, and complex (non)conclusions that press insistently—beautifully—against the decisive finality our minds have been trained to crave and accept as 'reality.' Unafraid to eschew norms and walk funky, and armed with a whip-smart arsenal of vernacular language (I dare any reader not to laugh aloud at the original portmanteau *swirlboss*), Asim presents a vision of love—grounded, humorous, and, perhaps most importantly, aspirational—one need not be a romantic to fall for."

—ARIANA BENSON, author of *Black Pastoral*,
winner of the Cave Canem Poetry Prize

"*99 Problems Finding the 1* is the best book about love I've read in years. It's the 1, you might say, because, like a great relationship, it takes itself both very seriously and with a mischievous, what-are-we-doing-here wink. That combination is irresistible. But to call G'Ra Asim's latest a book about looking for love is to shortchange it. It's a book about race, gender, politics, time, friendship, family, blind spots, projection, punk, basketball, French absurdist theater—and why playing it too cool is its own kind of heartbreak. It's a call to live ethically, earnestly, and joyfully. It's a triumph."

—BENOIT DENIZET-LEWIS, *New York Times Magazine*
contributing writer and author of *You've Changed:*
The Promise and Price of Self-Transformation

"*99 Problems Finding the 1* is a tour de force . . . a kaleidoscopic descent into love's endless labyrinths and one of the smartest portraits of loving while Black put to page."

—JUNOT DÍAZ, Pulitzer Prize–winning author
of *This Is How You Lose Her*

"There is more pleasure, hope, humanity, and intertextual intelligence in a single G'Ra Asim sentence than in most books. With the openhearted vision of Laymon, the kinetic connection-forging of Crenshaw, and the playful post-punk earnestness he's known for in his songs, Asim casts us as companions on a quest for love—not just with a romantic partner but with the world. Deep, audacious, provocative, and fun, *99 Problems Finding the 1* is a feat of the modern essay form."

—ELEANOR HENDERSON, author of
Everything I Have Is Yours: A Marriage

"On its surface, G'Ra Asim's *99 Problems Finding the 1* is about Asim's complicated quest for a lifelong romantic partnership, but under the surface, this is a book about race and gender, about music and psychology and pop culture. Shaquille O'Neal pops in, so does W. E. B. Du Bois. Reading this book is like sitting down with one of your coolest and smartest friends as they unspool tales of love and loss, as they interrogate attitudes toward Blackness and gender roles, as they make you laugh out loud."

—DANIEL A. HOYT, author of
Shit List and *This Book Is Not for You*

"*99 Problems Finding the 1* is no standard lament of the lovelorn. It's a trenchantly wise and wisecracking how-to manual for maintenance of the human heart in the face of bleak indifference and ruthlessly organized hatreds. It's also a deeply felt, wonder-full affirmation of the unlikely head rush of being alive—as well as a dispassionate inventory of the ever-wider race-addled, socioeconomic conspiracy to render that awareness unthinkable. It may be an ambivalent, unresolved chronicle of G'Ra Asim's own quest for abiding love, but it's an amazingly generous and indispensable work of what he calls 'thinkful wishing'—and thus an act of writerly love that legions of readers should joyfully requite."

—CHRIS LEHMANN, DC bureau chief of
The Nation and contributing editor at *The Baffler*

"*99 Problems Finding the 1* is a sublime illumination of what it means to be young, gifted, Black, and exasperatingly single. For Asim, finding a soulmate is the ultimate riddle, and in his quest to solve it, he masterfully draws clues from an artistic, intellectual, and cultural landscape so vast that references to Jay-Z, W. E. B. Du Bois, and Ntozake Shange feel as essential as those to Carl Sagan, Simone de Beauvoir, and Kierkegaard—to say nothing of OKCupid and Tinder. A virtuoso performance by a writer at the top of his game. Asim has written a timely manifesto on romantic love that will define a generation. Easily among the best books I've read in years."

—JERALD WALKER, author of *How to Make a Slave and Other Essays*

"G'Ra Asim turns his wide-ranging poetic sensibility toward the search for true love in the twenty-first century. At the same time, he holds up and honors his own models for love's possibilities in the lives of his twentieth-century grandparents and parents. This book both astutely signifies on contemporary culture and also dreams of a future with enough room for the tried and true. Since Asim's first love is probably language, the book is a joy to read, riffing and spinning off the pleasures of the word, reveling in the philosophical questions he finds in everyday interactions, from the wilds of the dating world to the halls of academe.

Asim frames his quest for love against the historical, political, and social backdrops that shape our lives, always keeping track of the way 'the behavior of the state at the macro level shapes the choreography of desire at the micro level.' Summing up the difficulties of one particular relationship, Asim writes, 'The entire imbroglio was somehow personal and structural at the same time.' This line also neatly addresses why *99 Problems* is so much more than a memoir. Asim's deft and nuanced depiction of this combination of the personal and the structural is what makes this book so readable and so smart."

—WENDY W. WALTERS, author of *Archives of the Black Atlantic: Reading Between Literature and History*

99 PROBLEMS FINDING THE 1

99 PROBLEMS FINDING THE 1

A LOVE STORY (SORT OF)

G'RA ASIM

BEACON PRESS, BOSTON

BEACON PRESS
24 Farnsworth Street
Boston, Massachusetts
www.beacon.org

Beacon Press books
are published under the auspices of
the Unitarian Universalist Association of Congregations.

© 2026 by G'Ra Asim

All rights reserved
Printed in the United States of America

29 28 27 26 8 7 6 5 4 3 2 1

This book is printed on acid-free paper that meets the uncoated paper ANSI/NISO specifications for permanence as revised in 1992.

Text design and composition by Kim Arney

Library of Congress Cataloging-in-Publication Data is available for this title.
ISBN: 978-0-8070-1778-4;
e-book: 978-0-8070-1777-7;
audiobook: 978-0-8070-2461-4

The authorized representative in the EU for product safety and compliance is Easy Access System Europe 16879218, Mustamäe tee 50, 10621 Tallinn, Estonia: https://beacon.org/eu-contact.

The thing that
makes you exceptional,
if you are at all,
is inevitably that which
must also make you lonely.

—LORRAINE HANSBERRY

For my grandparents

CONTENTS

INTRODUCTION

The second line of my home address, Apt. 1N, is a euphemistic account of who lives inside. As if the post office wants to cut to the chase. *There's one, childless, unmarried, late-thirties—ahem*—black person *kicking it solo dolo in here.* I can't decide whether this state of affairs is cause for celebration, complaint, or some combination. Of course, the *N* more literally stands for north, the hallowed destination of my emancipated ancestors. The freedom of middle-class bachelorhood is fittingly first rate. Few in my line have experienced it in the way I do now. At the same time, that freedom is coextensive with loneliness, as an expanse of ocean seems to shadow the sky.

When I think about having someone to dote on in my dotage, I inevitably ponder how much I'd like to live in a more supportive world. For good reason, I find it difficult to separate one aspiration from the other. The notion that hurt people hurt people is one of folk sociology's greatest hits. It rings just as true on its flip side: Beloved people be loving. A world with fewer slings and arrows leaves more for Cupid's quiver.

I concede from the outset that my accusation sounds like a confession. Someone who has 99 Problems Finding the 1 might well be the problem himself. You could reasonably try to picture me and conclude that the author is nasty, brutish, and short; a sullen, unhygienic layabout who thinks dating app height filters are the signal injustice of modern life. A loathsome layer of

Cheeto dust accumulates on the keyboard as he types. Except, of course, that being nasty, brutish and short(-tempered) is a posture more admired in twenty-first-century America than we like to admit.

The rap song from which this book borrows its name lionizes exactly that behavior. Ice-T's 1993 track "99 Problems" and the more popular version released by Jay-Z in 2004 both contain an element of self-fulfilling prophecy. Finding "a bitch" is a lot simpler than finding the one. If you subscribe to the idea that women are bitches, that shallow, transactional relationships are adequate, and that deep intimacy and mutual support are pipe dreams, then love isn't likely to be among one's 99 problems.

So, if I *am* the problem, it might be because I'm superbad and I got soul. But I'm not a "Soldier," the romantic ideal touted in Destiny's Child's 2004 chart-topper. The chorus demands that eligible men "better be street" no less than three times in a span of twenty-four seconds. "Soldier" fuses militarism with street cred. So seamlessly that listeners hardly notice what odd bedfellows they make. Destiny's Child hails from a minority group terrorized and subjugated by the very forces embodied in the American soldier. They make no bones about the fact that those are the only fellas welcome in their beds. The group might as well be called Manifest Destiny's Child. Beyoncé and crew are, perversely, more patriotic than the (then-Dixie) Chicks, that towheaded trio of harmonizing Southern belles publicly censured for their criticism of the Bush administration a few months before "Soldier" deployed. "Soldier" declares that the very pawns of the American empire—or at least their inner-city mimics—are the vaunted complement to Beyoncé, Kelly, and Michelle's queendom. You could even surmise from the track that DC personifies the state itself. The men who "don't mind taking" a bullet for them are laying down their lives for Lady Liberty.

Musically speaking, "Soldier" earns all the medals from me. It was a rumbling tank of a pop song when it came out. It still packs a wallop now. But more than twenty years on from its release, our social landscape reflects the fallout of a vision of love so closely bound up with imperialism. Destiny's Child is from Houston, a glimmering promised land of SUVs, megachurches, and prosperity theology. It's a setting that would nurture the illusion that America's opulent glow is the product of good karma, that domination is a mark of virtue rather than ruthlessness.

"The West won the world not by the superiority of its ideas or values or religion . . . but rather by its superiority in applying organized violence," political scientist Samuel P. Huntington writes.[1] "Westerners often forget this fact."

Where might we begin to remedy this amnesia, to define and pursue superior ideas and values rather than accept whatever detritus American exceptionalism leaves lying around? I'd start with love. Where organized violence is a cultural linchpin, bloodlust and the other kind cross-pollinate. Where soldiers are the most sought-after suitors, hawkishness hijacks the heart. "Soldier" is not just a smash hit but a direct one. It pinpoints how the behavior of the state at the macro level shapes the choreography of desire at the micro level. The settler-colonial history and economic precarity of the American project emotionally disfigures those who live on its soil. Neither the hustle to survive nor the values that motivate such competition lend themselves to the cultivation of trust, patience, compassion, or gentleness. Living on land taken by force and tilled under the lash does not a tender heart make. I don't mean to say that this impairment affects us all equally, or that no one eludes it. I'm just saying that taking up arms is met with more fanfare than wrapping arms around someone who needs them, and the disparity matters.

Imagining a more lovable and more loving future is on my mind lately because of the voids in my own family. I have no praying grandmothers left alive. Likewise, I haven't yet put my mother in a position to be one. Black grandmothers are like science fiction. They see it as their job to value the future on timescales that exceed their own. In the same way, speculative fiction has historically anticipated innovations and discoveries in real-life science. The sci-fi writer performs the dreamwork for our technological future. It's the secular version of the longstanding African American tradition of praying for unseen generations. As a literary nonfiction writer, I take on the heart's dreamwork for our interpersonal future. I call it "thinkful wishing."

To help us see our place in time and space more intuitively, Carl Sagan popularized the Cosmic Calendar.[2] It scales the chronology of the universe from its consensus age of 13.8 billion years to a single year. In this visualization, each month represents just over a billion years. The Big Bang takes place on January 1 at midnight. Our historical present occurs at the end of December 31 just before midnight. At scale with the Cosmic Calendar, a seventy-to-eighty-year human life maps onto roughly .16 cosmic seconds. I'm thinking about love and its potential to ennoble the human race from this vantage point. Humankind's behavior is easier to understand and to some extent forgive when I recall that we're in our cosmological infancy. Instead of aiming to move us into adulthood with my measly .16 seconds, I use thinkful wishing to envision the steps we might take to simply get out of the Terrible Twos.

What design specs of the heart will humankind need a hundred years from now? What can we do to make sure those blueprints are passed down? Broad credulity about love will be necessary to build a more equitable social order. What story should we tell ourselves about love to endear it to future generations as a resource?

As fashionable as righteousness may seem, most people are driven to garner the most social approval for the minimum amount of effort. Social media's grasp on the collective psyche extends beyond the limits of our screen time. Even when we deign to look up from our phones, we conduct ourselves as if they're surveilling us. Largely because they are. An aggressively moralizing culture, especially one oriented toward punishment, isn't necessarily a more compassionate one.

I'll use thinkful wishing to address these concerns. The goal is to offer tools that help us all link and build. The chapters that follow are discussions for a different day—a process of turning over the norms of now to hatch new horizons for tomorrow. They are intended to be collaborative. As I'm looking closely at the textbook cases of love and loathing in my own life, you, the reader, are invited to complete the same exercises.

The spirit of literary nonfiction serves that end. There are two expectations we have of each other and ourselves that diminish the love we can give and receive. We think we should be perfect, and we think we should be coherent. An art form like this one, custom-made for dramatizing the author's ambivalence without insisting on a resolution, embraces the human experience as a parade of contradictory desires and sensations. The widespread adoption of this view would be a boon for love. By the same token, the essay is a medium that champions the spirited pursuit of goals more than their attainment. The form follows my intended function: to encourage readers and myself to recognize shortcomings as inevitable and even charming. Scientists joke that even when a rocket blows up on the launchpad, NASA doesn't call that a tragedy. It's a "data-rich environment." We need this energy in the heart space.

Incisive and necessary critiques of misogyny and heterosexism have popularized the view that straight romantic love is a doomed endeavor. It isn't. But it is a data-rich environment worth poring over carefully. If we accept the premise that heterosexuality is in acute crisis, the handwringing is unlikely to stop there. The sense that gender difference is essentially unnavigable may well snowball into fatalism about historical divisions in general. Against the backdrop of a global rightward drift, the earnest striving for harmony within heterogeneity needs as much affirmation as it can get.

It ain't trans people's fault. But the paradox is that their rising visibility makes everyone double down on gender orthodoxy. There's a lot of Men Are from Mars, Women Are from Venus happening, even though the discourse purports to be the opposite. I don't trust the framing where "straight" and "queer" people are stable identities with rare overlap. The idea that those groups are completely distinct from one another muddies thinking about love—of wariness about it, of the expectations we have for each party in a pairing. Some maintain that straightness itself reinforces and is defined by adherence to traditional gender roles. From my observation, though, the most successful straight couples invert the old-school pigeonholes. Through an essentialist lens, these couples are "gender swapped" in the sense that the woman is more assertive and opinionated and the man is quieter and more deferential.

Popular recognition that biological sex and gender can but don't always correspond is a net positive. But even having acknowledged sex as hardware and gender as software, it's common to think of the latter only in terms of the most rigid stereotypes. The gender standards we often have in mind—let's call them Dick and Jane—are caricatures. Dick is an oafish, hypersexual he-man. Jane is a shrinking violet. She's sweet, simple, shy, submissive. Both are too cartoonish to live up to. Most people feel pressure to approximate Dick if they're assigned male at birth. Jane is the model if they're assigned female at birth. But only a deranged minority really feels completely at home in these camps. Something like nine out of ten cis ladies I've ever dated eventually say something like, *I have to let you know that I outwardly present a lot more feminine than I actually feel inside.* They disclose this like it's a dark admission sure to make me run screaming for the hills. To my eyes, androgyny is much closer to the rule than the exception. As psychologist Alfred Kinsey writes, "The living world is a continuum in each and every one of its aspects.[3]"

Race informs my relationship to love as much as gender does. My peoples are the inventors of soul music. We are the vanguard of American nonviolent protest. Seventy-nine percent of our community identifies as Christian,[4] a faith in which love is viewed as a reflection of God's nature. The stumbling blocks between us and love are legion nonetheless. Even with stand-up parents, a black person is likely to go their entire life without being assured of their intrinsic value. We are unlikely to be told that whether or not we achieve things, embarrass the race, have the right politics, avoid lockdown, or have children out of wedlock, we are precious, singular, and irreplaceable. Regardless of the strength or sincerity of our support systems, black people are generally coaxed toward the premise that they are starting at negative fifty humanity points. Accordingly, we must sweat and suffer and sacrifice to maybe, perhaps, if we're real lucky, get to zero. This deficit might begin as a description of how black folks are regarded by the broader society. But since minding that deficit is critical to survival, the quote marks around it often fade from view.

This is the context in which I search in vain for a suitable person to list as my emergency contact. It's not a story I can tell in linear fashion. The digressions and asides are as much the point as they are beside it. Linearity has no place in love anyway. Hearts don't queue in single file. Only an essayistic account could trace the torrid, twisted entangling of heartstrings. And I'm trying to be like NASA, too, those sanguine seekers of loftier ground. You'd think a rocket would fly in a straight line to exit Earth's atmosphere and reach the stars. But actually, the best way to achieve escape velocity is to fly at a tangent.[5]

A SUBSTITUTION OFF THE BENCH

I once texted a short video interview with Philadelphia 76ers point guard Tyrese Maxey to a woman I loved. In the clip, Maxey credits his then-teammate, shooting guard Buddy Hield, for offering encouragement and picking Maxey up during a low moment. After a pep talk from his backcourt partner, Maxey busted out of a slump. In the text to the woman I loved, I captioned the video by saying, "You're T Max and I'm Buddy Hield (and sometimes it's the inverse)." I was reminding her that I believed in her. I was thanking her for believing in me.

When we sense that a special someone is in our corner, we're more likely to pay it forward. The solidarity between Maxey and Hield is reciprocal. Maxey had a notable scoring night, which is why he was invited to speak to the reporters at the podium. When he was asked about his big game, he took the opportunity to shout-out Hield so that the public knew about the latter's contribution beyond the box score. Fiona Apple told us evil is a relay sport. Maxey and Hield exchanged a different kind of baton that is no less impactful. Yes, hurt people hurt people, but beloved people be loving.

Buddy Hield's own name sounds like a description of his function. My friend helped to heal me. Buddy healed. Personally, I want all my buddies to heal. I also want to be a restorative presence myself—a buddy that heals others. Romantic love is, in a best-case scenario, a form of healing facilitated through a buddy system. Two people mutually agree to look after one another. They reach a level of holistic wellness they wouldn't scratch alone. Ideally, I'd like every buddy to heal and no buddy brought to heel. All right, all right. I'll see myself out.

My motives are partially selfish. The fewer aggrieved souls there are in the world, the more hospitable the world will be to me and the people I love most. I later learned that Buddy Hield's given first name is Chavano. I collect terms of endearment—some of the main ones in my rotation are rosebud, primo, big dogg, honey bee, lovely one, big time, ace, starlet, blue chips—but I don't particularly like calling people "buddy." It's vaguely smarmy even when you don't mean it to be. Chavano is a way cooler name than his nickname, anyway. I've adopted it as a synonym for buddy. It's mysterious, but chummy sounding.

When I use direct address in this book, I will refer to you, reader, as Chavano. This is its own form of thinkful wishing. Maybe you will encounter other people who've read this book in the wild, and you can call each other Chavano. Maybe you will attend an event about the book where you and I meet in public, and we'll know to call each other Chavano. Chavano can act as a secret handshake, except with the goal of dissolving, rather than consolidating, insularity. Every time you say it, it's a spell. A charm that summons recuperative power. Turning an NBA sixth man into a talisman is a favor to the future, where camaraderie is as good a proposition as a corner three-point shot.

CONDUCT DETRIMENTAL TO THE MEME

99.

Why should anyone take anything my father has to say about anti-black racism seriously if he has a white wife? On its face, it's a reasonable if perhaps dogmatic question.

The race of a given black person's romantic partner is not a perfectly reliable index of the person's pro-black solidarity. But it is widely presumed to be one, and in that respect, it doesn't surprise my mother when the question comes up. My dad is a writing professor and the author of several books. When he appears in public, he is often asked about race and racism. His responses invariably invite some version of the okay-but-what-about-your-white-wife retort. Sometimes someone brings it up one on one, when my father is signing their copy of one of his books. Other times, a person in the audience raises the question during the Q&A session at the conclusion of my dad's remarks.

I'm amazed at how much attention this spectral white woman generates. Faith in her presumed existence is so strong that it can overshadow my mother's observable presence at my father's side.

Though she is often mistaken for a white woman over the phone, my mother is unambiguously black in person. On a one-to-ten scale of identifiable blackness, if one is Rashida Jones and ten is Stacey Abrams, Mom is at least an eight. The Black

Momba has been married to my clearly black father for more than thirty years. Mom, a homemaker and theater maker who has not worked outside of the home full time since I was in elementary school, doesn't always accompany Baba during his book tours and speaking engagements. But he's questioned about a phantom Caucasian companion even when my mother is in the audience. It's mostly other black folks who jump to this conclusion out loud, probably because they believe they can level this accusation from the moral high ground. Non-black people may be prone to similar assumptions, but not having that "righteous" outrage, politely hold their tongues.

I take the persistence of this charade as an indication of how tightly we cling to racial and gendered stereotypes. It's an intersectional counterpart to the old riddle about a father and a son in a terrible car crash that kills the father. The son is rushed to the hospital, where the surgeon exclaims, "I can't operate. That boy is my son!" Research shows that most are stumped by this riddle, likely because they can't imagine that the surgeon could be the boy's mother.[1]

Somewhere in the collective unconscious, there's a tablet bearing a commandment that surgeons are men. Etched alongside it is a rule that indicates that successful, articulate black men are married to white women, and that brown-skinned, unassuming black women aren't married at all. We don't commit to these ideas based on evidence alone. Often, our commitment to these ideas invisibilizes evidence that plainly contravenes them. Basic legibility eludes those whose existence and experiences run counter to these schemas. The mother who becomes a surgeon and the black woman who sustains a loving partnership with a black man both triumph over what sociologist C. Wright Mills calls "the problems of history, of biography and their intersections." In all the discussion of sexism and racism as "systemic" phenomena, it's easy to lose sight of their more mundane perils. Like how stereotypes about the groups we belong to shape the contours of our interpersonal relationships.

This difficulty synthesizing woman with surgeon and blackness with love points at a confluence between heteropessimism and Afropessimism, two discourses with rising purchase. These glass-half-empty takes on heterosexuality and blackness, respectively, frame each as problems that by their very nature defy all possible solutions. Heteropessimism holds that warm relations between men and women are structurally untenable, and that straightness itself is a pathology. Afropessimism is more of a philosophical school than a viral meme, but it holds that the condition of the ex-slave is subject to a similarly unchangeable predicament. As Afropessimists see it, anti-black racism is the mortar with which human societies are built. Colonialism, racism, and the echoes of enslavement are not only endemic to American life; they are foundational to it.

As Frank Wilderson, the writer and scholar sometimes known as the godfather of Afropessimism, puts it, the theory highlights an "essential antagonism between Blacks (Slaves) and Humans (masters)."[2] Heteropessimism conceives of women and men as beset by differences no less intractable. Both heteropessimism and Afropessimism are performative in the sense that they involve using language as a form of social action. The dour forecasts about straight people's pursuit of love and black people's pursuit of humanity are meant to emphasize the scale and resilience of the impediments to those pursuits. A non-exhaustive list of those obstacles, in the latter case, would include things like the school-to-prison pipeline, high rates of discrimination in primary health care, and voter disenfranchisement. Literal hopelessness is not quite the point of Afropessimism or heteropessimism; it's more that the seductiveness of hope tends to skew analysis. In his essay "Afro-Pessimism: The Unclear Word," University of California at Irvine African American studies professor Jared Sexton argues that Afropessimism illuminates the consequences of trying "to delimit the 'bad news' of black life."[3] Heteropessimism is guided by a similar conviction, namely that to delimit the bad news is to misrepresent the conundrum. All of this resonates with the disinclination to recognize my parents as a couple. Where love is concerned, does one truly see more clearly by taking off their rose-colored glasses?

Here's where Afropessimism and heteropessimism are interventions against different kinds of understatement. Soft-pedaling anti-black racism plays into the hands of racism's beneficiaries. Which means that refusing to soft-pedal it has at least some empowering benefit for black people. We might be tempted, then, to conclude that tamping down the bad news of straight life serves the interests of sexism's beneficiaries (that is, men), and that refusing to tamp it down specifically empowers women. There's something to this. Heteropessimism raises collective consciousness that bad romantic experiences with sexist men are reflective of a larger social problem rather than isolated incidents.

98.

But there's a reason *hetero*pessimism—and not something more like *gender*pessimism—is a robust online subculture: *The idea that misogyny is baked into heterosexuality is a tremendous coalition builder.* A number of identity groups who might not agree on much else can get behind it. Straight men buy in because we can claim that our backward ideas about women are normal. Heteropessimism gives queer men and women license to believe they're more enlightened about gender just by virtue of being gay. Believing that romance and sex between men and women is necessarily dysfunctional can feel validating to straight women, and also allows them to downplay their own agency and responsibility. A heteropessimist stiff-arms heartbreak, attenuates the pain of rejection, eschews the burden of self-scrutiny. Straight romantic destiny is immutable, and once you've absorbed the permanence of this bad news, you don't have to bother getting your hopes up. In a digital landscape that rewards snark and ideological purity, fatalism about heterosexual love thrives because it dulls feeling and absolves blame.

Women who date men are often, understandably, so aware of their structural disadvantages in the broader world that they sometimes assume they are in every way the romantic underdogs in their relationships. No reasonable person would deny that patriarchy creates a power disparity in heterosexual couples. But heteropessimism can obscure the fact that that disparity can be something without being everything. To be a fully accountable romantic partner to someone else, you must recognize that your own words and actions influence the quality of a relationship regardless of your gender. The downside of heteropessimism is that it can encourage the view that love channels toward a fixed outcome where one person is the bad actor and the other person is their victim. It can become a mock-conscientious objection to emotional risk; a specious justification for being so careful that you can't bear to be care-full or cared for. An equitable relationship is unlikely, if not impossible, when one party goes into it with the expectation that they are the default, exclusive, and permanent possessor of the moral high ground. Any hope of an anti-sexist heterosexuality would turn on the recognition of two concurrent truths: there's a long and sordid history of male domination and exploitation that shapes how men and women interact regardless of everyone's good intentions, and each day presents a suite of choices that can shape the interface you have with your partner just as much as that history. Keeping both of these facts in front of mind can help you to make choices that are informed by that history but that don't rehearse it.

When romantic feelings ratchet up, it's like climbing the hill on a roller-coaster track. You could experience that as exhilarating because going up the hill means there's a drop coming on the other side. If you're more afraid of the drop than thrilled by it, then you experience climbing the hill as dread rather than anticipation. To wit, the drop is more or less ruined if your primary concern is whether the other person is more scared of it than you are.

Anti-love confirmation bias doesn't usually prevent people from participating in dating and courtship. More often, it just makes them participate in bad faith. In his book *Good to Great*, Jim Collins popularized an idea called the Stockdale Paradox, a technique for confronting the reality of a brutal situation while maintaining ultimate and unwavering conviction that you can succeed in the end. I sometimes muse that perhaps in this one way I could heed Destiny's Child's call for a soldier. The concept is named after James Stockdale, a war hero and vice-presidential candidate who was the highest-ranking US military officer held captive in Hỏa Lò, known as the "Hanoi Hilton" prisoner-of-war camp during the Vietnam War. The Stockdale Paradox offers a compelling alternative to heteropessimism. One can acknowledge that the path to connecting with another person is often rife with trip wires and travails, and still remain determined to brave the journey with everyone's hearts and wrists intact. That's generally been a hard sell.

In one promising but ultimately doomed situationship, the person I was dating would habitually say, "I don't want the narrative of this to end up being that I wanted you and you didn't want me." Once smitten, thrice shy. An ex I dated for several years told me over and over that it's critical not to allow oneself to become "the more enamored of the two parties," and that she worried about being disempowered by caring more than I did. I found those fears understandable. I was sympathetic in both cases. In the moment, both of my former partners succeeded in making me feel responsible for their preemptive hurt feelings. I imagined myself as a moral failure for not providing an "emotional satisfaction guaranteed or your money back" coupon. (I wasn't being granted one in return, either.) Convinced that this made me a bad feminist, I was always trying to make up for that deficit. If not for a heteropessimist thumb on the scale, though, it's hard to believe that I was taking any less of a risk than the people I was dating.

97.

It seems wonky to compare straight people as a group with black people as a group. Far more than straightness, blackness is determinative of the structure of your family, where you live, your health, your wealth, and your relationship to the justice system. The list of things straight people share on the basis of their sexuality is much shorter, and most items on that list are privileges. A grim outlook is no real revelation to black folks, a group of people whose longevity has depended on making a way out of no way. Muting feelings of rage, indignation, hurt, and weariness are already long-standing black cultural imperatives. And blame tends to find us regardless of our chosen affective stances. Social media groupthink would have us believe heterosexuality is a prison, but blackness is actually shaped by various forms of ongoing unfreedom.

So what do you get when you combine the hyperbolic "imprisonment" of straightness with the factual reality of structural racism? *If straight culture is unconducive to love, and if Earth is inhospitable to black life, then black people face a doozy of a double bind.* The foreclosure of romantic possibility is costly even for black people who are not straight, as we've historically been stigmatized because of our perceived misalignment with normative family structures (e.g., the Moynihan Report).

For all that they might make visible when taken together, the latticework of Afropessimism and heteropessimism and the conditions that begat them push my parents' relationship out of view. As a black woman happily married to a black man, my mother has gotten the drop on the twin foes of misogyny and anti-black racism. These foes are so formidable that folks are often unable to recognize that my mother and father have bested them.

96.

Which makes my own genesis, as a product of this seemingly implausible and ongoing black love, an unthinkable event for many people.

Naturally this is a topical concern for me as a childless, single black person in his thirties. At some point I would like to have a happy marriage of my own. Thanks to my parents I'm fortunate to have grown up with an excellent model for how to do so. But it's a model that strains credulity for many of the people I would hope to replicate it with. Practically anybody single and dating in their thirties has absorbed their fair share of the conventional wisdom. They have developed the armor they are told is requisite: thickened skin and narrowed eyes and hesitance to suspend disbelief. They tiptoe toward romance with their inner drawbridges raised. The desires I would hope to fulfill by dating are scarcely recognized as extant.

In the dating world, heteropessimism and Afropessimism work together like that old medical school adage: If you hear hoofbeats behind you, think horse, not zebra. Just like doctors are taught to focus on typical possibilities rather than rare ones when making a diagnosis, single people are encouraged to see rules and not exceptions when assessing their suitors. This is prudent in a coldly mathematical sense.

But allowing the social equivalent of autofill and predictive text to dictate your love life is painfully unsexy.

It could be the sole credible defense of the much-maligned "not all men!" rejoinder. If you accept that men who aren't unbearably misogynist are so uncommon that they aren't worth mentioning, can you even recognize an exception when you see one? Of course, men interested in women are no less prone to using generalizations as a crutch. The self-pitying black male "nerd" narratives have their own misogynoir talking points. These, too, contribute to why my parents' relationship is seen as unlikely on multiple fronts: black women like my mother are presumed to only go for thugs, and black men like my father are presumed to prefer white women. Taking any of these stereotypes as gospel makes the heart a less than supple muscle. Love thrives in particularity.

Heteropessimism and Afropessimism, for all their uses, don't lend themselves to what the influential cultural theorist Stuart Hall calls a politics without guarantees. "If you think that race is a fixed biological characteristic, and that a whole number of other things: cultural qualities, intellectual qualities, emotional and expressive qualities follow from the fact of being genetically one race or another," says Hall, ". . . you will think then that the very fact of race can actually guarantee a whole range of things."[4] Protecting the very possibility of indeterminacy seems critical to any feminist and anti-racist project. And even more vital to any credibly romantic one. Love needs ellipses. Ambiguity nourishes intrigue. What is intimacy without open-ended questions?

The philosopher Daniel Dennett said that "the difference between a chimpanzee and a human brain is that the brain of a chimpanzee is largely unfurnished. Whereas we fill our heads with memes. We download hundreds of thousands of memes, and that's where we get our power from."

When someone behaves in ways that are contrary to the meme we have in mind about who they should be and how they should behave, our reflex is to dismiss or distrust what we're seeing. Heteropessimism is a meme no different from any of the others that furnish the human mind. Conduct detrimental to the meme is any behavior that counters heteropessimism's dreary prescience. It's the patient, thankless work of identifying and carrying out whatever conduct is beneficial to the *team*: building and maintaining a bond by taking a reparative rather than fatalistic view of the pitfalls that structural misogyny and heterosexism bring to bear in relationships.

As I type, my father is reading Dickens until he falls asleep. My mother reclines in bed next to him with her headphones in, a science fiction TV show flickering on her laptop screen. The sight of them together is domestic bliss personified. They don't just enjoy each other's company; they luxuriate in it. Two zebras were ingenuous enough to notice each other and team up, and to remain ecstatically teamed more than three decades later. If either of my parents had heard the other's approaching hoofbeats and thought horse, I might not be here.

95.

In early 2020, I landed a job as an assistant professor at a small liberal arts college in upstate New York. The job offered relative economic stability for the next six years, and possibly for longer if I managed to earn tenure. Since moving to New York City six years before, I had spent two years in an MFA program, two as a graduate teaching fellow, and eighteen months on staff at a gender and racial justice think tank. I'd long since resolved to make a living writing, reading, and thinking, but I also racked up a six-figure student debt in the process.

The professor gig was the break I had been waiting for. It felt like a level-up moment for my entire genealogical line. My parents had children young and came from blue-collar backgrounds. Though my father was a prolific author and eventually became a professor himself once I was an adult, our family lived below the poverty line for a significant chunk of my childhood. My future children would be the first generation born into the middle class. There was, of course, one hitch in the plan I had not considered: I was thirty-three years old, single, and childless. Taking the job meant that for the foreseeable future, I would spend at least nine months out of the year in a freezing upstate college town that was only 7 percent black. I had finally secured a level of income where having a family wouldn't feel irresponsible—in exchange for landing in a milieu unlikely to harbor a partner for starting one.

My parents' marriage had always been the prototype for the eventual emotional centerpiece of my own adult life. I'd had only a few girlfriends you could call serious but dated often enough to have a decent sense of the New York City singles scene. None of these experiences seemed to portend even a loose simulacrum of what my parents modeled. Was it something I'd been doing wrong?

94.

Sasha Bonét, my best friend from grad school, predicted that we'd become best friends—and not romantic partners—early in our acquaintance. Or rather, she relayed a theory that a white professor in our MFA program had devised based on years of experience presiding over an elite academic environment with few black folks in it. Having dated a number of black women, the professor fancied himself an authority. Though Sasha regarded him as more of a mentor figure, he appeared quite smitten with her right away. Maybe this was his way of deterring some of his competition.

The professor's theory went like this: In a predominantly white setting, black women and men intuitively look at each other like family rather than as potential paramours because they have such few reliable allies. The sight of another black person among the alabaster throng is the sound of sirens to a house on fire. The urgent need for intraracial social contact and limited opportunities for it encourage a scarcity mindset. We prioritize forming resilient, mutually protective and affirming connections with one another rather than taking on the risks that accompany romance. For black folks in the rare air of elite professional and educational spaces, the appeal of dating non-black people might stem from the calculation that they are people we can afford to alienate. This chimes with heteropessimism in that the ultimate result is that black women and men in such contexts don't link and live happily ever after. It's a departure from heteropessimism because the professor's theory posits familial comity rather than enmity as the impasse. On the other hand, it's classically Afropessimist in that racism truncates the spectrum of social possibilities for even ascendant black people.

Naturally, I bristled when Sasha summarized the professor's hypothesis. Who was he, I thought to myself, to play armchair sociologist with lives he couldn't possibly understand? Whatever the worth of his theory overall, the case of Sasha and me played out much like he predicted. In his essay "On Heteropessimism," heterosexuality theorist Asa Seresin cites the podcast *why do i like men* as the rare example of an outlet for heterosexual enthusiasm. On it, guest and filmmaker Theda Hammel offers the following answer:

> The reason that a woman likes men—or a trans woman maybe in particular likes men—is not necessarily because men are all that likeable . . . but just that they bring out qualities that you like in yourself, by virtue of being different from you.[5]

If the primary incentive for heterosexual companionship is contrast that accentuates positive difference, then maybe Sasha's professor friend is on to something. Black women and men's similarity feels more salient than their difference in a historically white university setting. Perhaps for the same reason, my friendship with Sasha allows for something far more dynamic than what Hammel describes. Sasha and I are alike in terms of interests, temperament, humor, and, yes, race. We each mirror qualities in the other that we like about our respective selves. This in turn allows us to experience the ways that we are different from a position of safety.

The rapport between Sasha and me works because it functions how relational theorist Emily Style argues the ideal curriculum should: as both window and mirror.

"If the student is understood as occupying a dwelling of self," says Style, "education needs to enable the student to look through window frames in order to see the realities of others and into mirrors in order to see her/his own reality reflected."[6]

To the heteropessimist, the dwelling of self is too seldom mirrored in a woman-man pairing. The view through the available windows is often unsightly. These realities are not immutable, and the heteropessimist bears some responsibility for the disrepair. If teachers can, through trial and error, gradually perfect their curriculum, then women and men can perfect their unions.

Style's windows and mirrors are trickier to reconcile with Afropessimism. The Afropessimist read might conclude that for the ex-slave, mirrors will reify abjection. Windows into other black people's realities will do the same. Non-black people's purview will only tantalize the black dwelling of self, since it depicts possibilities that anti-blackness forecloses. If this sounds solipsistic, it gets worse. Afropessimism holds that the experiences of black people can't be credibly analogized to those of other social outgroups. Not to go full John and Yoko, who released the apt but ham-handed protest song "Woman Is the Nigger of the World" with backing band Elephant's Memory in 1972, but women as a group seem to occupy a station similar to black people as a group. Reluctance to validate symmetries between racism and sexism (let alone fully conceptualize the position of people subject to both) informs so-called straight culture. It's part of why black men and black women so often lock horns over who is "more" oppressed.

The bad news of black life is certainly more bearable when I can commiserate with someone whose chains may be slightly different from my own. To frame my travails as so singular that they defy analogy is to compound them. All the hardships that heteropessimism and Afropessimism call our attention to are best attended to in coalition, not by retreating to silos. With Sasha and me, what makes our dynamic satisfying is something worth striving for—and something I fervently believe is possible—in all human connections: mutual identification, curiosity, and generosity toward one another.

93.

The pandemic struck New York City soon after I accepted the tenure-track position that would take me upstate. In the second week of March 2020, COVID's severity was still relatively unknown, but when I ventured out of my modest Harlem apartment share to stock up on necessities, it was the first time I detected "disaster movie" energy in the uptown ether. I trusted the instinct and moved in with my parents in Brookline, Massachusetts. As deaths and case totals climbed that spring, romantic desolation initially seemed like a petty grievance.

My predicament became obvious during a catch-up call with a childhood friend. She had just gotten an interview for her dream position. If she landed the position, she'd be able to move away from the Bay Area and relocate to Birmingham, Alabama. She'd longed to move to the South for years. Seeing one long-standing aspiration move tantalizingly within reach, she began musing about realizing another line item on her list sometime soon.

We should think about a marriage pact, she told me. If neither of us gets hitched in the next five or so years, maybe we should get married to each other. She and I were both staring down our Jesus year. We were in roughly parallel positions in our careers. I told her marriage was on my mind, too, which was not quite the truth. I had actually been thinking about love. Old-school love. Resilient love. I was imagining being a cherished member of a blissful, adaptable tandem. I had been thinking about the kind of love where marriage would be a mere formality. My goal wasn't really to be married. I'd be happy if marriage was a byproduct of successfully cultivating that kind of love.

My friend seemed surprised.

"Do you have any prospects on that front?" she asked me.

I began a quick mental inventory: There were two exes who, were it not for expiring visas and unfavorable geography, might still be in the picture. There was a family friend I had recently been on a handful of promising dates with right before the pandemic struck. With travel restrictions in place and coronavirus continuing to ravage the country nearly unchecked, none of these women seemed likely to walk down as much as a supermarket aisle with me in the near future.

"Uh," I groaned into the phone. "Not so much."

92.

In school, I would often turn down a corridor and catch Sasha in lively conversation with another fellow student. She would toss her hair and laugh loudly and easily, her broad, fetchingly monodimpled smile shining like a beacon across the hall. It was often the case that her (usually non-black) interlocutor was standing a curious distance away from her, in rapt attention but also perhaps a bit nervous.

I'd joke that Sasha's very presence in our MFA cohort was a visual aid. She was a convenient instantiation of Edmund Burke's conception of the sublime. Sasha is whip-smart and statuesque, but warm enough to offset the ways that she's intimidating. She's one of the only people I know as good at talking as she is at listening. Gracious and understated in her reception of compliments and quick to return them in kind. These winning qualities are, of course, nevertheless filtered through the prism of her womanhood and her blackness.

"Whatever is fitted in any sort to excite the ideas of pain, and danger, that is to say whatever is in any sort terrible, or is conversant about terrible objects, or operates in a manner analogous to terror, is a source of the sublime," Burke writes.[7]

I'm sure Burke wasn't thinking of us, but most of the time that black people are represented in popular culture, we're depicted as either suffering pain and danger or inflicting it. Attractive black people's appeal is complicated but nonetheless amplified by their association with threat. "When danger or pain press too nearly, they are incapable of giving any delight, and are simply terrible," Burke notes.[8] "But at certain distances, and with certain modifications, they may be, and they are, delightful as we every day experience." Womanhood itself foments its own share of passionate ambivalence, so black women are especially likely to occupy a nexus encompassing both desire and fear. For Sasha and me both, the collision of history and biography yields a capacity to draw others to us and at the same time an innate propensity to keep them at arm's length. Through a heteropessimist lens, this is yet another obstacle to the cultivation of sustainable romantic bonds. It's also resonant with the Afropessimist argument that an underlying racial antagonism structures social realities. Even when we are sublime, we remain repellent.

These structures of feeling are at work between and among black people, both in ways that are consistent with heteropessimism and in ways that heteropessimism can't fully account for. Intraracial patriarchy presents an array of challenges. Racism affects how black people think of each other as well. Calling black people's anti-black behavior "internalized racism" is like describing breath as internalized oxygen. When a given element saturates the environment like anti-blackness does, we can take it as a given that everyone has internalized it to some degree.

This calls into question whether black people even have access to heteronormativity. After all, Afropessimism posits that the world is organized by anti-black solidarity. Which means that even for straight black folks, we can't really embody what is normal, default, or preferred. Controlling black women's reproduction and black people's sexuality is a cornerstone of the American social order. One of the country's earliest laws codified black procreation as the wellspring of chattel slavery. In her landmark essay "Whiteness as Property," Cheryl Harris writes that "in 1662, the Virginia colonial assembly provided that 'children got by an Englishman upon a negro woman shall be bond or free according to the condition of the mother.' In reversing the usual common law presumption that the status of the child was determined by the father, the rule facilitated the reproduction of one's own labor force."[9]

"Because the children of Black women assumed the status of their mother," Harris writes, "slaves were bred through Black women's bodies."[10]

Carrying out a biological imperative—ensuring the longevity of your own people—would necessarily reinforce the institution that oppressed them. If "straightness" and "normalcy" connote compatibility with the state, heterosexual partnerships with even one black person involved have never enjoyed that status.

As Sasha and I each swashbuckled through various dating misadventures throughout grad school and in the time since, we always circled back to one another and compared notes. To put it in terms of attachment theory, we each served as the platonic "secure base" from which the other could depart and explore freely.

91.

The barriers between black women and black men are always simultaneously raced and gendered. A season two episode of Donald Glover's television show *Atlanta* (2018) offers an illuminating case study. During a party scene, a white woman notices that Candi, a black woman, is staring at her pointedly.[11] When the white woman asks if there's a problem, Candi describes the white woman as "saddled over there with your black accessory—and I'm just tired of that story." (Could this be the same story that is often projected on my father and used to invisibilize my mother?) The white woman's boyfriend is a successful black actor, and Candi insinuates that the white girlfriend is a status symbol.

"Maybe I'm just a good woman," the white girlfriend shoots back, defending her relationship. "I've been with him since he was doing community theater."

The white woman wants Candi to know that she supported her boyfriend before he was a success by conventional standards, and that maybe "two good people just found each other." Candi takes a moment to absorb the argument before ultimately dismissing it. She points out that the white woman's advantages make it easier for her to be a good woman.

"You can afford to invest early," Candi says. "I don't got time to be sitting out here with no community theater ass nigga for eight years."

It's hard to imagine a more succinct fusion of Afropessimism and heteropessimism. Candi's take boils down to the romantic version of "It takes money to make money." Privilege makes gambling on a promising but unproven man a lower-risk proposition. And Candi's suspicion that the actor chose his partner as a trophy, while obviously not accurate in all cases, is more than defensible. It's common for people in general to choose partners based on whom they believe will impress their friends. The prevalence of white beauty standards rigs the pageant. I don't dismiss the idea that whiteness makes romantic optimism affordable. But black love—romantic, familial, and otherwise—has faced long odds since we arrived on these shores, and black people have a track record of rising to the occasion.

In her book *Killing the Black Body: Race, Reproduction, and the Meaning of Liberty*, scholar Dorothy Roberts confirms as much:

> Black women, along with Black men, succeeded remarkably often in maintaining the integrity of their family life despite slavery's traumas. . . . Amazingly, despite forced mating, sale of loved ones, and other brutalities of bondage, many slaves lived in settled, intimate families for a good part of their lives.[12]

I'm not invoking the bloody legacy of enslavement to wag my finger at a fictional black woman. In fact, there's an argument to be made that opting not to spend eight years on a community theater ass nigga is the sound of freedom ringing. I just think that it's easy to forget that African Americans are heirs to a tradition of loving through struggle. Waiting for a safe bet before wagering is a *choice.*

90.

No matter how promising a young black person seems, they are always at the same time an at-risk youth. Sometimes it's precociousness itself that marks you as at risk, or at least, at risk of one day being married to a white person.

My dad and his sister were discussing a section of Barack Obama's memoir. They were speculating about whether the forty-fourth president foresaw that he needed to be married to a black woman to realize his full political potential. Like most Democratic candidates, he'd need near unanimous black support to be elected president. Maybe especially because of his biracial parentage, "black wife" was a box he needed to check en route to the White House. The conversation between my father and my aunt is in some ways the inverse of the *Atlanta* scene. Both clearly recognized Michelle Obama as a status symbol herself—a feather in Barack's "race man" cap. I don't think my aunt and my father would evaluate Barack's candidacy on this basis themselves so much as that they were imagining the criteria that black America at large might use. *Okay, he's a light-skinned Harvard Law product raised by his white mother and her family,* the thinking would go. *But we know he's down because of his wife, who is not only black but notably also not light skinned*—and *from the Southside of Chicago.*

I was twenty-two, and a long way from thinking seriously about marriage. But somehow Obama's quest to be an optimally palatable black presidential candidate had something to do with me. "G'Ra," my aunt began, apropos of nothing in particular. "I just want you to know that if that's something you wanted to do—if you married a white woman—that would be okay. And no one would hold it against you."

I didn't covet this: preemptive amnesty for an outcome I didn't see as a foregone conclusion, or even something I'd need to be forgiven for if it did come to pass. What I mainly took from the comment was that I was already marked as a racial defector in waiting before I'd even accumulated any substantial romantic experience. "I don't think this is something we have to worry about, actually," I replied, a bit flippantly. "Because I want to be president, too."

Here was the hubris of youth talking—my ambition to be head of state was extremely short-lived. I was probably only a few years removed from grudgingly accepting that my grown-up job wasn't going to be "ninja." But the core of what I was saying was true. I was determined to be a person who didn't alienate himself from the only community who felt some obligation to embrace him. The notion of pandering to the "white gaze" takes up so much conceptual real estate that the import of the black gaze is hardly considered. Whereas calibrating one's image to the white gaze is crucial to sustenance in the public sphere, catering to the black gaze is central to the private one. These two color-coded viewfinders aren't symmetrical, though. The white gaze, buttressed by institutions, laws, and norms, is easy to generalize about. The black gaze is more situational. In this particular case I knew my audience well; both my aunt and my dad were and are in happy, long-lasting marriages to black people. I thought that a similar future was well within the realm of possibility for me. But more importantly, I didn't want to be sorted into a category of people who found the prospect unappealing.

When I tell Sasha that I'm considering writing about the search for love in the valueless abyss of modernity, we spitball ideas about it together, as we usually do. She relates to some of the challenges that I enumerate but is for the moment unconcerned with surmounting them.

"I really think that you and Elle are my soulmates," Sasha tells me. Elle is another black woman and NYC-based artist we know. "I'm happy with that."

A few days later Sasha texts me a link to an *Atlantic* article called "What If Friendship, Not Marriage, Was at the Center of Life?" None of the featured "best friends" who've centered their lives on a single, emotionally satisfying platonic relationship are of different genders.[13] From the looks of it you might surmise that men and women are only non-romantic soulmates if it's the first act of a rom-com, a waystation en route to becoming something else. I'm not surprised that my particular scenario isn't mentioned. It's only the latest in a lifelong succession of hints from my society that I'm doing gender wrong. The article's framing makes me curl my lip, not because I've never asked myself the same question, but because in the context of the earlier discussion Sasha and I had about searching for love, it carries a whiff of meek surrender.

ANSWER KEY

This answer key takes Audre Lorde's observation that "what's going on between us is related to what's going on between us and other people" as its point of departure. Lorde said this in a conversation with James Baldwin in 1984.[14] Originally published in *Essence* magazine, the exchange between two generational black minds showed that even among those mutually committed to anti-racism, there are still broad gaps in understanding about how patriarchy shapes and maintains power disparities between black men and black women.

"I don't want to break all this down, then have to stop at the wall of male/female division," Lorde says. "When we admit and deal with difference; when we deal with the deep bitterness; when we deal with the horror of our different nightmares; when we turn and look at them, it's like looking at death: hard but possible."

The alternatives to heteropessimism and Afropessimism begin with recognition of the hard but possible. Most people are not well practiced in thinking about sexism, racism, and heterosexism at the same time, and yet it's hard to imagine that any of the three can be properly understood independent of the others. What would it mean to deconstruct that wall of male/female division, particularly as it pertains to race and sexuality? Can black women and black men do the difficult work that Lorde alludes to, and look honestly and unflinchingly at our separate but deeply entwined nightmares?

For a possible route forward, I looked to Mandy Len Catron's Modern Love essay, "To Fall in Love with Anyone, Do This."[15] The essay refers to a study in which psychologists sought to find out if two strangers can form a bond by asking each other a series of specific personal questions. The study includes thirty-six questions divided into three sets, with each set of questions intended to be more revealing than the last. I wondered if the same format could be used to scaffold the kind of mutual self-disclosure that could meaningfully advance feminist anti-racist solidarity. I set out to write questions that could encourage two people to expand upon and investigate some of the gaps and silences in the Lorde-Baldwin conversation. The exercise is designed to suit any two black people willing to be receptive, self-critical, and accountable. As pivotal as those three qualities are in the pursuit of solidarity across social difference, they are even more vital to the possibility of love. I often think of my generation's smug refrain: "We are not our ancestors!" To which I say, yes, we should be learning a lot more from our forebears than we do. As things stand now, we may need to discover from scratch the wisdom that should have been inherited. I offer the below not only in the spirit of retracing the steps to the recipes we've lost but in fashioning new ones too.

SET 1:

1. About when did you become conscious of your assigned gender? What caused you to become conscious of it?
2. When was the first time you realized you were black?
3. Tell me about a time when you became aware of expectations placed on you about sexuality and what kinds of desire were "allowed."

4. When was the first time you thought about the relationship between your race and your gender? If you can't remember, how about the most recent time?
5. How do you think your gender influences/d your relationship with your father?
6. How do you think your gender influences/d your relationship with your mother?
7. If you could change anything about the way you were raised, what would it be?
8. What does the American Dream mean to you, and do you believe in it?
9. Do your race and your gender have any bearing on what you think of the American Dream? If so, how?
10. When was the first time you recognized some form of anti-blackness in yourself?
11. When was the last time you had to check yourself on being sexist?
12. In what ways do you feel empowered? In what ways do you feel disempowered?

SET II

1. Respond to this James Baldwin quote: "Don't you realize that in this republic the only real crime is to be a black man?"
2. Respond to this Audre Lorde quote: "It's not Black women who are shedding Black men's blood on the street—yet. We're not cleaving your head open with axes. We're not shooting you down. We're saying, 'Listen, what's going on between us is related to what's going on between us and other people,' but we have to solve our own shit at

the same time as we're protecting our Black asses, because if we don't, we are wasting energy that we need for joint survival."

3. Pick a pivotal moment in your life. Narrate how you think it might be different if you were still black, but not the gender that you are now.
4. Narrate the same moment, but this time imagine how you think it might be different if you were the same gender that you are now, but not black.
5. Audre Lorde tells James Baldwin that "the boot is on both of our necks. Let's talk about getting it off." If we were to hatch a plan together about how to get the boot to budge even an inch, where do you think we should start?
6. What is the most common misconception about who you are that you face? Why do you think that misconception persists?
7. Tell me one thing that you think would be incredibly important for black people of a gender other than your own to know. Pick something that they are unlikely to know or learn otherwise.
8. What's a positive stereotype about the groups you belong to that, even when well-intended, gets on your nerves? How does it affect you?
9. Be honest: Do you have any grievances with black people of genders other than your own? What are they?
10. Describe how you feel in environments where black people of a gender other than your own are the numerical majority.
11. Do you think eagerness to blame one another is a contributing factor to discord between black women and men? What would getting past blame mean to you?

12. How important is it to you to show strength? Is your attitude about being strong in any way connected to your gender and/or race?

SET III

1. Describe how you feel in environments where black people of your gender are the numerical majority.
2. Who was the first black person in popular culture that you aspired to be like? Why did you want to emulate them?
3. Who was the first black person in popular culture that you admired romantically or felt attracted to? Why did they appeal to you?
4. Do you date or have you dated interracially? Has the decision caused you any inner turmoil?
5. How do you feel when you see black people dating people who are not black? Do your feelings vary based on the genders involved?
6. If you looked forward to starting a family when you were young, what did you imagine that family would look like? Who did you imagine as the other members?
7. What's one thing that you can do to help spread awareness that brute force is not a legitimate way of dealing across sex difference? What's your idea of a first step toward, as Lorde puts it, "setting up some different paradigms"?
8. Finish this sentence: "Let's make a mutual commitment to . . ."
9. Tell me about a kind of freedom that you are grateful to have. Then describe a freedom that you long for or wish that future generations could have.

10. Describe a time when another black person made you feel loved.
11. Share one way in which you would like to be supported, encouraged, or assisted that is otherwise lacking in your life.
12. Share one way in which you, personally, could stand to be more compassionate.

LONGING FOR THE CROOKED CROWN

Whenever I have a social interaction that feels entirely rote, like everyone's lines and blocking are memorized verbatim from an Instagram infographic, I mentally recite this litany before I can stop myself: "iced coffee, fit checks, podcasts, biggest flex." This is my shamefully patronizing way of thinking about mass culture, and the supplied opinions people use to make decisions and shape conversation. Iced coffee, fit checks, podcasts, biggest flex. My tic is a reaction to people who are living and narrating their lives in ways that are perfect reflections of the zeitgeist. Like they're moving dutifully through a grocery list of attitudes and activities, lest they fail to qualify as a credibly contemporary person.

A guitar YouTuber named Brandon D'Eon has a way of describing this that I particularly enjoy. When an intermediate guitarist plays a solo, they're often guilty of what D'Eon calls being "too scalar." Instead of their solo sounding like music, it sounds like someone performing a guitar exercise—applying a template without ingenuity, originality, or verve. A guitar solo is supposed to involve scales, sure, but it should consist of the scales plus your soul, with emphasis on the latter. People whose lives and lingo are too scalar depress me. I experience heteropessimism as one form of being too scalar with interpersonal life, a way of confusing the gift of a guideline for the leadenness of law.

Of course, heteropessimism is just one expression of a broader trend where hip, left-leaning young people suppose that humanity's faults and liabilities are unique to (or at least most pronounced in) society's most advantaged groups. For example, X is a straight-people problem because queer people *would never.* Black kids who accuse their high-achieving peers of "acting/talking white" don't do so because they scorn succeeding in school, or for the same sheer pleasure that white kids get from bullying others. No, they're just calling out the classmates who purposefully distance themselves from black culture.

I hear this kind of reasoning from my undergraduate students fairly often, but I don't think it's limited to Gen Z. Sometimes, I suspect older people make these remarks to signal that they're with it. Not long ago it was far more socially acceptable to make unflattering generalizations about women and sexual and racial minorities. (And obviously in conservative spaces—including, tragically, the federal government under the second Trump regime—it's still the order of the day.) Fully abandoning the well-worn practice of judging individuals by the groups they belong to would be a lot harder than simply using the same road to drive in the opposite direction. And this is America—give us convenience or give us death. It would be inaccurate to call this behavior reverse racism, reverse sexism, or the like. There is no institutional or political capital reinforcing these sentiments. Sneering that straight people are wayward certainly doesn't amount to oppressing them. But there is a retaliatory impulse behind it, as if hierarchy doesn't need to be dismantled but merely inverted.

Aspiring to the power that has been used to marginalize and denigrate you is almost always misguided. And pretty much everyone does it. I call it longing for the crooked crown. The term draws on an iconic picture of Biggie Smalls in which the legendary Brooklyn emcee faces the camera with his brows furrowed and a plastic crown cocked at a jaunty angle atop his dome.[1] His pose and costume are a way of installing himself as countercultural royalty. The photo was taken a few months before Biggie's death in 1997, when the Bad Boy Records prodigy was enjoying his imperial phase. Perched comfortably atop rap's pecking order, Biggie wielded all the power of a traditional ruler but shed the provinciality. At a surface level there is something radical and transgressive about a colonial subject seizing the symbol of his disempowerment and repurposing it for his own ends. Biggie is having all the fun playing the rabbit who grabbed the gun. Trading places with the oppressor and leaving the system of domination essentially unchanged is not liberation. But it is a powerfully seductive notion for people fated to catch hell from cradle to casket simply for being who they are.

I was, in some sense, vying for the crooked crown by attending Columbia University for graduate school. Being accepted there seemed like the beginning of the most heartwarming chapter in the improbable black progress narrative my parents kickstarted before I was born. My mother became pregnant as an undergraduate student at Northwestern University and, along with my father, dropped out to support and raise me. Neither of my parents reenrolled. Completing my graduate degree at a school comparable to Northwestern was a momentous closing of the loop. As much as Columbia's vibrant intellectual community and considerable resources appealed to me, the prestige and access was a selling point, too. Like many of my black classmates, I wanted the satisfaction of knowing that a black kid from one of the most lethal ghettos in the US managed to earn credentials from a top institution. I didn't fully clock that the school was named after Christopher Columbus until I got there. Conquest and domination suffuse the school's branding. For most prospective students these colonial overtones are not deterrents; they're incentives. The insufferably smug university logo is a tiny, ice-blue crown. It's totally revolting. And I made a beeline to purchase a snapback with that logo and slant it saucily on my skull. I was eager to rock it for probably the same reasons that hip-hop audiences found that photo of Biggie so captivating. The Columbia University snapback announced to the world that I had ascended into an echelon of status and exclusivity that few people of my origin ever would or could. The cap's off-kilter placement asterisked that message. It signified that yes, I rubbed shoulders with run-of-the-mill squares native to the corridors of power, but I retained the rugged flexibility of the outsider. The crooked crown promises, deceptively, that not only can you make the system work for you; you can launder and redeem the system by doing so.

I romanticize the crooked crown least when I think about a harrowing sequence in Zora Neale Hurston's *Barracoon: The Story of the Last "Black Cargo."* The book is based on interviews Hurston conducted with Oluale Kossola, a man believed to be the final survivor of the Middle Passage. Kossola's perspective is unique. He remembers his time on the African soil as well as his years in America as human chattel. Before he was brought to American shores in chains, Kossola saw his family and all of the elders in his community slaughtered at the order of the king of Dahomey, an African slave trader.

Writes Deborah G. Plant in the introduction:

> Kossola described to Hurston the mayhem that ensued in the predawn raid when his townspeople awoke to Dahomey's female warriors, who slaughtered them in their daze.

> Those who tried to escape through the eight gates that surrounded the town were beheaded by the male warriors who were posted there. Kossola recalled the horror of seeing decapitated heads hanging about the belts of the warriors, and how on the second day, the warriors stopped the march in order to smoke the heads. Through the clouds of smoke, he missed seeing the heads of his family and townspeople.[2]

Women in male-dominated fields and black people in white-dominant fields sent Kossola to the cotton fields. You don't preclude phenomena like black cargo just by changing who licks the stamp. I don't blame anyone with the boot on their neck for imagining the shoe on the other foot. But we shouldn't confuse replacing the oppressor with replacing oppression. Everyone you meet contains the seeds of revolution and empire alike. Which potential they fulfill turns, in large part, on how and by whom they are loved.

THE JIG IS UP AND DOWN

I didn't give him a penny. But still he gave me his thoughts. "If I had just heard your voice without seeing you, man, I'd have sworn I was talking to a white person."

So said a man who described himself as homeless as he approached me on the street. He was a roughly forty-something white dude. Noticeably fit, well-fed and clean-looking for someone down on his luck. I explained that I could buy him some food but I didn't have any cash on me. He said thanks, but he'd eaten very recently. That's when he volunteered his assessment of my racial conformity.

The overfamiliarity of this reaction does not make it less annoying. But it doesn't throw me off balance, either. The blackest thing I can do is reject the limitations of anti-black thinking.

A lot of my social life is shaped by the perception that my get up (the body I'm in) and my get down (how I carry myself) don't match. Dating back to elementary school, I've been told that I am somehow "against type" in terms of my race *and* my gender. The racial dissonance is more obvious and easier to explain: Both anti-blackness and well-intentioned responses to it can foster the idea that black people act, talk, and think in one particular way.

The gender dissonance is more complicated. Even though men are the most advantaged gender, many people hold narrow ideas about how they act, talk, and think as well. For the most part, I ignore those standards. My get up and my get down are barely related in terms of race. Maybe that makes it easier for me to disentangle them in terms of gender.

I think of gender more like shirts and skins in PE class. When you show up, somebody assigns you to stand in either this line or that line. If it's this line, you're supposed to take off your shirt. You are now a skin. However you may have felt about your classmates in totality, you are now to regard the other skins as your teammates. The people in the line across from you are your prescribed opponents. In that line, you're supposed to keep your shirt on. You might not have been fond of the other shirts. But now that you have the same assignment, it's time to squad up. A sweaty man in mesh shorts with a whistle around his neck is the great arbiter. He makes the knee-jerk decision about who you should help and who you should hinder. He prescribes your get down based on your get up.

The experience of being a shirt or a skin, and working together with one to defeat the other, can (but doesn't always) create a sense of allegiance to your assigned side. Some people feel that their get up correctly predicted their get down. In that case, they may not resent the sweaty man in mesh shorts for his decision. Other people feel that their get up and their get down are inverted. They got shoved into the shirts line when they actually felt locked in with skins, or vice versa. Like a *y* that moonlights as a vowel, I have no more consonance with one group than the other. I do recognize, however, that I'm marked by my experience on the skins side. My tenure on the team affects me in ways I'm conscious of and in ways I can never fully unpack. For one thing, the sweaty man in mesh shorts has generally given the skins a friendlier whistle. The shirts' frustration with and even rage about that has always made sense to me. Since I experience my get up and my get down as largely independent of one another, the shirts vs. skins fault line feels suspect.

All of this comes to a head in love. Relationships challenge us to navigate differences, and how we do so at the group level informs how we settle differences between individuals. In love, gender difference is seen as normal but racial difference is not, and this is perhaps more arbitrary than it seems. Consider how it might alter our perception of interracial and queer romance if we used terms that emphasized difference in straight relationships and sameness in intraracial ones. A straight couple is just as accurately called intergender. The prefix "homo" is understood as a shorthand for gay, but a same-race couple is homochromatic. These simple rebrands undermine the apparent normalcy of those choices, even though the shift in adjectives has no material impact.

Toeing the various race and gender lines without stumbling is like doing a two-step to the Dramatics' 1971 funk classic "Get Up and Get Down." Your get up seems to take precedence most of the time. Then suddenly it's your get down that raises eyebrows. It's a dizzying dance. It never lacks for dramatics.

GET UP

I had just moved to Harlem, and my good friend Chris, whom I'd grown up with in suburban Maryland, was in the Apple for the weekend. Chris met a photographer, Ron (not his real name), at a retail job they worked together. It turned out that like me, Ron was in an MFA program in the Northeast, and he often found himself in NYC. Ron remarked that he liked Chris's look. He asked Chris to model in a project he was working on for grad school.

I met up with the two of them in Chelsea thinking Ron would have my boy posing and looking handsome in hip clothes or something. Instead, Ron asked me to appear in the pictures too. Specifically, he wanted Chris and me to act out a series of fight scenes in the rain. A surge of misplaced solidarity overwhelmed my better judgment. Ron and I were both young black artists plying our respective trades in the Ivy League. I granted him some creative latitude I wouldn't readily allow someone else.

With Ron directing us, Chris and I pantomimed squaring up, choking each other, bobbing and weaving and exchanging pulled punches. I was typically instructed to be the throttler and not the throttled, the uppercut thrower and not its target. Ron muttered something about his project making a visual commentary about "masculinity and aggression." His camera clicked rapidly. Even as we cooperated, I locked eyes with Chris, wiggled my brows and tilted my head warily in a body-language approximation of "the fuck?"

Chris is half Asian and half white but often perceived as either white or racially ambiguous. He is taller and skinnier than me. It was not hard to imagine how a third party might regard the photos Ron staged, especially if they were taken out of whatever "subversive" context he had in mind. We were doubtless generating ammunition for the Republican attack machine.

"These photos," I whispered to Chris out of the corner of my mouth, "are definitely going to resurface on the internet when I run for office one day."

While I don't think Chris was as uncomfortable as I was, he definitely seemed hesitant. There was a largely unspoken subplot between Ron and Chris that made Chris even more reluctant to object. Ron is a soft-spoken gay dude. Chris is a straight pretty boy with a history of attracting admirers of various genders. Earlier that week, Chris and I had entertained the possibility that Ron's invitation to model was a pretext for something else. We ultimately dismissed it. Both of us were well aware of the homophobic cliché in which straight bros assume all gay men find them attractive. Neither of us would be caught dead acting so unenlightened. But then . . . being photographed mock–kung fu fighting your man fifty grand as lightning crackles overhead can make you rethink your life decisions. When the shoot was over, Ron promised to share the photos with us at a later date. We took turns grinning, shaking Ron's hand, and thanking him for including us.

"Not sure what we'd do with those photos if we ever see them," Chris quipped when we were out of earshot.

"Other than burn them," I added.

We debriefed on the train back uptown. Chris's intuition told him that we were both being sexualized, but he didn't dare confront Ron about it directly. What if Chris was wrong, and we were both just being bigots? I tried to imagine what turn the photo shoot might have taken if Chris had shown up without a plus one, as was the original plan. It seemed unlikely Ron had envisioned shots of Chris punching and choking himself. Would masculinity and aggression still have been a theme? Or did the unexpected appearance of a black subject make those topics resonant?

Ron reached out to Chris a few weeks later. He didn't mention the photos—or how they'd turned out—at all.

"I was wondering if you could put me in touch with your friend," Ron wrote. "For creative reasons."

At first, Chris wasn't sure which friend Ron was talking about. He tried to find out what Ron wanted before he handed over any contact information.

"Oh . . . it's fine," Ron typed back. "I just wanted to talk to him about literature. But since I'm too gay I'll pass."

Chris was flummoxed. He was now being accused of exactly the faux pas he'd taken pains to avoid. Hoping to smooth things over, he apologized and suggested that Ron follow me on socials. Ron volunteered that I was his type. He told Chris I had denied an earlier friend request. To my knowledge, I hadn't been sent one.

Soon after, a note from Ron appeared in my inbox.

"How are you? I'd like to talk to you a little in detail about your writing, and some of my writing as well. I'm in New York sometimes on the weekends. Do you have a space that you use specifically for writing? I would imagine that you don't have a 'studio space' but if so I would like to meet you there and talk to you a little, if possible. Take care!"

For the most part, the correspondence seemed innocuous. If our first meeting hadn't spun wildly out of control, I'd probably have been eager to connect with Ron about art and our respective MFA experiences. What little I knew about him before we met portended an organic friendship. But his preferred meeting place struck a discordant note. New acquaintances usually suggested coffee or drinks in a public setting. Women who have read me as straight and responded positively to my own flirtation never insisted on meeting alone right away. Honestly, I'd probably have left Ron on read and not thought much more about it. But it turned out that what Ron had politely euphemized for my benefit was made explicit to Chris.

Chris messaged me a screenshot of his own conversation thread with Ron, who had been combing through my public Facebook pictures and sending a select few to Chris with annotations. In one of the photos, I'm cradling a microphone in mid-croon, bobbing along atop a sea of outstretched hands at what punk rockers call a "house show" in Huntingtown, Maryland.

"I'm not lurking lol," Ron wrote beneath the image. "I'm sure he'd be bi for me."

In Ron's eyes, whatever thousand words the photo was worth, he'd seen receptivity to his advances within it like an answer to a crossword puzzle. It made no difference that Chris had gently reminded Ron that I didn't date men. A black kid who fronts a punk band and comfortably crowd-surfs waves of whiteness *must* be sexually available to him. For all my eye-rolling at the primacy of identity labels, scenarios like this one reveal why they're so central at this cultural moment. Our digital footprints take on more significance than our corporeal selves.

Under mass surveillance, your live studio audience comprises more than just the blasé NSA agent peering through your webcam. Suitors' snap judgments are ongoing. Covers might as well be the book. Presumptuous as Ron's assessments happened to be, they weren't entirely off the mark.

"It looks like he was surrounded by white people a huge part of his life," Ron went on. "And even if that is the norm for you, you still feel a sense of otherness."

Present-day me actually finds his intrusive close reading more compassionate than creepy. It's not often that anyone is tender toward me about that specific aspect of my life. It's usually something people cite to justify their suspicion or contempt. That said, I didn't exactly work up a heady rush of warm and fuzzies. Would Ron extend this same gentleness to me if I rebuffed him in the (nonexistent) private writing space he'd invited himself to? I thought of the classic street harasser. One who greets an attractive passerby with, "Hey beautiful, how's your day?" only to ditch the genial veneer by spitting, "Fuck you then, bitch!" when she winces in reply. Ron's certainty that I'd "be bi for" him could be harmless bravado, but it might also represent indifference to my consent.

In the time since we met, Ron has become an increasingly notable figure in African American photography. Critics laud his work for humanizing black male figures that are more often positioned as passive erotic objects. A black artist who makes inroads with a white audience that has chronically under-imagined him tends to acquire a unique form of capital. He's often welcomed into exclusive institutions as a supposedly credible spokesperson for the underrepresented group. I don't doubt that Ron brings a cannier eye to black life than, say, Robert Mapplethorpe did. At the same time, it would be easy to overestimate the difference in their critical and artistic reflexes. Ron appointed me as his vision's resident brute practically on sight. We'd barely exchanged hellos before I was conscripted into a tired tableau as the raging black buck. It's completely plausible Ron was still honing his creative instincts at the time, and maybe his subsequent oeuvre reflects a more imaginative approach. But resorting to racist caricature and overwriting my sexual agency don't seem incidental to one another. It's easier to impose your will on someone you're attracted to if you flatten them into a trope.

Ron's photography gave him the power to stage a mise-en-scène that served his fantasy. While heteropessimism emphasizes that inequality is part and parcel with heterosexual attraction, anti-black racism ensures that queerness is no refuge from predation, either. Far from it, Chavano—if men are aroused by women's vulnerability, how irresistibly steamy is the slave? To be black is to reliably invite a desire that leaves much to be desired.

GET DOWN

By the Black Momba's decree, I went to a hippie-dippie elementary school from pre-K through third grade. The school's philosophy was based on Howard Gardner's theory of multiple intelligences. Our lessons were tailored to hone and support what our instructors called logical mathematical, spatial, musical, bodily-kinesthetic, linguistic, interpersonal, and intrapersonal intelligences. (The theory has since been updated to include an eighth form of intelligence called naturalistic.) As a child, I thought interpersonal and intrapersonal intelligences seemed utterly useless, and worse, dull. I sighed any time my teachers fixed their lips to mention those two. I later came to recognize intrapersonal and interpersonal awareness as the most consequential threads in Gardner's theory. There's one class activity on the subject that I've been turning over in my mind for years.

The instructor told the class that she would read to us two different prompts. She asked us to perform a wordless charade to demonstrate the idea described in the prompt. The first prompt was "Act like a lady." Most of the boys in the class, myself included, affected a comically high femme demeanor. We hooked elbows and formed a chain of limp wrists, coquettish smiles, and angled hips. The second prompt was "Be a man." The boys, still playing the activity for laughs, saw this as their cue to emulate professional wrestlers. We preened and flexed. We poked out our puny preadolescent chests.

One student out of the entire class struck the same pose for both phrases. When she heard the instructions, she made a skeptical expression and shrugged. For my classmate, "acting like a lady" and "being a man" looked just alike: She stood relatively still, looking straight ahead, with her hands pressed casually into her pockets. Watching this classmate, even in the moment I suddenly understood that I'd completely missed the point of the assignment. I had been too busy clowning to absorb it, but the instructor had put emphasis on the terms *act* and *be*. To my adult mind, *be* confers a level of permanence and authenticity to the condition of manhood. *Act* frames being a lady as an elaborate ruse. I don't think this disparity was lost on my classmate at the time, even if she wouldn't be able to articulate it right then. She probably also sensed that overestimating the differences between men and women played into patriarchy's hands. At that age, she was already identifiable as our class's budding feminist. She was sporty and no-nonsense, a proto-badass. A number of my young friends admitted they were afraid of her.

I wasn't quite friends with this classmate, but we'd been in the same homeroom for three straight years. She was the first to call out any sexist double standard on the playground or in a lesson plan. At our school, we were taught and encouraged to use terms like *discrimination* and *exclusion*. This person was the most adept at putting those terms to use in pointedly girl-powered fashion. Peering across the classroom at her nonchalant stance as I grimaced and raged in my best impersonation of the Incredible Hulk, I felt the vague sense that I'd betrayed her.

GET UP

In Greta Gerwig's *Barbie* and Amy Poehler's *Moxie*, the battle lines in the gender wars are drawn along a single axis: men of all races are united in their determination to oppress women, who are united across race in their resistance to sexism. This isn't a complete mischaracterization of the real-life state of affairs—all men benefit from patriarchy to varying degrees. In turn, patriarchy disadvantages women across the board.

Admittedly, any film that takes on a giant, gnarly social problem like sexism must necessarily simplify the issue to make it digestible and entertaining to a mass audience. In *Moxie* and *Barbie*, the simplification shares a common formula.

De-emphasizing race and its impact on how, when, and which women experience sexism allows both movies to champion a deceptive, ahistorical sisterhood. It also spares the white protagonists from having to wrangle with the complexity of being disadvantaged in terms of gender and privileged in terms of race at the same time. The plots of the two films largely ignore the racial tensions that tend to arise between black and non-black women in the pursuit of a feminist project that serves them all. The peripheral black women characters appear to enjoy strong solidarity from white women and no solidarity from black men. Instead, the black men are busy being bootlicking acolytes of the primary antagonists, Ryan Gosling as Ken and Patrick Schwarzenegger as star jock Mitchell Wilson, respectively. These gleeful cosigners of white patriarchy are the only black men represented, which feeds the misconception that all of us are more committed to the interests of men than to the welfare of black people.

Depicting this type as the most common form of black man is a selective and opportunistic vision of feminism. Couldn't a white character's feminist awakening also heighten her consciousness about anti-racism, since most women on earth are of color? Might black women's feminist striving not only improve their relationships with non-black women, but also strengthen mutual understanding within the black community, which is overwhelmingly where black women live, work, and partner romantically?

In modern liberal circles, it's taken as a given that gender is not binary. The illusion of a villain–victim binary, wherein one is either complicit in systemic oppression or aggrieved because of it, is largely unchallenged. In one memorable *Barbie* scene, Margot Robbie's character Stereotypical Barbie remarks that she's reluctant to hurt Ken, even if he's made mistakes. Gloria, a self-described boring mom with a boring life, chimes in with a summary of all the ways that Ken has done her wrong. Her point is that Ken has it coming. Nearly everything that Gloria rightly holds Ken accountable for is analogous to some historical atrocity that people who look like Margot Robbie (they don't *really* look like her but phenotypically speaking) have done to people who look like me. If Ken's exploits represent the misconduct of men throughout time, and Gloria argues that his track record warrants some measure of revenge, then thin, blue-eyed Stereotypical Barbie's flaxen-haired noggin is just about equally deserving of the chopping block.

This didn't distract me from absorbing the film's trenchant critique of gender inequality. It did make me look forward to an iteration of mainstream feminism dynamic enough to problematize white supremacy and patriarchy at the same time without treating either as small potatoes. As trendy as the word *intersectionality* has become, it's mostly used in pop culture to signal a feminist storyline that has some queer and non-white people involved. It's still relatively rare to see storytelling that rigorously engages how other forms of social difference intersect with gender.

In another poignant scene, Ken quips to a businessman that the man's company isn't "doing patriarchy very well." The suit-clad white man shoots back that they are doing patriarchy well, but they're just hiding it better now. The scene wryly tweaks businesses that pay lip service to diversity, equity, and inclusion while mostly maintaining the status quo save for a few strategically placed tokens. Yet *Barbie* itself is pulling a related stunt with whiteness. When Stereotypical Barbie asks if any women work at Mattel, a low-level employee answers the question with a question: "I'm a man with no power; does that make me the woman?"

The one-liner obviously isn't meant to be literal, but the glib insinuation that powerlessness might be an essential feature of womanhood glosses over two relevant facts: 1) that whiteness empowers some women at the direct expense of others and 2) that some women are structurally advantaged in ways that some men are not. Isn't Stereotypical Barbie's status as the default—the image one conjures when prompted to visualize a Barbie—a source of considerable power? By using Stereotypical Barbie as the narrative vehicle for exploring sexism, the film reinforces the centrality of whiteness without examining it. The story foregrounds all the ways white women suffer for being women and leaves aside the ways they benefit from being white. Mainstream feminism is doing white supremacy well, but hiding it better than in the past.

Barbie made over a billion dollars at the box office. These portrayals influence how the relationship between race and gender is commonly understood. Ken's multicultural coterie of backslapping yes-men is what a lot of people picture as standard-issue guys.

GET DOWN

I always feel skittish about overstating how my subtle, subjective gender nonconformity has exposed me to real harm. I have a clear memory of a formative time when it did. The year was 2003 and I was a high school student in suburban Maryland. It was far less socially acceptable for black kids to dress punk or engage with skate culture than it would be a decade later. I was posted up at a local mall in Wheaton, Maryland, with some friends. Two members of the crew I was with were white and one was Asian. The four of us were leaning over the handrail looking down at the food court, people watching and making jokes, when I noticed a group of black dudes from my high school approaching us. Their faces were familiar but I didn't know many of them by name. A couple of fellas in the group craned their necks at me and squinted.

I had dyed my hair, which was styled in a nappy bob, bright red. My outfit that night consisted of black Chuck Taylors, a studded belt that was fashionable among punk and emo kids of the era, a white "work shirt" tucked into black jeans, and a skinny black tie. My sixteen-year-old self regarded the fit as smooth and subversive. The tie and work shirt represented the dreary adult future that threatened to arrive in a few short years. The Chucks, the belt, and the tight jeans signaled my connection with punk culture, which I saw as a potential antidote to exactly that future. All of this was lost on Robert, the apparent ringleader of the pack of sneering, social-promotion beneficiaries who had me in their sights.

"Look at this faggot ass nigga," Robert cracked. His gang did as they were directed. Then they laughed.

A handful of change sailed through the air and hit me in my grill. Two of the friends who'd accompanied me to the mall that night slumped into separate corners, making themselves as small as possible, as if they hoped to become invisible. I only faintly resented their dereliction. It was instinctively clear to me that while those two guys might catch some strays if they intervened, I was the true target. I ducked and hunched my shoulders to protect my face as more coins whizzed past. One of Robert's boys somehow had rocks and pebbles handy. He launched and only a few of them connected, but the humiliation stung much more than the contact. Watching his crew pelt me with miscellaneous makeshift missiles made Robert howl.

"Little bitch!" he cackled.

"Flamer," one of Robert's cronies snorted at me, emboldened. "You a bitch ass nigga."

Rocks and coins—alongside a steady chorus of slurs—rained down for what felt like several minutes. My assailants lost interest in my torment once they'd walked by. A security guard at the far end of the mall bellowed at them to move along, and they did. I shook off my friends' reassurances. It wasn't their business. Embarrassing as the encounter had been, it felt like a family matter that was better off kept in-house.

Years later, I incorporated this incident into a lesson plan for a creative writing class. The anecdote served as a model for how to write about something painful in a comedic fashion. My students absorbed the larger point, but they were puzzled by some of the details in the story itself. Why did the boys at the mall target the black person, while mainly leaving the two white people and the Asian person alone? The students hadn't read their instructor as gay or trans; why did his antagonists use those particular slurs against him? Listening to their questions, I realized I hadn't fully made sense of the experience yet for myself. At the time I didn't have a heartwarming coda to offer. There was no empowering epilogue in which I'd fled the provincial confines of my hometown, been gathered up in the arms of an affirming community, and mustered enough cheery self-possession to clutch a struggling young counterpart by the shoulder and with twinkling eyes declare that "it gets better." The slurs in question had been chucked at me often enough in life to prompt some pointed introspection. Did I feel any buried inclination to date, sleep with, or fall in love with cis men? No. What about becoming a woman? Longer pause, but still no.

The worrisome racial implications of a group of young black men targeting and harassing another, visibly eccentric young black man seemed more straightforward. In the eyes of some other black men, I was subject to a narrower standard of decorum than the clique I was hanging with that night. For them, black men's adherence to this more stringent code is the backbone of our social role and identity. It's what makes us distinguishable from men of other races and from women broadly. By dyeing my hair and dressing punk (which is, not coincidentally, a synonym for sissy) I had bucked this standard twofold. Not only did these transgressions warrant my ouster from the in-group; they also signaled an opportunity for Robert and his boys. The jeering that ensued consolidated each of those young men's own blackness and manhood. Accentuating and exploiting my vulnerability is how they assured themselves and each other that they were strong.

Experiences like that night at Wheaton Mall can influence some men to cling more tightly to machismo. The very behaviors and characteristics that feminism entreats men to reject—belligerence, insensitivity, cruelty, and predation—are the same ones black men are sometimes pressured to perform and embody to strengthen their sense of belonging. I see it as the social equivalent of terraforming, the science fiction trope in which futuristic characters transform other planets to resemble Earth. Many people cultivate personalities and appearances that align with the conventional wisdom about their gender and their race for the same reason: They're emulating the most successful model of a foundation to support life. Coherence with these norms (even harmful ones) is like the oxygen, hydrogen, nitrogen, and phosphorus of sociality.

Prevailing thinking about gender and race often places straightness, blackness, and masculinity on one side and queerness, whiteness, and femininity on the other. This tendency influences how we terraform ourselves. Most savvy people develop social identities that signal their connection to the groups they want to be associated with. No small part of that process involves conforming to the dominant ideas about our races and genders. With few exceptions, we intuitively recognize the danger of being too different, and shape ourselves accordingly.

As for me, Robert and his crew's assessment indicated that I'd made some wrong turns at Albuquerque. I hadn't terraformed well enough to deflect the negative attention they'd gleefully directed my way. Instead, I'd made the laughable mistake of being myself and hoping for the best. This is the clear limitation of gender and race terraforming. To usher in the world that could be, you have to endure some positive maladjustment with the world that is.

GET UP ≠ GET DOWN

Even those of us who take a more expansive view of our gender don't necessarily recognize anti-sexism as an obligation. In middle school, I obsessed over Black Star, the collaboration between Rawkus Records staples Talib Kweli and Yasiin Bey (who was then called Mos Def). There's a cut on their first record named "Twice Inna Lifetime," on which Kweli raps: "you stopping us is preposterous / like an androgynous misogynist." It instantly became my favorite bar. The pure sonic umami of the phrase and its witty wordplay were irresistible. The quip became a hallmark of my teenage lexicon. Any time something struck me as buck wild, crazy, unbelievable, or absurd, I would crow, "That's preposterous as an androgynous misogynist." After the umpteenth time my parents overheard it, Baba asked where I'd gotten it from. He also pointed out that the punchline relied on what he saw as a false opposition. Androgyny and misogyny can and often do coincide, he insisted.

"What about Dennis Rodman?" my dad cracked, referencing the San Antonio Spurs' flamboyant forward known as much for his litany of off-court domestic violence incidents as his rebounding prowess. "Doesn't that guy from Outkast who dresses up like a woman also rap about bitches and hos?"

He was right, of course, and the realization alarmed me. Hypermasculine men did not have a monopoly on disdain for women. It shouldn't have really shocked me, given how obvious this dynamic is when transposed to questions of race. Many of the white folks who idolize and even emulate figures like Rodman and Andre 3000 are no less prone to bias against black folks. The Black Star lyric and my father's reaction to it informed my still-processing sense of my place in the world. Resembling, admiring, or identifying with the thing that is othered does not make one immune to othering. Whatever likeness I might or might not share with the girls I grew up with wasn't absolution for participating in their oppression.

At times the dance floor instructions are slowed and reverbed. Exhortations to get up or get down become indistinct. The two-step gets frenetic.

There's only so long I can cut a rug as it's pulled out from underneath my feet. As the Dramatics pulse at ear-splitting volume, I'm not so much seeking a partner as someone to take by the hand and dip from this dance floor altogether.

PUTTING THE FUN IN FUNGIBILITY

A few years ago I was perusing a Harlem grocery store with a friend of mine and her son. Three different people who know my friend and her son came up to me and started talking to me as if we had met before. They addressed me as if my friend's son was also *my* son, and spoke as if I knew them and their kids from a nearby day care. The child's actual father, who was not present at the time, is black and roughly my age and height. The "resemblance" between us ends there. There was never a moment of recognition where the acquaintances of the child's father accepted that I am, in fact, a completely different person.

I'm not what you'd call a naive observer of American race relations, but the experience still prompted a kind of revelation: Black people are uncannily interchangeable. Someone who has never seen you before can instantly substitute you for someone they actually know, provided the person you're replacing is also black. This would explain a lot—maybe Ben Carson made a covert switcheroo with a lobotomy patient around 2013; maybe the real Lauryn Hill retired after *Miseducation* and drafted a random sister from the block to pose in her stead. If I'm on to something, somebody put me in touch with A$AP Rocky. If he is down to slum it as a broke writer, I would love to try being Less Pretty Flacko for a spell. Come to think of it, Whitney and Chaka are actually singing about this phenomenon in "I'm Every Woman." They're just reminding you they can serve as understudy for any black woman alive at any time.

And in this way, when you can red-rover your way into any existing configuration of black folks and snag a place at their side without much ceremony, the project of family making feels evergreen.

MOTION CAPTURE

In most informal settings, if someone greets me with some variation of, “What’s up?” I’m going to say, “Chilling.” What I mean when I say that is, I’m luxuriating in the great statistical improbability of existence. My heart rate is low and my spirits are high. I’m in placid communion with the very essence of being. In academia, though, everyone is obsessed with productivity. Now, chilling and productivity are not mutually exclusive; the kid can be fully frigid and fecund at the same time. But I don’t think acknowledging that I’m “chilling” will be properly understood within those ivy-covered walls. It may be received as confirmation that I’m exactly the feckless, half-stepping DEI hire that my inquisitor already suspected. So, if I’m on campus and somebody says how’s it going or how’s your day, I like to go with, “Getting after it.”

Telling everybody I’m getting after it can feel grotesquely puritan. But it’s a multiple entendre, I guess, in the sense that I do be having motion. Motion is slang for momentum, clout, action, go-getter spirit. In my case a lot of that motion is happening on foot, because I never learned to drive. That’s why I’m in the backseat of a car with my friend Mikiel and his girlfriend Amber. I’ve recently undergone a breakup that is only three weeks back in the rearview mirror. And now I’m third-wheeling for the first time in a couple of years. We’re on tour, traveling from a gig at a Hartford, Connecticut, pizza shop and headed to another show in New York City.

I'm the oldest person in the usual lineup of my band by six years. Maybe due to being an itinerant male spinster whose only hobbies are literature and music, for about 40 percent of the shows that we're offered, I'm the only person available to play. I wrangle ringer members so that I can turn down as few show offers as possible. The word *spinster* originated in the fourteenth century. It came to be a generally demeaning term for an unmarried woman, but it was initially used to describe a woman who spun thread and yarn.[1] The word codifies a perceived connection between motion and lovelessness. Yarn spinning is one of my primary vocations, sometimes on laptop screens and other times over a yearning chord progression. *Spinster* feels like a more fitting and functional epithet than *bachelor*.

The word *bachelor* better suits the character Hov is playing in his immortal anthem "99 Problems." It came out when I was a junior in high school. The verses itemized the Brooklyn emcee's hardships while the chorus bragged that despite grumbling music critics, drug-sniffing canines, and racist district attorneys, Jay-Z's sex life, at least, remained blissfully problem-free. Twenty years later, I'm beginning to notice that some of my friends and I are facing the opposite predicament. We've got the degrees, the budding careers, and relative economic security that we were told were central to stable adulthood. Finding and sustaining fulfilling relationships, on the other hand, is a taller order. The unrepentant womanizing that Jay-Z boasted about is far more attainable than what I aspire to. My parents have been married thirty-eight years. My grandparents on my father's side were married for seventy years. My maternal grandmother outlived my maternal grandfather by thirty years, but they were together for twenty, and Grandma remained very much in love with her late husband until she passed. Those three couples are my models, but they weren't navigating the gender wars, dating app overload, or tweet-length attention spans.

Of the musicians playing on this tour, I'm the only one who is not in a relationship. Over the span of the five tour dates, three different iterations of my band are performing: an acoustic duo, a quintet, and a quartet, composed of a total of seven different musicians. Before the tour is over I will alternate between acting as acoustic guitarist and backing vocalist, electric guitarist and co-lead vocalist, and then return to my typical job as frontperson-bassist. If you catch me at the right moment, I might claim that playing a variety of roles is a nuisance, and that if my collaborators were as consistently available as I'd like, I'd much prefer to experience each show from the same vantage point. But of course, a part of me relishes the chance to stretch out, to contort myself into new shapes and positions depending on the night. In its date-to-date fluctuation, the composition of the band mirrors the fluidity of the self. What is the modern existential situation if not staggering in the dark with few solid footholds to rely on, where making ourselves up moment to moment is an adaptive reaction.

Mikiel is one of the musicians joining me tonight. He and I have been friends since high school. We've been in bands together before, and this week he's helping me out with a couple of gigs as a co-vocalist. Right now, that means learning the words to the song we plan to open tonight's show with.

The song in question is blaring from the speakers of his girlfriend's car.

"That reminds me," Mikiel says. "When I was first going over the lyrics, Amber wasn't a big fan of this verse." He means it lightheartedly. Amber nods, a sly smile spreading over her face. There's something startling about another person close-reading your lyrics in real time. It's not as overtly mystical as visiting a psychic, but no less revealing. A third-party reader—and particularly one who knows the songwriter—can pick up themes and preoccupations that reflect the mind that made them.

Mikiel is referring to a verse that goes like this:

Will I end up satisfied
With a wife and a mortgage
And a tire swing outside
With the dreams that I orphaned

I can imagine why Amber might not be enthused with it, and particularly with hearing her boyfriend crooning it at the top of his lungs. The speaker in the song associates family with domestication and domestication with complacency. The three of us are all in our mid-to-late thirties. They're a happy couple trending toward permanence and trying to work out their own pathway to settling down.

"I didn't mean to say that wives and mortgages have a causal relationship with orphaned dreams," I pipe up from the backseat. "I was more thinking about people using their relationships and their financial obligations as an excuse for giving up, rather than those things posing insurmountable obstacles."

It sounds good, but I'm not sure I believe me. My unconscious has probably given something away. There can be a sedentary quality to family life that doesn't, to my mind, jibe easily with getting after it. But do I really see jumping the broom as my personal jumping the shark?

Playfully or not, the two front-seat occupants have ganged up against me and the song. It calls to mind Viriginia Woolf's essay "How Should One Read a Book?" Woolf suggests that the astute reader has motion, too. Good reading asks us to hone a certain interpretive flexibility. "To read a book well, one should read as if one were writing it," Woolf writes.[2] "Begin not by sitting on the bench among the judges but by standing in the dock with the criminal."

Even if my lyrics weren't being parsed by the wary eyes of my bandmate's girlfriend, I'd find the court metaphor apt. A person who ventures to create art and release it to the world is more or less on trial. You plead a case to the globe through your work. You use your wile and guile to rally judge and jury to your side before the gavel goes down. Woolf's framework resonates with me just as much, if not more, as a consumer of art. Joining the artist in the dock before copping a squat next to the judge is a skill that you can practice. Passionate engagement with art and art making has helped me to retain a toggle switch between wide-eyed suggestibility and sober discernment. Maybe I'm biased, but it seems to me that the same mobility of perspective is an asset in love.

Hannah Arendt's theory of "representative thinking" and Woolf's views on reading share a common foundation. They're ways of putting your own personal viewfinder on a dolly. Dolly shots are our best chance at seeing something in other people besides hell. There are some who'd say that empathy is the vehicle for doing so. Representative thinking is distinct from empathy in the sense that it's less acquisitive and more inquisitive. You use your own mind from another person's position. As Arendt puts it, "One trains one's imagination to go visiting."[3] Books can act as critical tools in that training regimen.

So can ghostwriting in rap music. The composition process behind Dr. Dre and Snoop Dogg's 1999 hit "Still D.R.E." is an example of representative thinking in practice. Jay-Z penned the tune as a comeback single announcing Dr. Dre's turn-of-the-century resurgence. The song's lyrics anticipate and disarm detractors who might view the seven-year layoff after 1992's *The Chronic* as evidence that Dre had lost his touch. By stepping up to the microphone again for the first time in nearly a decade, Dre is once more the criminal in the dock. Dre's ghostwriter not only stands beside him in the dock but trains an eye on the judge and addresses his rhymes accordingly. Jay's ability to think from Dr. Dre's position is particularly impressive when you consider the regional affinities of each rapper. Jay-Z's handle comes from the conjunction of the J and Z subway lines near Brooklyn's Marcy Projects. His geography is minted into his brand. In hip-hop annals, New York City and Los Angeles traditionally represent opposing camps. The J and Z rails stretch far enough to traverse the country in Hov's imagination. "Still D.R.E." bounces along on a G-funk cadence and swaggers with West Coast imagery.

"Jay-Z is a great writer himself," Snoop said during an interview with the Breakfast Club.[4] "So imagine him striking it for someone he truly loves and appreciates. He loves Dr. Dre and that's what his pen showed you, that I can't write for you if I don't love you."

Mobility of perspective is like reverse projection. When you project, you take something that's going on with you and saddle another person with it, usually without their consent and often without their knowledge. It figures that there'd be a more generous, outward-looking corollary. A mobile perspective allows you to take what someone else tells you is going on with them and provisionally saddle yourself with it—while bearing in mind that it ultimately doesn't belong to you.

Hip-hop is often viewed as a hotbed of toxic masculinity, but here we are with a hit song that low-key affirms the power of love. Awww. But wait a tick. Why is Jay-Z's mobility of perspective so useful for flowing on beats by Dre but impotent when it comes to *beatings by Dre*? Woolf's criminal in the dock metaphor is apropos in a few ways. The gangsta rap ethos has always rested on criminality. Outlaw figures in rap music are often real-life possessors of considerable rap sheets. In Dre's case, his extracurricular activities have included viciously assaulting ex-girlfriend and fellow musician Michel'le Toussaint and rap pioneer and television personality Dee Barnes.[5] Dre has largely eluded any lasting culpability for either misdeed. Could someone like Jay-Z, with his traveling imagination, think from Barnes's or Toussaint's position? And if he could, how might that exercise alter the love he had for Dre? A mobile perspective and the most pernicious edition of the bro code can apparently coexist, if not reinforce one another. Love is often a form of unwavering partisanship.

In that sense I'm glad to see my bandmate and his girlfriend on the same side about my own song lyrics. It bodes well that they're partisan to each other. What am I partisan to? The road. The chase. The mission. Not necessarily a destination. We use the phrase "settling down" to describe when two people commit to each other and choose a base of operations. Which might suggest that having motion and a steady relationship is a conflict of interest. The genesis of the band All reflects the members' refusal to settle down. After releasing and touring behind seminal album *Milo Goes to College*, Descendents vocalist Milo Aukerman fulfilled the album's prophetic title by pursuing a biology degree full time. He became less available for band activities as a result. The remaining members of Descendents recruited a series of alternate vocalists and relaunched Descendents as a band called All. The name of the new band stemmed from a maximalist philosophy invented by drummer

Bill Stevenson, which centered on achieving one's goals to "the total extent."

All is "a way that I created in dealing with achievement and satisfaction and how the two relate," Stevenson said in an interview with Ragged Press.[6] "Basically just to avoid stagnation. Going for 'ALL' and never being satisfied and just wallowing in your sameness." My admiration for Stevenson's credo influences my life choices to date. I front a band based in New York City and I teach creative writing in St. Louis. Striving for all means grading papers at punk clubs. It means tweaking lesson plans on the plane and heading straight to campus from the airport. It means booking a tour with a rotating lineup because most of the people in my musical orbit are weekend warriors at best. And in love, avoiding stagnation often seems to land me between punk rock and a hard place.

Pursuing my own self-actualization as an artist and thinker has had an admittedly exacting toll on my relationships. During one stretch of my twenties, I lived in five different states in five years. Financing my education and playing in bands more or less necessitated it. I left a trail of dashed romantic hopes in each locale. If I didn't fulfill my potential, I suspected I'd be an ineligible mate, a classically disappointing black male underachiever. At the same time, staying in one place long enough to be with someone would make it difficult to fulfill my potential.

Between all of us serving the endlessly rapacious economic system of capitalism and black people serving a god of abundance, as the Great Bureaucrat is commonly known in African America, the culture I live in does not often acknowledge the existence of finitude.

Maybe that's why Kenneth Koch's poem "You Want a Social Life with Friends" feels like a guiding subtext of my thirties. It's the rebuttal to Stevenson's vision of infinite growth. The poem's speaker warns that there simply isn't enough time in one's life to enjoy romantic love, hard work, and robust friendships all at once. At best, you can have two of the three. I moved to the Midwest for the teaching job about a year and a half into the pandemic. As one might expect, the initial months in a new state were brutally lonely. When I complained to my father, he seemed surprised that I was affected.

"I didn't know you needed people that much, G," he told me, almost sheepishly. Instantly, I felt like a weakling for whining. I knew what he meant. Artists are often loners. But a few hours after we got off the phone, I realized: When it came to Koch's formula, my father had chosen work and love. My mother has been his primary company since he was in his early twenties. My four siblings and I provide backup. When I was growing up, my pops had a signature boast: "All my favorite people live in my house." (Thumping his own chest and affirming the people around him in one fell swoop is one of his best and most characteristic magic tricks.) Baba had designed his life to prevent the scenario I found myself in. I had relocated to a new city for work while single, and during a time when people avoided gathering in large groups for fear of dying. It might not be the case that I "need people" any more than the average person; the social and emotional deficit I was dealing with was, by most reasonable measures, extraordinary. My father's own lifestyle insulates him from loneliness almost comprehensively. So much so that a baseline amount of need for human contact—and keep it a buck, not just contact but love, support, intimacy—struck him as inordinate.

"You Want a Social Life with Friends" has always reminded me of Ned Vizzini's memoir in essays, *Teen Angst? Naaah . . .*[7] The young Vizzini attends Stuyvesant High School in NYC, a specialized college preparatory school with a 3 percent acceptance rate. Early in his high school career, Vizzini is told that surviving Stuy is easy as long as students remember that it comes down to grades, friends, and sleep. The rub lies in accepting that a given student can only have two of the three. Vizzini chooses grades and sleep. The decision models wisdom I admire but rarely muster: constructive submission to finitude.

Between my bandmates and the four people in the band that we're touring with, I have a vibrant social life for at least the next ten days. The verb of choice to describe making music is *play*, but organizing a tour as a DIY punk act in 2024 involves considerable work. Looking at my life through Koch's lens, I can't help but wonder: Did I choose friends and work as my two out of three by default? Or is my interest in (fine—obsession with) creative work a causal factor in my limited love life?

When the tour swings to the Midwest, I open the dating apps. For this leg of the tour, my band and the band we're touring with have rented a van that comfortably seats eight adults. We're somewhere in Iowa, flying down nondescript highways with cornfields on either side of us. I'm not expecting to match or meet up with anyone I might encounter on these apps; my purpose is almost anthropological. OKCupid uses a series of personal questions to recommend potential matches. One of my favorites is, "Would you rather have your dream job or your soulmate for the rest of your life?" I tend to have the highest "match percentage" with bookish, cosmopolitan types who work in arts or nonprofit sectors. A high number of such women indicate that they'd prefer to have their dream job. The import of this pattern is hard to determine without more context, but I have some working hypotheses.

An ex tells me that growing up, she was encouraged to believe that romantic success was largely a crapshoot, and that professional achievement was within her control. Racing after a dream job full tilt, then, was a better allocation of her energy than wishing for Prince Charming on a shooting star. Work represented independence and strength. Relationships connoted submission and immobility. Escaping patriarchy's thrall meant doubling down on capitalism. If my ex's upbringing is a representative sample, it illuminates a lot. For an ambitious, intellectual woman, placing a premium on having a soulmate might feel naive and antiquated. The strategic OKCupid user selects answers that they imagine will appeal to the kind of person they want to attract. Choosing a dream job over a soulmate might be a way to signal that they will not put men ahead of their own interests.

That's fine by me. But philosophically, at least, the question is a no-brainer on my end. I'll go for having a Thelma to my Louise, a snare to my kick drum, a skateboard to my handrail ten times out of ten. Are there actually people on their deathbeds moaning in regret that they didn't work more sixty-hour weeks? I'm not unambitious, pathologically needy, or a suction cup. I would not expect or even want a partner to shove everything in her life aside to accommodate me. Yet, people interest me a lot more than profits. My platonic relationships are more sustaining than anything that has ever happened at a department meeting. I would ideally partner with someone equally attuned to the merits of subjective experience. It's an old problem with some uniquely contemporary wrinkles.

Colloquially, we tend to describe ambitious people as "chasing" their dreams. You don't really hear about folks cultivating their dreams. Or nurturing their dreams. More often than not, having drive is a precondition for having motion. In a feverishly competitive attention economy—where focusing on a task at a time is unusual, let alone focusing on a person—seekers of vibrant, dynamic lives are prone to seeing moving on as moving forward. Consider the player-empowerment era in the National

Basketball Association. Half of the players in the 2017 All-Star Game switched teams within one eighteen-month span. Ever since the free-agent summer of 2010, when former Cleveland Cavaliers icon LeBron James fled Ohio to join a stacked roster in South Beach, elite hoopers jump from team to team with unprecedented regularity, searching for the perfect climate to maximize their endorsement deals and championship rings.

Many have framed this cultural sea change as workers overthrowing their management's despotic rule. Certainly there's something to that, but I doubt the phenomenon is entirely heroic. LeBron and those who followed in his footsteps are all products of the internet age. They, like me, are part of a generation hardwired to expect that there is always something better and brighter elsewhere. On one view, it means we tend to dwell in fairer houses than prose, as Emily Dickinson put it. We embrace boundless possibilities. On another, it means we're primed to sprint for the exits at the first sign of adversity.

The advent of college basketball's transfer portal reflects and encourages the same habits of mind. In 2019, the NCAA created a database that allows schools to confirm that a student-athlete is available to be recruited. Now, student athletes who are dissatisfied with their current schools can publicly signal their intention to transfer, and more immediately, to be courted by other schools. In 2025, more than a thousand Division I ballers entered the transfer portal during the first two days of the thirty-day offseason window alone.[8] When I hear phrases like "the male loneliness epidemic," I wonder how many of those doleful dudes hop into the sexual and romantic transfer portal too hastily. Or were partnered with people who did. Hyper-individualistic values short-circuit love as least as often as fumbling first dates. I think of love as the highest end of a spectrum of prosocial behavior. I'm skeptical that the non-romantic domains in people's lives encourage habits and impulses that are conducive to love.

When briskly dispensing with inadequate settings is evidence of high status, remaining steadfast is read as weakness. In the fall of 2020, my situationship disintegrated at the same time that premier shooting guard James Harden sabotaged his season with the Houston Rockets in the hopes of forcing a trade to his preferred destination. I noted the throughline between Harden's public issues and my private troubles. The prevalence of smartphones means everything is literally at your fingertips. It follows that impatience is a virtue. Whatever fails to immediately gratify is better slashed and burned than troubleshot. We had a few rocky weeks and just like that, dealing with me had gotten old to a woman I hoped to grow old with. Like Harden's soon to be ex-teammates, I couldn't compete with the allure of the other side of the fence. It's hard to bloom where you're supplanted.

Smartphones don't just seduce us with the promise of greener grass. They also disincentivize reflective solitude, without which we're far less likely to cultivate an inner life. In the household I grew up in, when landline phones were still commonplace, it was my responsibility to screen the family's calls. I spent a lot of time reciting the phrase: "I'm sorry, they aren't home right now. Would you like to leave a message?" The whole concept of being "not home" more or less evaporated when I was in high school. We should have fought for its dignity. Between email, text messages, social media, and the decisive erosion of the boundary between home and work, we are accountable to the world around the clock. The phrase *out of pocket* used to mean "unavailable," and now the kids use it to mean "inappropriate." As in, *Bro, I can't believe you said that. That was out of pocket.* The shift in meaning is telling, since it's now inappropriate to be unavailable. I wonder if being on tour is, in some humble and largely symbolic way, a means of being an out-of-pocket conservationist. Introspection improves with remove. Quality of thought surely declines when there are fewer occasions to be truly alone with one's thoughts. Idle hands might be the devil's workshop, but idle time is the heart's renovation project. Chilling in an oversized van carrying two different rock bands, there has generally been more silent contemplation than chatter. The clamor of Midwestern highways and the thrum of the air conditioner deters all but the faintest conversation. When you're on tour, you spend your nights being aurally assaulted by thunderous amplifiers and drums, so you're naturally attracted to monkish quiet during the day to keep your balance. I welcome the opportunity for reverie.

Mobility was a prime consideration when my older brother and I would pick out action figures from the Sears catalog as children. We'd spend hours craning our necks and rotating the delicate Wish Book to see the grainy pictures of superhero toys from different angles. How much do the arms move on this Deadpool toy? Are these startlingly lifelike versions of the Teenage Mutant Ninja Turtles hearty enough to stand up to the elaborate fight sequences we plan to choreograph with them? These speculative exercises were at least as satisfying as actually owning the toys.

Dating apps are in many ways the counterpart of the Sears Wish Book. The same way the photos of clothes, toys, and appliances stirred the yearnings of the wide-eyed consumer, the selfies and bite-size self summaries provide fodder for romantic fantasies. It could explain how scrolling through OKCupid or Tinder or Hinge makes me think about Kung Fu Grip. In 1974, Hasbro outfitted their popular line of toy soldiers with soft rubber hands.[9] The purpose of this design choice was to allow

G.I. Joes to hold their toy weapons better. It had nothing to do with martial arts, but I assume the toy makers named the innovation this way for obvious reasons: It sounds rad. Suddenly, the Joes were better suited for action poses. The added mobility of Kung Fu Grip made the Joes more functional rather than merely ornamental.

I would analogize a G.I. Joe action figure's Kung Fu Grip to a love interest's emotional and intellectual range of motion. When a person is compressed into pixels on a screen, the first thing I wonder about is the degree to which they are limited to the poses they present in. How much can this person move around beyond the confines of the Wish Book? Relational Kung Fu Grip might encompass things like knowing how to ask somebody questions to keep a conversation going, rather than only answering them. It could include the willingness to show vulnerability, or express contrition, or revise one's perception of something when presented with new evidence. A soldier's job is to fight. Kung Fu Grip makes it easier to carry out their raison d'être. Relational Kung Fu Grip likewise streamlines a lover's lot in life. I imagine it as a functional sensitivity, a repertoire of capacities and reflexes that make you a scene partner who can advance the plot. As much as clear skin and a svelte figure are what's hot in the streets, we might all be better off cultivating soft rubber hands.

Remember Curley in John Steinbeck's *Of Mice and Men*? He's the story's antagonist, a boss's son with a Napoleon complex. He gets his shit rocked by otherwise gentle giant Lennie in the book's climax. One of Curley's calling cards is a forerunner to Kung Fu Grip. Curley wears a glove filled with Vaseline on his left hand, supposedly so that some part of him remains soft for his wife. This was, I suppose, the opposite of keeping his pimp hand strong. To some extent I think he has the right idea.

He reconciles two conflicting imperatives: On one hand he's expected to materially provide for his wife, and on the other he must remain supple enough to offer her care and compassion. The arduous life of a migrant ranch worker blunts sensitivity. Preserving some vestige of tenderness in himself would take intention.

Curley's life hack speaks to black men's embattled relationship with softness. In slang, we brandish "soft" as a categorical insult. "Being sensitive" is colloquially understood as being irrational and weak. "Hard" is an all-purpose superlative. It's tempting to believe that African Americans place a heightened emphasis on strength relative to other groups, given the scale of our unique hardships. This framing gives other groups undue credit, though. Earth is a sketchy neighborhood. Some scientists estimate that more than 99 percent of all life that has ever existed on Earth has become extinct. The survival value of grit can cause us to overlook sensitivity's merits, to our collective detriment. The notion that sensitivity and resilience are at odds is a misguided one. All of my favorite people are both sensitive and resilient. I doubt that's a coincidence.

Part of having motion is having range. Maybe it's easier to visit other perspectives when you don't view your identities as pigeonholes. A pliable sense of my race and gender help my imagination mosey. My hands are equally at home rocking the glove filled with Vaseline as they are a set of boxing gloves, sequined gloves, or handcuffs (assuming they are clipped to a headboard and not to a policeman's desk). More importantly, I feel most myself when I can oscillate between these accessories. But to whom is this flexibility a flex, and to whom is it a fault?

In the romantic world and elsewhere, a man willing to behave in unmanly ways is often lauded for being secure with his masculinity. He's so assured of who he is, the thinking goes, that he's comfortable doing things that seemingly contradict who he is. This is funny because masculinity *is* fragile. If masculinity is a social identity, something contingent on both one's self-concept and how one is viewed by others, it's about as solid as soft serve. People will look askance at your manhood for not finishing your french fries.

The popular understanding of masculine security doesn't map onto blackness, which is anything but fragile. A black person who confounds black stereotypes is not credited as secure with his race. He's more likely to be viewed as aspiring to whiteness, fleeing from his blackness, or otherwise betraying his true nature. This is funny because blackness is something you can't actually eschew. You can go full Candace Owens or Tim Scott if you wanna. The security guard still needs to see your receipt. The loan officer still doubts your proof of income. The ER doctor still thinks you're less susceptible to physical pain. Your individual choices can't really attenuate the social and political reality of blackness. The stigma is sticky. You needn't retain your "black card" to get blackballed or blacklisted with the same frequency and intensity as the rest of the melanin contingent.

In terms of criteria for membership, there's a tighter perimeter around manhood. It's like playing hopscotch while bound and gagged. You must plod to particular steps or you lose, but you can't look too balletic while you're at it. (That would be soft, right?) Meanwhile, you can tread anywhere and remain black, but every step is a crack that could break your mother's back. These are treacherous beats to walk. How do you stay footloose enough to love someone?

And yet I want to say I have. The major intersectional dilemma of my life is that I'm magical and a Negro, but definitely not a Magical Negro. Some of us are brave. Spike Lee popularized the term *Magical Negro* on a 2001 lecture tour, during which he noted characters in films like *The Legend of Bagger Vance* and *The Green Mile* as examples of the trope.[10] A Magical Negro is a stock character with unusual insight or seemingly mystical powers who is less a fully dimensional being than a moral tutor for white protagonists. I can see why central casting might dial me up. Their call will always go to voicemail, though. Outwardly I'm one of these furrowed brow types, but most mornings I wake up humming Isaac Hanson's harmonies from "MMMBop."

Later in the week, the van arrives in Lawrence, Kansas. We're playing a late-night show at a bar near the Kansas University campus. Six years ago, I had agreed to come to KU to start a PhD in American studies. I withdrew at the eleventh hour on the admittedly woo-woo basis that something didn't feel quite right. Returning to Lawrence now, more than a half decade later, is like being zapped onto the road not taken. AB, the doctoral student who showed me around during my campus visit back in the day, pulls up to the gig and watches us play. We dap each other and hug as if we've been grad school buddies for years. Maybe it's because of a palpable sense of the alternate universe where that happened.

When I look into the crowd from the stage that night and lock eyes with AB, I feel the collision of what could have been and what is. The twinge is familiar and not entirely unpleasant. In moments of upheaval, people can experience what Kierkegaard called the dizziness of freedom. Breakups have been known to cause that dizziness to spike. It's the overwhelming sensation of authorship; the queasy awareness that many lives are possible, and your decisions will extinguish countless possibilities and actualize just a few.

Those toy workshops at the mall represent the problem in miniature. Instead of Build-A-Bear, it's Build-A-Bearable-Life.

Build-A-Bear workshops present the consumer with four sets of choices. First you choose a furry friend. Which stuffed animal are you going to dress and accessorize? In the second step you pick out clothes and shoes. Then you choose sounds and scents for your bear, and last you choose accessories. As the assembly line chugs along, the customer must commit to one possibility at the expense of another. The threat of buyer's remorse looms at every turn. What if the other furry friend was more suitable for cuddles? Would these accessories actually look better with different clothes and shoes than the ones you snagged? The knowledge that you're creating a toy, and that you'll have to live with the consequences of your own design, makes the process more fraught than going the prefab route.

I suspect that what people call awkwardness is a way of taking a peripheral glance at the dizziness of freedom. Because looking at it head-on would be terrifying, of course. From Issa Rae's memoir *The Misadventures of Awkward Black Girl* to MTV's comedy series *Awkward* to Michael Cera's entire filmography and aura, the state of social discomfort and uncertainty has been played for laughs to great commercial success. But awkwardness always struck me as something more sinister, or at least more serious. It functions like the interpersonal equivalent of rumble strips: You know that you've drifted out of the preferred discursive or behavioral lane when you feel awkwardness creeping in.

Anxiety and awkwardness are understandably dominant headwinds in the digital era. We are more surveilled, more policed, and held to more strenuous standards of perceived virtue than ever. The norms that govern how we're expected to interact are in a state of ever-accelerating flux. Words that have fallen out of favor now aren't merely dated, but problematic. Adhering to tradition is less reliably interpreted as polite, and more often as retrograde.

There's a significant link between awkwardness and what some researchers call homophily, the notion that people tend to prefer and seek out companions they view as similar to themselves. That can include a predisposition to cluster with members of the same gender, race, or perceived social class. This preference is why exchanges across class and race boundaries can often produce feelings of discomfort, stress, and anxiety. Which means that where diversity, equity, and inclusion are points of emphasis, awkwardness is sure to follow.

A black writer and rock musician risks enclosure in a condiment bottle labeled "diversity." I land in samey settings as if yanked from a cupboard, turned upside down, and drizzled liberally to taste. Rather than accept awkwardness as an occupational hazard, I'm keen to see it as an opportunity. Or even, perhaps, a transfer portal through which we might build more bearable lives. The world that could be shimmers at the edge of the world that is, and awkwardness separates the two.

I know it sounds like I'm lecturing from a Sesame Street stoop when I channel Uncle Walt, the ultimate agony aunt. Being curious and not judgmental is a sure route to being more loving and more lovable. That hairy old sage was on to something. In many cases the American preoccupation with awkwardness guarantees that we don't take Unc's advice. If we stigmatize all behavior that isn't immediately comprehensible or situationally appropriate, we privilege judgment as the right and just mode of response and deter curiosity. It's convenience addiction taken to its logical conclusion: We see others as either instantly gratifying or not worth the trouble.

People usually need to feel their feelings to move through them. The prevailing view of awkwardness poses it as a dead end rather than a yellow light. We should grow up. A settler-colonial nation has too many skeletons in its closet to get shook at the rattling of bones.

Before I started teaching full-time, I was a lackey for one of the leading thinkers in intersectionality theory. Comparing converging forms of social difference to an intersection has revolutionized anti-discrimination law. I suggest that another metaphor might forward our ideas about difference and democracy in new and constructive ways.

The longer-term goal should be to view the grid of social difference as a walkable city. You live in a house or an apartment, but your way of life requires access to things like the grocery store, the post office, and the bank. The presence of manageable routes to each of these places raises your overall quality of life, because you don't need to expend tremendous amounts of time or energy to access the things that you need. Hoofing it from place to place creates the opportunity for incidental contact with other community members, which studies show is a key amenity for initiating and strengthening friendships. Living in a city where you need to drive to secure resources means you spend most of your time in a car. Cars are isolating for their occupants and destructive to the broader environment. Car-centric cities breed solipsism, and how could they not? Your mode of transport is a silo.

Sociologists use the term *social location* to describe the combination of factors like an individual's race, gender, economic class, and sexual orientation. Suppose that the various social locations map onto buildings and establishments in a city. To make that city walkable, we'd need to train our imaginations to go visiting the way we'd prime our bodies for pedestrian activity.

No one has a social location that your imagination couldn't visit. Creating a more loving society means figuring out a way to not only view the walk as viable but salutary, because walking is good for your heart.

On the last night of the tour, I spot the frontperson of one of the other touring bands as I'm walking into the venue. I greet her and tell her how excited I am to be sharing a bill tonight. As the two of us load in gear and set up our respective merchandise tables, we talk about a recent interview her band did with a popular punk music publication. In the interview, the singer-guitarist championed an app called How We Feel. The app sends the user prompts a couple times per day that ask the user to assess their emotions. Over time, these self-reports accumulate data and patterns emerge. The app helps users strategize ways for navigating their emotions in the moment.

"I just got a notification from How We Feel a few minutes ago," the singer-guitarist tells me. "I ignored it. At this point in the tour, it's probably better not to check in."

Tonight is her band's last show on the road for the month. I'm too exhausted to index and confront every single negative emotion right now, the lead singer says. The other bands begin setting up their equipment in the front of the house. The lead singer and I discuss how songwriting and performing are ways of sublimating negative emotions.

Like many artists—including the one I'm talking to now—I find that despair and malaise are often catalysts for my songwriting. On stage, I might be performing a song that stems from a deep wound. But once that turmoil has been transposed into song, the pain is allayed with the pleasure of changing tension into resolution. The lead singer agrees.

"Yeah, because whatever chaos might be lurking underneath the song, now that chaos is tempered by a harmonic structure."

Doing justice to the song when I perform it requires me to exist in affective superposition, to embody two seemingly contradictory states at once. I have to inhabit both the angst and its antibodies.

"Sometimes I think about how much healthier it could be to actually identify and deal with those negative emotions when they happen—rather than putting them into songs," the other band's frontperson says.

I actually squint when she says this. It's hard for me to see sublimation as avoidant. To me, she's selling our mutual coping mechanism short. We live under a number of constraints that make it untenable to exhaustively inventory our negative emotions. For the time being, tapping our grief, rage, loneliness, and guilt with Gibson Les Paul magic wands and humming *presto chango* until lightning strikes seems like it'll have to do.

But I'm on the bench with the judge and I haven't yet stood in the dock with the accused. Catching myself, I reorient. The singer-songwriter I'm speaking with is white. The cultural messages that inundate me as a black person tell me, in short, that I stand outside the human circle until further notice. That moral arc I keep hearing about hasn't bent sharply enough to reach justice, so I'm bending six nickel-wound strings to compensate.

The cultural messages addressed to my compatriot here are likely quite different. She's told that the grand game is fixed in her favor, and if she's dissatisfied with it, she needs to fix herself. Of course, it's true that the border between inner and outer turmoil is more porous than that. We are all awash in reasons to turn our lives of quiet desperation into deafening catharsis. But the immensity and permanence of anti-blackness deny me the illusion that a clear enough mind could somehow transcend the need for distorted guitars.

At the end of the night, I review the tour with my drummer. Going forward, he wants to plow through the set list with fewer breaks between songs.

"The main thing I'm trying to avoid up there," he says thoughtfully, "is any amount of dead air. Primarily because the silence makes *me* uncomfortable."

I dare him to lean into it.

SCREEN-TIME REPORT

I periodically rewatch the Showtime television series *Dexter*. In grad school I developed a habit of revisiting it whenever I go through a breakup. These binge watches cause my screen time to skyrocket. The post-pandemic 2020s are an epoch of atomization, a term sociologists use to describe when ties to family, community, and collective identity weaken, leaving detached, self-interested individuals in their wake. Few things encapsulate contemporary atomization like screen-time reports, those unsolicited tallies of slack-jawed inertia. A notification pops up unbidden in the corner of your browser. The irretrievable fraction of your life that you've spent glued to a device, unmoored from the world, is expressed in a statistic, like on the back of a baseball card. The dispatch that follows is another kind of screen-time report, Chavano, but more like one from the front lines of isolation.

On the surface, *Dexter* explores the paradox of a scrupulous serial killer. By day, Dexter Morgan is a thirty-something blood-spatter analyst for the Miami Metro Police Department. By night, he stalks, captures, and kills the city's bad guys. Dexter was forced to witness the gory dismemberment of his mother when he was a toddler. The trauma imprinted him with an irrepressible urge to kill, but with a few exceptions he limits himself to evildoers whom he believes deserve the ultimate punishment. I experience the show as a heavy-handed parable about white supremacy, and a commentary on how the emotional disfigurement of the American psyche stunts our capacity for love. The show makes use of extensive voiceovers because Dexter keeps his serial-killer identity secret. In his internal monologues, Dexter describes himself as empty inside. He repeatedly justifies his bloodlust by claiming that inflicting doom upon villains is the only way he can feel alive. All of which rings to me as a dramatization of the heart-numbing experience of American whiteness. You can't live as the primary beneficiaries *or* victims of brutally repressive structural racism without strip-mining your nervous system. *Dexter* is a reflection of this truth told slant. Watching the show contextualizes the social climate I live in and the conditions that heighten the difficulty of finding and sustaining human connection.

Since debuting in 2006, the show has amassed more than 125 episodes across its four iterations: the original Showtime series, the *New Blood* miniseries, the prequel series *Original Sin*, and the sequel *Resurrection*. The story's central ruse is a delicate one. For his adventures to continue, Dexter must retain a facade of innocence while racking up an ever larger and more conspicuous body count. This would not be possible without quite a bit of what critics call plot armor, the phenomenon in fictional stories where protagonists are allowed to survive threats because the narrative would otherwise die with them. Dexter's industrial-strength plot armor represents the resilience and longevity of white supremacy. He's a symbol of the perceived invincibility of white masculine power.

Of the four principal characters of color, three figure out that Dexter is a serial killer and lose their lives for trying to hold Dexter accountable for his crimes. While these characters of color are presented in a sympathetic light, the mechanics of the plot require their destruction to insulate Dexter from ever experiencing proportionate consequences for his actions. The first character to see through Dexter's affable guise is Sergeant James Doakes, a fierce detective and military vet known for his rippling biceps and bombastic personality. He's one of two black male employees of Miami Metro with speaking roles. Both of them die violently in ways that protect Dexter's secret and advance the plot.

Their deaths parallel what comic book writer and critic Gail Simone calls *fridging*. Simone coined the term in 1999 to describe a trend in comics in which female characters endure gratuitous harms like maiming, torture, and death as plot devices to serve the male hero's journey. The word *fridging* stems from a tragic incident in "Forced Entry," *Green Lantern* vol. 3, #54, in which the ring-wielding superhero comes home to find that an adversary has murdered Green Lantern's girlfriend and stuffed her into a refrigerator. The fridging phenomenon in comics speaks to the ways that women and girl characters are often positioned as afterthoughts, intuitive targets for graphic and irreversible injury, and mere means to other characters' ends rather than ends in themselves. It may seem counterintuitive that two black *men* on *Dexter* are vulnerable to fridging, but white patriarchy often disempowers black men and boys in ways that resemble travesties perpetrated against women of all races. It's ironic and lamentable that this shared predicament rarely foments a feminist anti-racist solidarity between black men and women broadly.

As early as the pilot episode, Doakes recognizes Dexter's phony smile and habitual purchase of donuts for his colleagues as deceptive tactics. Doakes is viscerally affected by Dexter's insincerity: The titular character gives him "the fucking creeps." The sense that something is off, even if it's not clear exactly what, recalls the experience of being a black child in an anti-black environment. You might not have yet developed the critical consciousness to explain why the people around you feel vaguely distant and conniving, but the gut-level awareness is there. By the middle of season two, Doakes has substantiated his suspicions about Dexter when he catches the latter disposing of a corpse in the swamp.

Doakes and Dexter parallel critics of racism and racism's deniers. When Dexter's season-two love interest, Lila West, realizes that Dexter is a serial killer and that Doakes is onto him, she fridges Doakes rather than allow him to bring Dexter to justice. The brief conversation between Doakes and Lila before she offs him is chilling. Lila finds Doakes locked in a cage inside a cabin in the Everglades. Doakes explains that he urgently needs help. Dexter has trapped him there because Doakes has evidence that Dexter is a serial killer.

"Poor thing," Lila oozes. "All alone."

Doakes reassures her that he's fine, but he just needs her to open the cage.

"Not you," Lila corrects him. "Dexter."

Lila fully absorbs that her boyfriend is an unrepentant murderer, and her heart swells with pathos for him. She has no such sympathy for the black man that her boyfriend has wrongfully imprisoned. Doakes, who has been chained up like a dog for several days, is too exhausted to act particularly outraged. He asks if Lila is Dexter's accomplice, and she tells him that she's Dexter's soulmate. Though white women, who suffer under white patriarchy themselves, are sometimes framed as idle bystanders in a system of racial oppression that advantages men, the scene demonstrates how and why they often enter the fray with frightening zeal. Not only are many members of American society conditioned to more readily empathize with a white kidnapper than a black captive; racial chauvinism can and often does motivate white women to deliberately protect the interests of a white criminal at the expense of a black victim.

Dexter himself is reluctant to kill Doakes without cause aside from pure self-preservation. In an example of the title character's extensive plot armor, Lila conveniently eliminates the threat so Dexter can maintain a pretense of nobility. Some fans argue that Doakes deserves his fate because of morally questionable activity during his time as an operative for the US Army Rangers, which occurs off screen before the Showtime series' chronology begins. In season one, Doakes takes out a Haitian military officer and later, a fellow former operative. Both killings occur in the line of duty and are ruled as self-defense. Dexter doesn't personally see Doakes's death as warranted, so he's relieved that Lila took the dilemma out of his hands.

"[My father] always said there were plenty of people who deserved to die," Dexter recalls. "But no matter how hard I close my eyes and wish, Doakes isn't one of them."

When viewers insist otherwise, I'm reminded of the *New York Times* article that described teenager Michael Brown of Ferguson, Missouri, who was shot to death by police officer Darren Wilson in the summer of 2014, as "no angel." Anything short of cherubic innocence exonerates a white person for killing a black person, even if both are fictional characters.

Partially due to Dexter's own frame job, the Miami Metro Police Department determines that the late Doakes, not Dexter, was the serial killer known as the Bay Harbor Butcher. Dexter's ability and willingness to pawn decades of his personal misdeeds off on a slain black man mirrors the racist civilization that blames centuries of subjugation and terror on black inferiority instead of white depravity.

The lore about *Dexter* suggests that, initially, some people in the television industry were skeptical that viewers could connect with a character who teeters on a bloody knife's edge between murderer and vigilante antihero. The creators imagined they were pushing the envelope. But only someone with an ahistorical reading of the US could legitimately view Dexter's popularity as a surprise. A settler-colonial country is predisposed to root for a serial killer who fancies himself a do-gooder. When it comes to the variety of psychic gymnastics necessary to convince yourself that one who seeks out and enjoys avoidable, self-serving violence is actually heroic, Americans are Simone Biles.

One of the most baldly allegorical scenes in the show's history takes place in season two. Doakes confronts Dexter in the latter's private lab at the police station. The two men are alone, and the other Miami Metro employees are out of earshot for the moment, so Dexter allows himself to unmask and taunt Doakes candidly.

"No matter what you try, no matter when, no matter how hard you work," Dexter says smugly, "I'll always be a step ahead of you for one simple reason."

"And what's that?" Doakes asks.

"I own you," Dexter says, punctuating the pronouncement by viciously headbutting Doakes in the face.

As Doakes recoils in pain and shock, Dexter exits his lab and calmly strolls past his colleagues en route to the elevator. Doakes recovers and sprints after Dexter in a blind rage. Against his better judgment, he suplexes a cowering, fake-whimpering Dexter and rains blows down on him until two fellow police break it up. As the onlookers see it, the muscular, perpetually scowling Doakes is the aggressor. Dexter masquerades as a self-described "lab geek." This persona predisposes Lieutenant María LaGuerta, the show's most prominent black Latina character, to interpret the skirmish unfolding in front of her office door as a case of brawn-on-brains crime. María takes Doakes's gun, badge, and police ID and punishes him with administrative leave.

Doakes and María are close friends outside of work, and it's strongly hinted that they're former flames. Just as Lila, Dexter's girlfriend during this season, instantly falls into step with Dexter's caper against Doakes, María aids and abets the title character as well, albeit for vastly different reasons. Male characters on the show consistently question the merit of her professional ascension. At least two other high-performing woman cops angle to topple and replace María in side plots throughout the show. It's clear that María feels some amount of sexist pressure to steer the department with an unwavering hand. Between that context and the typical credulity extended to white folks when it is their word against a black person's, María has ample incentive to ask minimal questions about the showdown between Dexter and Doakes, and to come down hard on the sergeant in front of his peers. Whatever racial chauvinism might otherwise induce María to take Doakes's side is for the moment tempered by other variables. *Dexter* grants us no access to Doakes's interiority, so we don't know if the supposition that he is Dexter's possession rang to Doakes as a racist dog whistle. When he says his ownership of Doakes is permanent and insurmountable, Dexter essentially breaks the fourth wall and echoes writer and theorist Saidiya Hartman, who coined the phrase "the afterlife of slavery" to describe how the chattel regime's lengthy tentacles continue to throttle black life in the present.

People of color looking for love in America do so while balancing their responsibilities as supporting characters in a 250-year-old *Dexter* episode. White people seeking the same are hardly unscathed. Their own hearts wither under the weight of being conscripted from birth into the elaborate and enervating project of getting away with murder.

SHTICK SHIFT

Sometimes when people are talking about their difficulty locating themselves in some kind of dyad—are they an introvert or an extrovert, are they more masc or more femme, are they from where they are born or better understood as part of a diaspora, are they poor because they grew up poor or middle class as they are now, sheesh how confounding—I feel like we almost forget that we came from two parents. You're at the very least a synthesis of two immediate ancestors. You wouldn't say, "I feel so trapped between worlds—it's like I'm part my father and part my mother!" It should be obvious and actually regular to be not quite A and not quite B but some indeterminate combination that in one moment more resembles this and in another favors that. Yet it's so common to behave as if someone not being flush with various neat poles is some striking novelty or vexing conundrum. Being chimerical isn't freakish. It's the baseline.

Maybe for the same reason, I struggle with the concept of personal authenticity. In the punk scene, the worst thing you could be in the late '90s and early 2000s was a poser. Posers lacked cred. They were unthinking copycats who mimicked whatever was socially expedient to align with. I was seldom called one; there wasn't much social capital to be gained from pretending to be a black punk. But I was skeptical that posers deserved so much vitriol. Couldn't posing be a way of learning by doing? What begins as a pose might become a comportment that feels as true and real as a home. Adherence to a trend can express an honest part of someone's inner world, even if it isn't the whole. As for those of us who resonated deeply with the punk ethos, we probably developed our lingo, clothes, record collection, and philosophy by first cribbing from some admired elder in the scene. Posing can be a route to refining a sense of personal taste. Maybe more importantly, it can be fun. Why not rent an identity you're not ready to own? There's room for imaginative play between Halloweens.

Poser has gone the way of *sellout* in the 2020s. No one playing the dozens is launching either term to demoralize their opponent. Neither insult can retain its bite with everyone archiving selfies and consolidating their personal brands. Calling something "performative" has emerged as a substitute. It's the fashionable term for deriding behavior that seems too contrived, calibrated for the approval of an audience, or conscious of how it's likely to be received.

I often get the sense that other people see the self as something that exists in platonic form. There's a nonphysical, immutable, absolute identity somewhere outside of reality. The corporeal you is responsible for representing that platonic form with perfect fidelity. When you fail to do so, you're being performative.

But I'm performative, and a poser, and a sellout. The self isn't something I can just be. It's more like a vehicle I pilot manually, shifting shticks when the road calls for it. Or when I can't help it.

What follows is like a cross between a self-interview and a parlor game. Below you will find a series of prompts that frame personality as a set of gears, as well as my answers. I invite my readers to fill out shtick shifts of their own. May it help you to discover the fellow travelers who are most your speed. Or at least share the road graciously with those who aren't.

1ST GEAR—0 TO 10 MILES PER HOUR

When driving a manual, you use first gear each time you start the vehicle from a stop. Choose a piece of media—a poem, a song, a scene from a movie, a meme, etc.—that you see as a point of departure for your personality.

If a high number of total lifetime hours spent listening to Christian pop punk is a boon to my chances of acceptance at the pearly gates, I've got a shot. It's probably my strongest argument for making the cut. I've been an ardent fan of MxPx, a scrappy melodic punk trio from Bremerton, Washington, since middle school. The members of MxPx assembled and earned renown during their own tween years, when all three were still Sunday school regulars. They've kept pumping out songs and going on tours for thirty-two years and running. Over the course of their twelve studio albums, you can track their ideological evolution (er . . . intelligent designs?) from being hardcore Bible-thumpers, to wishy-washy spiritualists, to outright nonbelievers. Their discography is like if your buddy from homeroom kept a journal for three decades and let you read it. You can hear the gradual movement from songs of innocence to songs of experience. As their catalog of the latter grew, traditional faith phased out.

I was particularly taken with an early MxPx track called "The Aspect" back in the day. I knew that in the song's grungy chorus, vocalist/bassist Mike Herrera meant to say that because he is a friend of Jesus, he will never be lonely, regardless of whether he is embraced by his peer group. It was, to me, a startlingly acute sentiment for a tenth grader. The members of MxPx are about ten years older than I am. I read up on the band

and learned that Herrera had written the song when he was around sixteen, the same age I was as a listener. At that time in life, most people I knew seemed to be curating their personalities based on whatever they thought would earn a consistent seat at the coolest lunch table in our cafeteria. I was powerfully moved by "The Aspect," but a more secular twist on the basic idea was what resonated. I interpreted the song to say that my seeming isolation in the present was an illusion because I walked in the footsteps of countless like-minded others. (Who were the others? I didn't know, but I sensed them.)

Don't fear the social costs of nonconformity, I heard Herrera saying, because what might alienate you from your surroundings brings you closer to who you're supposed to be. I bought it. This conviction acted for me as a kind of spiritual wealth. To this day I move through the world with the sensation of having a spectral cohort as backup. Maybe these furtive tagalongs are ethereal ancestors, descendants, compatriots, and omens of friends I've yet to meet. Hearing "The Aspect" helped me to give these feelings a name.

I spent the first half of my childhood in urban North St. Louis and the second half in a coastal suburb. Much later, I returned to St. Louis as an adult. I now reside within walking distance from the ritzy, exclusive school where I teach. When you escape the tendrils of Moloch draining energy, resources, and hope from the old neighborhood, you owe at least a sidelong glance at those still writhing in its clutches. Suppose fortune had frowned upon you in some instance when it happened to crack a smile. You might be in their place and they might be in yours.

An older black man pacing the street caught my eye on my way to work one morning. We struck up a conversation and he told me that he'd recently finished doing a bid. The man had been arrested for selling weed in his teens. Because of a series of legal complications and his inability to pay for a proper lawyer, he'd been locked up for nearly forty years. Now he'd returned to the outside for the first time in decades, where earning money legally proved difficult. He described the Kafkaesque riddle of trying to find legitimate work as an ex-con. A potential employer had offered to bring him on if he could provide identification. It was hard to get identification at the DMV without a permanent address, and having a permanent address was tricky to secure without a job.

The simplest solution, he told me, would be to find a wealthy elderly woman and knock her over the head before robbing her. Occam's Razor wouldn't cut it, though.

"I can't do that, because there is no way to hurt her without hurting all of us," he concluded.

I nodded, rapt by this pavement prophet who went from living behind bars to dropping them. Humanity's interconnectedness preoccupies me, too. A felt sense that violence begets violence, that malice multiplies itself, is part of what I can only describe as spiritual wealth. The MxPx song came back to my mind in a new light, this time as a credo of transcendental unity. What's perpetrated against the few comes back on the many. Shunting people aside into the carceral system affects those of us on the outside. Families and support networks suffer most immediately, but that suffering reverberates. Criminalizing and imprisoning more of our own people than any other country in the history of the world coarsens our collective character.

I wondered how this man knew what he knew. Did his time in prison refine his vision? Does losing access to the soil heighten access to the soul? It's hard to believe that incarceration is in any way rehabilitative. At the same time, if deep reverence for human interdependence—as this newly freed person seemed to have—permeated the United States, there would be less of a need for prisons in general. Where does someone go in this country to acquire the spiritual know-how that this man brought home from the joint? What do we lose when there's no consensus stronghold of that consciousness? Christian pop punk isn't going to do it for everyone.

CLUTCH

The clutch pedal is what enables a driver to switch gears smoothly. Tell me something about you that defies summary or generalization. Own up to your versatility, your both-and, neither-nor qualities that might otherwise escape the eye.

It would be so clutch to have a sexual orientation. As in, a counterpart to freshman orientation. Not one of those increasingly byzantine modifiers like demisexual or pansexual or sapiosexual. No. See, a big, introductory meeting about sex orchestrated by experts would fix me. Charts, graphs, helpful hints, tips and tricks conveyed with a hortatory tone. Public school health class ain't that. I need something more like the beginning of the music video for Prince's 1994 Valentine's Day release, "The Most Beautiful Girl in the World." In the video's opening scene, a futuristic voice promises a beautiful experience of comprehensive instruction on everything from courtship to fetishes to love and hate.[1] A learning module arranged and facilitated by Prince, who used gender as a playground and defied categories like straight and gay, would be expansive enough to cover the gamut.

The *Q* in LGBTQIA is sometimes understood to mean "questioning." I've been aware of being in that bucket for a number of years. I thought that question mark would turn into a period eventually. Frantz Fanon famously concludes *Black Skin, White Masks* with the prayer, "O my body, make of me always a man who questions!"[2] My body has clearly endeavored to do that, but somehow I don't think this is what Fanon meant.

In the title sequence of the sci-fi television series *The Greatest American Hero*, protagonist Ralph Hinkley loses the instructions to a superpowered suit provided to him by benevolent aliens. The suit gives him special abilities. Without the instructions, though, he's flying by the seat of his extraterrestrial pants. In one episode, he accidentally discovers that he can use the suit to make himself invisible. In another, he realizes he can start fires with his mind. These properties of the suit only reveal themselves when Ralph stumbles into circumstances that activate them. My experience of sexuality mirrors Ralph's experience with his suit. Like the suit, my body responds unpredictably to the scenarios I find myself in, usually without pattern or warning. Trial and error has helped me to recover some semblance of what the instruction manual might have conveyed. Just as Ralph faced an array of unknown unknowns every time he tapped into hero mode, I'm still never totally sure what I'm in for when I date. Over the course of his various adventures, Hinkley's superpowered alter ego never gets a handle. He experiments with calling himself "Captain Crash" and "Captain Gonzo" but a label never sticks.

Predictably, my touch-and-go relationship with touching mostly didn't go well. Beautiful Experiences were rare. The second or third time I had sex, I thought I could grit my teeth and get through it without incident.

"What are you doing?" the woman I dated all through college asked me. I stood with my back to her in the spartan scenery of my Harlem apartment share. She propped herself up on one elbow in my bed. We'd been together for several years but mostly avoided having intercourse. This was one of the few occasions where we tried to do so. *Tried* being the operative word because instead of being excited about the encounter, I was having a panic attack. And then, mid-attack, scolding myself for not being able to perform a function that mass culture swore all men were champing at the bit to indulge in, at all times.

"Self-flagellating," I told her darkly.

"Oh. Farting?" she said, giggling.

"If only," I muttered, unable to meet her gaze.

Flatulence would be an easier fix. Instead, we had a missed connection on two fronts. How fitting that verbal misunderstanding and sexual misalignment coincided so neatly. As above, so below.

For much of my twenties and early thirties, my partners entertained various explanations for our low-voltage sex lives. The possibility that I might be asexual and/or agender usually came up, but I was disinclined to see sexual identity as a static category.

In most of these thought experiments, the problem was implicitly . . . me. Maybe I didn't fully identify with the body I lived in, which made it hard to express myself physically. Maybe I didn't experience attraction in the normative way. In New York City, this was a popular and nearly ubiquitous way of theorizing by the mid-2010s. Never mind that patriarchy is what makes us imagine cis men as unconditionally ravenous for sex. Can I both capitulate to this trend and criticize it?

Yes, of course. I'm knocking it and trying it at the same time. I'm not binary.

2ND GEAR—3 TO 25 MILES PER HOUR

As you begin to accelerate and get in the stride of your journey, you might use second gear as a transitional mode. What's a shtick you shift into when you're starting to rev up? Name something you've nicked from someone else that has since become a standard part of your repertoire.

There's a tradition where guys who peaked in high school continue to call a middle-aged ex-quarterback the initials QB after they are decades removed from their gridiron glory years. Or at least I think it's a tradition. Maybe I'm making a faulty extrapolation from the *Friday Night Lights* TV show. I can't say I actually gather round at local watering holes with burly men in scuffed letterman jackets often enough to know for sure. In either case, I have schemed to caricaturize that idea by continuing to call one of my dear friends "EIC" well into adulthood. Because all sports clichés need nerdy counterparts. This friend was editor in chief of the *Blake Beat*, the award-winning high school newspaper we both worked on for three years as teens. In truth, though, our mutual connection to journalism began even before that. EIC and I met as eleven-year-olds when we attended a "humanities and communication magnet program" together in middle school. The magnet metaphor referred to the fact that the school drew promising humanities-minded students from across the school system, rather than from the elementary school that fed directly into ours. Since we lived near each other, EIC and I took multiple buses to and from school every day, and our friendship ripened through the solidarity of those rides. EIC had a hilarious and slightly annoying habit of pretending to stick a microphone in your face after she asked you a question.

"Who do *you* think our best candidate is for class president this year?" she'd say, extending her hand and curling her fingers around the mic's imaginary handle.

We're all made up of bits of other people, consciously or not, and I've nicked this move from EIC quite deliberately. Mid-conversation my wrist will shoot out before I can stop it, like the mandible of a discursive Venus flytrap. My interlocutors tend to pause in confusion. Then they aim their words a few inches above my cupped hand. If they know me well, the pause is often followed by a knowing and playfully exasperated smirk. I emulate EIC in this way for a few reasons. First, it's a tribute. EIC grew up to become, among other things, a Public Media Journalists Association editor of the year winner. She's a badass and I admire her. Second, I'm a subjectivity voyeur. I catch myself staring at the temples of other people's heads the way an oversexed teenager lingers at the threshold of the girls' locker room. *So this is where it all happens.* I picture everybody's brain as the inside of a cockpit. I want to know what switches and knobs are on everyone's inner central console. To whatever extent possible I would like to know how it feels to occupy that cockpit, to manage its fuel, hydraulics, and pressurization. You may have heard of the philosophical problem of other minds, which supposes that because you don't have direct access to anybody's interiority except your own, you can't be entirely sure that anybody else has consciousness at all.

I think about this a lot, except to me the condition it describes is less a problem than a prism through which other minds become exotic, alluring frontiers. Teeing up the microphone EIC-style is a request for access to that frontier. It's body language meant to say, ahem, raise the blinds on your inner life, please. Okay yes, maybe I'm a cognitive Peeping Tom, but in a harmless, not-creepy way, I promise. Which, of course, speaks to the third reason I use EIC's move so often. The invisible microphone gag is strange and off-putting. When much of your time is spent cornering people and asking them probing questions, you need a reliable source of comic relief.

3RD GEAR—15 TO 45 MILES PER HOUR

3rd gear is the one you use when driving at medium speed. It's best for cruising or passing other cars on the road. Share something that you've done to put distance between yourself and others.

Any time I'm involved with a surprise party, I'm constantly amazed at how bad other people are at hiding and being quiet. I choose to see this as heartening. It might mean that if and when my friends conspire to murder me, the scheme will be sloppy and poorly executed.

I'm guilty of losing the plot myself sometimes. For example, the social scripts at jobs always confuse me. I have trouble forgetting that my colleagues have many impersonal reasons to tolerate each other. All of our interactions feel like they're taking place on a sitcom set or something. It's not the artificiality itself that bothers me; it's when the artificiality goes completely unacknowledged. Once, I was a part of an office culture in which the small number of people on deck would coordinate celebrations for each colleague's birthday. I had great fun helping to plan and carry out festive activities for other people's birthdays. But when my own birthday approached, I was filled with dread. I was nervous about pretending to be honored that a group of people thought of me when I knew they felt obligated to do so. Simulating intimacy with people I didn't choose to be close with gave me the heebie-jeebies.

I decided to head off my own office birthday party at the pass by writing a play about it. In drafting the play, I drew on my passing familiarity with playwrights like Eugène Ionesco and Tom Stoppard. I could never quite wrap my head around the notion that their work was "absurdist." They just seemed like perceptive realists.

About two weeks before my birthday, I circulated the script in an email chain and asked my colleagues to begin learning their lines. They generally weren't thrilled with the idea. Some bristled at taking on unnecessary labor. Others appeared to recognize and resent the ploy for what it was: a stylized stiff-arm deflecting even the faint possibility of genuine connection. I might not be as good at hiding and being quiet as I'd like to think.

WORK BIRTHDAY

K: He should be here any minute. Let's arrange ourselves now so that when he walks in, we're all poised to shout "happy birthday" and do so with a tone and affect that indicates that we care about him, and that we're certainly not going through the motions of performing a ritual or observing a norm just because we work with this person every day and it could be professionally costly to alienate him. Okay? Muster some "oomph" behind these scripted words. Conjure up some luster in your eyes when you say them.

N: Well, I appreciate you raising that, but my participation in this is definitely phoned in. I mean, if I could be anywhere else, doing anything else, I would. But we do work with him and because of the way this society is set up, I have to make money, and since I have to make money, I have to be here, and since I have to be here I might as well fucking plaster a smile on and cosplay some modicum of warmth.

J: Samesies.

M: This is a professional development opportunity for you all. After all my years in this business, method acting my way through public displays of affection is my love language. So for those of you who still have fully functional limbic systems, think of this as like a Duolingo activity to help you get fluent.

K: Indeed! Tell those pheromones to let my people go.

J: I prefer to approach it like emotional karaoke. The familiarity with the real thing allows the spectator to mentally compensate for the inevitable deficiency of the imitation. The point is not to achieve perfect correspondence with the genuine article, but to bastardize it gently enough that a drooling, buzzed person could plausibly confuse the two. Light work.

M: OW, OW!

N: Shh, shh, here this motherfucker comes! Places, people.

J: Whose birthday is it again?

M: I believe it's Cambridge Analytica.

Enter G.

G: Morning, all—whoa!

M: You've been selected to lead the conference call this afternoon! I don't feel like doing it!

K: No, that's not it.

N: Surprise—you're undergoing an impromptu performance review!

K: Also wrong. What they mean is, your ass is fired!

G: Uh—I guess I thought . . . you were surprising me for my birthday.

J: Sweet baby ISIS, it's his birthday!

M: Happy birthday! We've demonstrated our appreciation for you by hanging decorations and screaming at you in unison upon your arrival at a destination you're required to come to. Do you yet feel Loved Sufficiently? Can we abandon this pretense and restore our undivided attention to profit making? No rush, take your time!

N: Wait, it's his birthday? That's all? I had my hopes up for an active shooter situation.

BLACKOUT

4TH GEAR—30 TO 65 MILES PER HOUR

The penultimate gear is suited for town and city driving. Describe an instance when you were tempted to floor it but ultimately held back to navigate the traffic. Tell me about a time when you were a little truer to yourself than was appropriate for the setting.

At a job interview, one of the interviewers mentioned how much he enjoyed Paul Beatty's novel *The Sellout*. His co-interviewer quickly agreed.

"Oh yes, a classic," she said breathlessly.

"I'm always interested in what people mean when they say that," I blurted, against my better judgment. "A black author writes a book that deals in part with a black drug dealer reviving slavery, and the book is applauded far and wide. If that's not an enthusiasm that calls for some unpacking, I don't know what is."

Chatty Interviewer blinked rapidly, exchanged an uneasy glance with Less Chatty Interviewer.

"Well, I imagine everyone is responding to Paul's genius," one of them began slowly.

"That's what captivated me about the book," the other put in.

"Genius at communicating what?" I pressed, like a dummy. "I wonder if, in everyone's eagerness to show us that they're in on the joke, they pass up any scrupulous examination of what the joke actually is."

Chatty Interviewer cleared his throat.

"Mr. Asim, if I may, uh—let's go over your CV, shall we?"

I guess I don't need to tell you that I didn't get the job.

5TH GEAR—45 MILES PER HOUR OR OVER

This gear is ideal for open road driving. What does it look like when you're in overdrive? Tell a story depicting your full-throttle personality.

A few months into the first Trump presidency, I was studying at the campus writing center one afternoon when an Israeli classmate sidled up to me. She was eager to recount a dream she'd had the previous night. I can't explain to you how I knew what the dream was going to be about, but I had a hair-raising proleptic moment where I was instantly sure the dream would involve two things: white enslavement and a romantic subplot between myself and the classmate.

It was not the kind of story I wanted in my Netflix queue, but I readily granted her the floor. In general, I'd rather listen than talk, and maybe that's asking for trouble. My classmate began telling her tale. The dream took place in an apocalyptic world. The American social fabric had unraveled and white folks became public enemy #1. Militarized police began rounding up and exterminating white people. Those not eliminated on sight were forced into segregated labor camps. My classmate's husband became a casualty of this racial terror program, so she remarried and went into hiding with her new husband. Eventually, the anti-white gestapo discovered the couple's hiding place. Her alarm clock buzzed just when my classmate's tormentors were knocking furiously on her and her new husband's door. The part of "new husband" was played by one G'Ra Asim.

You don't need to be a scholar in Freudian analysis to grasp the relevance of this dream. It figures that someone born and raised in Israel would entertain an elaborate persecution fantasy. My classmate grew up in an ethno-nationalist state made possible by Palestinian dispossession. That state justifies its existence by rehearsing the bloody history of global antisemitism. Narratives of hard-earned survival and return underwrite the nation's ethos. In adulthood, my classmate came to the US to further her education, where she was absorbed into American whiteness. We were both in our late twenties when this conversation occurred. In my classmate's young life, she'd already been a patrician of two different settler-colonial projects famously adept at sweeping their origins and shadows under the rug. Some projection was inevitable. When her nocturnal writer's room got to work, they displaced her feelings about identity-based harm so that she was only the recipient and not the vessel. I waited until my classmate broke eye contact. Then I shook my head vigorously. It didn't dislodge the image of her mobilizing this dream in a speech at some bizarro March on Washington.

But then there was the matter of my cameo. There was no flirtation or chemistry between us as far as I knew. Yet, in the wake of her spouse's murder at the hands of the state, her subconscious called me up from the minors. Maybe marrying black was a defensive maneuver in the anti-white dystopia she cooked up. I didn't have to ask to find out.

"[My man] was dead," my classmate said simply. "You're the smartest guy I could think of, so you made sense as a successor."

This was towering condescension masked as flattery. I'd heard enough about her real-life incumbent to know he wasn't chosen based on his IQ. A black hopeful would have to meet different criteria, like being exceptional enough at something to compensate for his race. Of course, in reality, I wasn't hopeful in the first place. She'd breezily concluded that her whiteness alone would be too tantalizing to resist.

The entire imbroglio was somehow personal and structural at the same time. I'm often mistaken for what I call a *swirlboss*—a black person not only predisposed to date white people but one who imagines doing so is a progressive and righteous enterprise regardless of the terms under which such relationships take place. The term *girlboss* emerged in 2014 to describe accomplished women in traditionally male-dominated fields. It has since been ironized. Now, a girlboss is more commonly a would-be symbol of female empowerment who replicates the abusive and self-serving behaviors stereotypically associated with male leaders. The same way feminist progress isn't always what it seems, interracial relationships aren't necessarily anti-racist. Swirlbosses confuse mutual fetishization for the realization of MLK's dream. Though I have dated black as well as non-black people, I see the matter with considerable nuance. I'm like a post–*SFFA v. Harvard* admissions committee; I use holistic review. To the extent that anyone consciously controls the rubrics of their heart, I'm drawn to the individual as a whole. Nevertheless, the sum of my appearance and demeanor is taken as a tell promising otherwise. The least obtrusive blackness is easily transfigured into blankness, a smooth canvas beckoning to host shadows.

TRICKLE-DOWN EXCEPTIONALISM

One sweltering August day I stood in my parents' kitchen, where my older brother Joe and I were helping them move houses. My mother had hired movers, so Joe and I collaborated with those two men to pack the family's belongings onto a U-Haul truck. Afterward, my mother wanted to know if we'd noticed anything about the pair we'd been loading boxes with.

"Did the two movers seem like brothers to you?" my mother asked.

"They seemed like light-skinned dudes," Joe said. "Maybe they could be from Brazil or something."

There was a beat before Mom registered Joe's confusion.

"No. I mean, did they seem related? As in related to each other. Actual *brothers.*"

It turns out that they were. Mom was asking to determine whether her two sons had noticed that they were teamed up with another set of brothers. Joe had thought she was asking whether the movers were black men.

"That happens so often in this family," Mom said wryly. "We don't think like most other people."

A few days later I was loitering outside of a gig before my band's set began. My bandmate Rhiana, their boss Donna, and our friend and fellow musician Jamilah were chatting about the infused bakery that Donna and Rhiana operate together uptown. The air conditioner at the shop had broken earlier that day. The store's co-owner is a man of about forty-five. Donna, the other co-owner, was disappointed that the man was no help.

"I couldn't fix an air conditioner even in my prime," he'd told Donna dismissively.

"This man is forty-five. He's *in* his prime," Donna complained.

Rhiana, Jamilah, and I agreed.

"He's barely ten years older than I am," Donna went on. "You want to claim your prime was when you were twenty-two or some shit?"

Jamilah was wearing a T-shirt advertising a band called Middle-Aged Queers. I remarked that the band should actually be called Queers in Their Prime. Jamilah blinked, not comprehending. She started to explain the origin of the band. They're a supergroup of familiar names from the Bay Area punk scene who put in serious work in their previous bands, she told me. The band's handle is in reference to their veteran status.

I clarified that I was just connecting Jamilah's shirt to Donna's insistence that someone forty-five years old is in their prime.

"Oh," Jamilah said, laughing. "I definitely didn't get that but I get it now. Well, I have another shirt that says, 'Girls Love My Autistic Swag.' So, yeah."

This was a way of saying that she hadn't understood the (admittedly not hilarious) quip because of her autism. I wonder if the knee-jerk inclination to self-exceptionalize diminishes our ability to connect with others. Yes, Jamilah has autism, and yes, my family is unquestionably a bit unusual. But conversational miscues are a giant part of being around other people. Everyone is struggling to understand everyone else every day. Words are ambiguous. Well-intentioned communicators are often opaque without trying to be. Language is a pale shadow of our interior lives. At best, the most elegant sentence is a wispy filament connecting one mind to another. That connection can be blown asunder with the faintest breath. I can't shake the suspicion that we would hold each other a little tighter if we didn't confuse boilerplate human experience with extenuating circumstances (autism, weirdness). Being a person is the extenuating circumstance.

According to Andscape, as of 2020 "the number of love songs by black artists on the Hot 100 has fallen from one or two dozen per year in decades past to an average of five per year since 2015." Though the total number of black artists featured has risen, the fraction of black love songs dwindled from two-thirds in 1969, to half at the turn of the century, to around one-sixth in the late 2010s.[1] R&B music has not only reflected social realities but shaped them. If the crooners aren't celebrating love, who, if anyone, is singing its praises in the public sphere in general?

There is a vanguard compensating for the decline in lovestruck barbershop harmonies. I know this because I am so often found guilty of barbershop heresy: being a single black person approaching forty with no children and no spouse. People who cut hair are secretly the most stringent enforcers of heteronormativity. It's like these dudes will lose certification if they don't ask me when I'm getting married at least once per cut. Armed with the power to destroy your aesthetic confidence with a flick of their wrist, they propagandize as you sit hostage.

ME: Let me get a number two on top, low on the sides, taper in the back. Good looks.
BARBER: Fine, but you know what's really a good look?
ME: Er—
BARBER: A sacred covenant with your soulmate.

The most recent time I rocked up to my usual Harlem barbershop, my barber asked how many children I have, like he didn't know the answer. When I mumbled "zero," he looked aghast.

"You don't need to plan a family to have one!" he crowed. "You just let it happen. Are you waiting until you're married to have children?"

Well, no. Not really. I'm waiting for the one. Which, to the guy who buzzes my thinning pate down to a light glaze every few weeks, might as well be Godot.

SIX DEGREES OF DEROGATION

Nice is a commonplace word but niceness is a scarce commodity. Sometimes we use nice to describe the kind of restaurant or outfit we choose for a special occasion. The use of nice to mean lavish or chichi knits pleasantness together with luxury, but the most satisfying niceness is usually simple. To describe a person as nice is generally seen as either childish or dismissive. Nice guys are simpering losers; nice girls are prim, precious automatons. My mother is fond of saying that she's kind but not nice. Distinguishing between the two is usually meant to establish that a kind person offers substantive support and goodwill to others, whereas a nice person will merely feign kindness through empty gestures. Both kindness and niceness can be mistaken for weakness, but niceness is often despised by even those who are kind. I'm not in this camp. Is it greedy to want kindness and niceness to coincide, to fancy a performance of geniality alongside acts of generosity? I don't see why I couldn't speak to you warmly while I offer you a blanket.

Bizarrely, I hunger after niceness. Crave it. I relish an opportunity to go grandma mode, clasping my hands and extending my chin. *Isn't that nice?* When I use the word *nice* I picture sitting on a sunlit blacktop on a clear day, with a dandelion in my hand in the moment before I blow it and make a wish. I can only imagine myself alone in this tableau.

In many of my social interactions I sense not only a fear of sincerity but a discomfort with unmediated niceness. As if a bright, clean C major chord activates the gag reflex. As if positive sentiments are synonymous with sentimentality. I figure this aversion to niceness is related to the perception that negativity is more realistic than positivity, and thus that someone preaching positivity is less likely to be genuine.

I poke and prod at these norms in my personal life. For instance, when the rhythm guitarist in my band went on a trip to Europe with his wife last fall, the rest of the band played a few shows without him. When he returned, he asked me how the shows went.

"Sonically, everything was cool," I told the homie. My bandmate nodded, satisfied with that answer. "But emotionally there was an unfillable void without you onstage with us."

Our guitarist stared blankly for a second, then busied himself with setting up his pedal board. I'd made this bid for connection as an experiment; how would unguarded earnestness go over in this context? It reminded me of dividing by zero on a calculator.

Cathy Park Hong's 2020 book of essays *Minor Feelings* defines the book's title as the negative emotions felt by marginalized groups.[1] As she sees it, these emotions are minor in both key and importance; the feelings are "ugly" and generally disregarded or undermined. While that's certainly been true for the majority of American history, minor feelings actually have some currency in the zeitgeist. The 2024 Democratic National Convention was a parade of stylized minor feelings. Each of the speakers delivered rebukes of Donald Trump and critiques of the status quo in a slam poetry cadence. The ethos of slam poetry is simpatico with minor feelings. "Slam" is not an onomatopoeia that we think of as pretty. Using it to modify poetry suggests a form perfectly suited to weather and aestheticize ugliness. On virtually every social media platform today you can narrate your minor feelings in a spoken word poetry voice and a Greek chorus will materialize to hum *go off, sis*. Among the marginalized, we indulge each other's minor feelings because they confirm our reality. Society's dominant groups have some appetite for minor feelings for a host of reasons, schadenfreude not least among them.

In music theory minor notes have a relative major. The sixth note of a major scale is the root of its relative minor. For example, C is the relative major of A minor. At the risk of stretching the metaphor until it breaks, minor feelings likely have relative majors. I suspect that minor feelings stem in large part from disappointment and betrayal. They grow from resentment at not being able to access the dominant culture's wellspring of major feelings. Minor feelings intensify with the knowledge that an in-group's major feelings are made possible at your and your out-group's expense. Relative major feelings might include belonging, love, comfort, and pride.

CHORD—C

On New Year's Eve 2004, my neighbor Ryan and I threw a small gathering in his parents' basement to celebrate. As our teenage friends milled about making fumbling overtures with the opposite sex and nursing red Solo cups, Ryan, his crush Taylor, and I sat three abreast on the couch watching television. The relationship between Ryan and Taylor had been platonic before that night, but Ryan planned to change that when the witching hour struck.

"She's going to be my New Year's kiss girl," he'd told me confidently that morning as we plotted the guest list. Historically, Ryan had been a smooth operator. I didn't doubt him. During the party, the R & B superstar Usher Raymond came on the television screen.

"He would be so hot," Taylor remarked, "except for his nose. His nostrils are so big."

I didn't want to take it personally, but for me, the comment felt charged. Some people at my high school had even specifically compared my nose to Usher's. I couldn't help but note that Taylor had an undeniably prominent honker, too. But I could easily imagine why she felt she had room to look down hers at us: She was white and Jewish, and Usher and I were black. Ryan, too, sensed the alignment between Usher and his trusty token black friend. This made him register Taylor's caveated compliment as a threat.

"What? Black guys aren't hot!" Ryan quipped.

Taylor's eyes swiveled uneasily toward me, then back at Ryan. She broke into tentative giggles. Saying nothing, I excused myself from the room to fiddle with the stereo. Responding to Ryan's insult would only draw me into a fruitless war of words. We weren't even competing for Taylor's attention. He'd just made me, and "black guys" more broadly, into a rhetorical prop to advance his own quest. I was unsurprised to spot Ryan and Taylor locking lips as the Times Square ball dropped on television a few hours later.

RELATIVE MINOR—AM

The incident reflected a labyrinthine web of misplaced insecurities and projections. Taylor's insistence that Usher's nose made him unattractive was likely an implicit admission that she feared being written off on similar grounds. Securing the admiration of Ryan, a normatively attractive gentile boy, and making out with him was a kind of balm and perhaps more;

it was an assurance that she was not black adjacent. For Ryan's part, denigrating black people's sexual viability shored up his confidence in his own. Elevating his stock not coincidentally positioned him as sentry at the gate between Taylor and interracial attraction. I had no real horse in the race. It would be just dandy with me if the two hormone-addled teens could coalesce without sullying the honor of any gyrating black hitmakers in the process. Somehow, though, Usher and I became the foils by which both of these white people understood their worthiness.

Part of the reason that this anecdote has stuck in my craw is because of the way that racial tension is generally summed up as hate. The word *hate* can obscure rather than clarify the mechanics of racism. I happen to hate spaghetti. So, I avoid spaghetti entirely for the most part. I don't use spaghetti to buttress my self-esteem. Residing in a spaghetti-less universe makes my life better. What we call hate often involves using a maligned group for a psychic leg up. Anti-blackness usually isn't a desire to be rid of black folks so much as it is an attachment to keeping them in a subordinate position. In this way the object of so-called hate is a critical resource. Having undesirables around helps to define the parameters of desire. It's also a way to raise morale. The group is galvanized when a flattering contrast is drawn between the group's members and those outside of it. This dynamic shapes major and minor feelings.

CHORD—C#

There's a parallel between what happened at that New Year's party and Pause, the cheekily anti-gay charade some men carry out when a word or utterance doubles as homoerotic innuendo. If you've never played Pause, it's a lot like "That's what she said" in structure. In function it's closer to "No homo." First, a man says something that another man views as suggestive. The second man says, "Pause," to cue an imaginary rimshot. The joke is a comfortable way of admitting that another guy has made you uncomfortable. Their words alluded to or even created a transgressive intimacy. "Pause" nips that in the bud. In some instances, saying "pause" is understood to impugn the manhood of the person who made the suggestive comment. If you catch yourself saying something that could be misunderstood as homosexually suggestive, you can add "pause" to the middle of your sentence with a verbal em-dash. Doing that will grant you amnesty.

The game baffled me at first blush. If nothing untoward was intended, the fellas doth protest too much. Why give airtime to something that isn't relevant? Now I see saying "pause" like the beeping of an ankle monitor. One who is told to pause is in danger of leaving his allowed area, the boundary between "us" and "them." "Pause" offers a ritual reminder of this boundary. Through the game, straight men strengthen their sense of belonging by invoking its limits.

RELATIVE MINOR—A#M

Pause defenders claim that the humor is harmless. You pause to cut a pair of meanings down to one, not to stigmatize anyone's sexuality. This argument doesn't hold water. The very idea that homoerotic innuendo must be urgently disavowed is a form of stigma. But here, too, the word *hate* could be misleading. Even the most gleeful pause participant doesn't necessarily despise queer people. Rather, he needs them. Like Ryan telling Taylor that black guys aren't hot, pause is a case of creating polarity with another group to aggrandize your own.

CHORD—D

In the movie *Elf*, Will Ferrell's character, Buddy, is a human raised by Santa's helpers at the North Pole. Buddy is generally accepted by the elf community, but he doesn't have their knack for toy making. He struggles to keep up with productivity quotas that the other elves meet with ease. In a moment of frustration, he declares himself the worst toy maker in the world.

"I'm a cotton-headed ninny muggins," he whines. The elves around him gasp. A hush falls over the room as if he's blurted out a slur. And maybe he has. The colorful insult seems carefully engineered to sound antebellum alarms while swaddling its user in a patina of plausible deniability.

The word *ninny* recalls *pickaninny*, a dated and offensive term once used to describe black children. On the other hand, *ninny* is also British slang for a foolish person. Cotton-headed could be a mocking reference to tightly coiled or kinky hair. There's also a racist association between black people and cotton based on the fact that we picked it while enslaved. A generous reading, though, could surmise that Buddy is just comparing his brain to soft, fluffy fiber.

RELATIVE MINOR—BM

There are zero visible elves of color in Santa's employ. We only see black characters when Buddy's hero's journey takes him to New York City. If cotton-headed ninny muggins is what it undeniably sounds like—a coded swipe at an inferior race—what gives? Why mention people who are conspicuously absent from the mythological realm that Buddy resides in? It seems that even magical creatures need a subordinate group to define themselves against. Buddy's incompetence at toy making was causing him something akin to minor feelings. The only way he could capture the depth of his self-loathing was to compare himself to people redlined out of the North Pole.

CHORD—D#

A few semesters ago, one of my colleagues was a panelist in a public conversation about a novel from the 1960s. I logged into Zoom to check it out. A middle-aged woman dressed in business-casual attire materialized onscreen. Flanked by over-flowing bookshelves and stacks of corrugated boxes, it looked like she was Zooming in from some kind of industrial sup-ply closet.

"Don't worry—I'm not being held hostage by millennial women personal essayists," the woman joked. She'd been remote working from a bookstore and decided to take the Zoom call from a stockroom rather than driving home. The three other pan-elists in the discussion were all men, ranging in age from about mid-forties to early sixties. The writer seemed eager to establish her serious intellectual bona fides before the audience could write her off. She offered a non-sequitur jab at a demographic wholly unconnected to the event as a warrant for her credibility.

RELATIVE MINOR—CM

The stray insult distinguished the writer from what she clearly sees as a contemptible lot. Personal essayists are (unfairly) as-sociated with self-absorption and triviality. Millennial women are the whipping boys of Gen Xers, Gen Zers, and millennial men. Stirring two easy targets into the same pot didn't just coax a cheap laugh out of the Zoom audience; it inflated the writer's own gravitas in turn. The opposition between this writer and *those lightweights* was so fierce, in fact, that they might kidnap her to settle some scores.

CHORD—E

The term *rent-free* is used on social media to describe a situation where someone thinks obsessively about a person or thing that they claim to hate. If you bring up the target of your ire apropos of nothing, it's living rent-free in your head. I wonder if there actually is a form of rent being paid in this scenario. In *Black Reconstruction in America*, W. E. B. Du Bois writes that whiteness acts as a "public and psychological wage" that impedes the development of class solidarity between white and black workers.[2] The wage is most satisfying in view of the benighted hordes who lack it. DuBois notes that "news that flattered the poor whites and almost utterly ignored the Negro except in crime and ridicule" dramatized the status benefits of whiteness. That formula maps onto most hierarchies, not just racial ones. If infatuation with one's own status is a kind of hypnosis, the periodic invocation of lower-status groups acts as a swinging pocket watch.

RELATIVE MINOR—C#M

From low-level drug merchant Wallace on *The Wire* to football prodigy Vince Howard on *Friday Night Lights* to Rocky Balboa protege Adonis Creed, the throughline linking Michael B. Jordan's most iconic roles is his ability to sprinkle vulnerability into convincing representations of black masculinity. Wallace admits that seeing the badly burned and beaten corpse of a stickup boy upsets him. Vince eventually confesses his agony at knowing his crush has fallen for Vince's own teammate. The payoff of the first *Creed* film involves the title character overcoming an abandonment complex that began when his biological father died in the boxing ring. So, it figures that when *Morning Hustle* radio show host Lore'l told her listeners about attending middle school with the young Michael B., her cohost chimed in that the generational movie star was corny. Later, Lore'l interviewed Jordan at the red-carpet premiere of his directorial debut, *Creed III,* in which he also stars.[3] When Lore'l mentioned that she and the actor had once been classmates, Jordan got passive-aggressive.

"Oh yeah," Jordan said, smirking. "I was the corny kid, right?"

A clip of the confrontation between Lore'l and Jordan picked up steam on social media. The *Grio*'s Natasha S. Alford recognized it as a symptom of a larger problem.

"When are we going to stop trying to limit black boys and men's range of emotions, personalities, and possibilities? Why do people shame them for being so-called corny unless they conform to a certain identity?"

Lore'l maintains that Jordan was bullied for having the same name as His Airness, the now-retired NBA legend who starred for the Chicago Bulls when Lore'l was growing up. She acknowledges that preteen Michael B. was also mocked for carrying his headshots with him to school.

"We lived in Newark," Lore'l pointed out on *The Morning Hustle*.[4] "That's the hood. We would make fun of him like, 'What you gonna do with your stupid headshot?' And now look at him!"

CHORD—F

But I'd wager that the emotional suppleness that's made Jordan one of the most successful actors of the decade was on display even in childhood, which was part of what made him bully bait. To bring your headshots to school in the hood, you have to imagine that your aspirations are feasible despite the odds. You have to have some level of self-respect and hope, which fall under relative major feelings. Being consumed with minor feelings would actually be the preferred condition for a boy of his race, age, and circumstances. Jordan's corniness came down to being in the wrong key.

In early 2024, a photo of a black man looking vaguely pleasant after getting a fresh haircut went viral. I can't quite proclaim that the man in the photo is "smiling." I'd say if the corners of his mouth are like hands on a face clock, he's giving 2:46. His eyebrows are raised only slightly. To me his expression is placid but guarded, as if he is wary of appearing or being *too* happy. I wouldn't be surprised if he foresaw being mocked if his expression was north of neutral and carefully arranged his face so as to disarm potential detractors.

RELATIVE MINOR—DM

It didn't work, though. The photo went viral because of the comment section. Internet users lined up to roast the pictured man as if the photo is an unequivocal faux pas. The ribbing is good-natured, but there is an insinuation that looking so guileless in a photograph is something to be embarrassed about.

"Dude a sweetie pie" and "bro says hooray" are two of my favorite comments. Other commenters observed that the man in the picture looks like he's going to heaven, or like a good intention personified. Comedian Kevin Fredericks shared a video called "Black People Will Roast You For Anything" that commented on the meme.[5] I'm less convinced that black people will roast you for anything than I am chagrined that people will roast you for this thing. The socially acceptable margin for unironic sweetness and light is terrifyingly thin.

A sweetie pie who says "hooray" is likely much more emotionally available than one who sees that behavior as anathema. Lovelessness is the outcome of a circular process. It's a bleaker version of the punchline in "The Gift of the Magi." The classic short story follows a young couple with great love for each other but few funds to spend on Christmas gifts. Della sells her hair and uses the money to buy a platinum chain for her husband Jim's prized pocket watch. Jim sells his watch so he can afford to buy Della a set of ornamental combs. Irony ensues. What good is a set of combs to a shorn head? Who is psyched to own a platinum chain if there's no watch to put on it? In Della's and Jim's cases, at least, their gifts have inestimable symbolic value even if they aren't practically useful. The person who adopts cynical cultural norms in order to belong—only to reduce their capacity to be lovable and loving as a result—has no such consolation prize.

As long as we rely so heavily on contrast as a source meaning, lifting our spirits will be a zero-sum game in which we can only wax in proportion to another group's wane. It's common to be embarrassed and even disgusted by wholesomeness because brokenness is not only widespread but fetishized. We need sources of major feelings that don't create or intensify minor feelings for others. That probably means learning to endure mushiness, sappiness, and corniness. It probably means improving our stamina for niceness.

In today's digital self-help argot, everyone's ex seems to have been a pathological narcissist. Popular YouTuber Andrew Bustamante estimates that 10 percent of the American population has psychopathy, sociopathy, or narcissistic personality disorder.[6] Part of our fascination with these figures is their entertainment value. We picture psychopaths twisting their mustaches in dank basements. They cackle impishly and rub their hands together. They bedevil hapless ingenues the world over. If we want to position ourselves as victims, framing those that didn't love us right as members of that odious 10 percent can invite the sympathy we crave.

But the primary appeal of these cartoonish narcissists is that they flatter the rest of us by comparison. Sure, they occupy the extreme end of the sociality spectrum, but "the norm" is closer to narcissism than to behavior that is legitimately prosocial. Prosocial behavior (i.e., humility, openness, clear communication, respect for human dignity, slowness to judgment) has considerable overlap with niceness. It's for the most part discouraged and disdained. People want to make bids for connection that don't expose them to the possibility of rejection, and major/minoring jokes let them do that. Everyone could become less sensitive to rejection if we could affirm and adore each other with less trepidation about being judged for our earnestness.

When I think of repression, I tend to focus on the practice of censoring or redirecting my antisocial impulses. Healthy repression, at least, should center on containing my inclination to be violent, confrontational, or selfish. But the major-and-minor-feelings dynamic suggests that a lot of us are also censoring our prosocial tendencies for fear of being judged as soft, weak, or dependent. That kind of repression seems more tragic. While civilization may depend on the repression of antisocial impulses, it could be improved by diminishing the pressure to hold back prosocial ones. Some of society's loneliest and most attention-starved people become its most desperate and most violent.

Men with shameless enthusiasm and affection for their crushes or spouses are mocked as simps or wife guys. Women who are too receptive to male attention are dismissed as pick-mes or worse. One could argue that these put-downs are reserved for those who are excessively focused on validation from others. I submit that in American culture, the threshold for "excessive" emotional need is below sea level. What would it look like to change the Overton window for prosocial behavior?

HOME KEY

Suppose everyone had a pitch pipe. In a healthier society, we'd encourage people to develop an emotional point of reference that doesn't rely on derogation and exclusion to achieve a desired effect. The tonic, which is the note on a musical scale that the key is named after, is sometimes called the home key. It's the tone that makes a melody or song resolved or concluded. It offers a resounding sense of wholeness.

In the early 2000s, Hollywood got significant mileage out of a trite device in which a beloved secondary character leaves a voicemail on a protagonist's phone. The protagonist doesn't discover the voicemail message until after the caller has died, which gives the voicemail the valence of a farewell transmission, or parting shot. Kismet strikes: The content of the message proves spookily applicable to something the protagonist is going through in the narrative present. Playing the message at a timely moment in the plot simulates the effect of being comforted by a ghost.

My childhood best friend Jonathan married his wife, Anitha, on Zoom in the spring of 2021, and all the people who loved them got together in person to celebrate the nuptials a year later. I was the best man. We commenced a number of wedding-related exchanges through snail mail as the COVID-19 pandemic raged on. The thank-you note that Jonathan mailed to me in 2021 escaped my notice until fall 2023, when my parents sent a bunch of personal effects I'd left at their house in Boston to my campus office. And just like in the movies, I found and read the note at a serendipitous time. A grueling semester was still weeks away from completion and morale was low. Fortunately for me, though, the author of this galvanizing message is still alive.

> G'Ra,
> I look back at my life and legitimately cannot tell where my personality begins and yours ends. You have been such a part of my life that I don't know what kind of person I would be without you. As a kid I always felt stupid, you more than anyone made me believe in myself. Thank you for being you. I wish you could stand up there with me, but you have always stood with me so I know you'll be here, even if just in spirit.[7]

Jonathan's note is my tonic, my home key. It's a cleansing counter to minor feelings. At bottom, most of us just want to contribute. We want to know that something is better on this planet for our having set foot here. When I reread what Jonathan wrote, I feel like I could be a couch potato for the rest of my life and still go to my grave grinning. I become a generous tycoon of a swelling love fortune. In its simplicity and sincerity, the handwritten card offers replayable salvation.

It's fortunate that I have a home key handy, because I wouldn't say I'm nice, personally. What I am, mainly, is detached. I can extend myself to and for others because I'm not that invested in getting a return, which isn't to say that I'm especially altruistic. I'm like a rich person dribbling coins into the Salvation Army bucket on my way into the grocery store. I dole out a pittance while sitting on a nest egg. When I make an unsuccessful bid for connection, I'm never all that certain that anything I did penetrated the other person's thick husk of projection, distraction, insecurity, and self-absorption. This means that when I am rejected or ignored, I'm hesitant to take it personally. Maybe the other person took a good, hard look at me and recoiled—in which case, that's disappointing and painful. But it's generally more likely they never saw me in the first place. In most ways my awareness of these odds is more propulsive than disabling. Fishing for mutually affirming human contact is a venture with low risk and high potential for reward.

THE ONE

The first degree of a major scale is sometimes called the one. The people who raised me referred to the existence of another kind of one quite regularly and with complete conviction. It wasn't mystical. It was practical. I assumed I had a mate the way you figure the other sock will eventually turn up in the laundry. When couples who were friends of the family broke up, my mother would say "He wasn't the one" by way of explanation. When my folks would forecast a scene in the future in which I or one of my siblings gave them grandchildren, my father would add the caveat, "after you meet the one, of course."

Meeting someone ideally suited to journey through life with you was spoken about as if it was not only plausible but vital. Since both of my folks are artists, they each maintained that having a partner who understands and supports their creative practice had been central to their quality of life. I could picture what they meant. When I was in fifth grade, my dad became fascinated with Georges Perec's novel *A Void*. The book is written entirely without the letter *e*. Baba was working on his own first novel at the time. As an homage to Perec, he completed a chapter of the manuscript without using *e*. Baba narrated this experience to me over breakfast the way most dads probably bloviated about box scores. Being married to my mom, a woman who made up melodies to car side-view-mirror safety warnings for fun, had to be way more satisfying than if he'd partnered with a philistine. Today we'd say they matched each other's freak. But that doesn't quite capture it. There was a mutual magnification of each other's freak.

Being raised in that kind of home instilled high morale about a particular kind of love: two free people nurturing, encouraging, and keeping each other company. There was an in-house proof of concept. Gender-equitable love, specifically, was attainable. The functionality of a relationship turned on the two parties' choices and behavior. Not the genders involved. No one who knew my mother saw her as a pushover. It would be hard to imagine someone less inclined to languish in an extractive relationship as some kind of second-class citizen. If being married to a man earned my mother's seal of approval, men could love women well. We aren't biologically damned to be thoughtless ogres. We can learn and choose to behave as competent, emotionally present stewards.

"When I tell people I've been married for thirty-eight years, I'm sure they have the wrong idea," my mother has said to me. She calls herself a housewife, but she knows that it carries connotations that don't apply to her situation. A situation made possible by getting hitched to the one. "They're not imagining, for example, that I haven't done laundry since my early twenties because your father does it."

I never took this to mean my parents' relationship was perfect. Nor did I expect to meet a perfect person. But these persistent references to the one were affirmation that I had a complement out there in the world, and if we both acted in good faith, we could form and maintain a deeply life-affirming team. As a younger person, I didn't think that carefully about this. I blithely presumed life had positioned me to surf a cosmic conveyor belt that would land me next to some hyperverbal, socially conscious Lark Voorhies look-alike. Once fate had ensured our proximity, I would shoot my shot. In my twenties, it became clear that if such a conveyor belt existed, it wasn't going to deposit me where I expected. Connecting with someone as powerfully as I had envisioned would take a much more active process.

Eventually I came to believe in the possibility of the one in terms that resemble Pascal's wager. The seventeenth-century philosopher Blaise Pascal argued that one gamble shapes your life: the choice to believe in God or not. He reasoned that if you live as if you believe in God and it turns out you're wrong, you'll suffer no consequence but disappointment. If you live as if God doesn't exist and it turns out you're wrong, however, eternal consequences await. I'm wagering on the one. The great smorgasbord of majesty and misery bookended by oblivion is best enjoyed at a two-top. If the opportunity cost is protection from disappointment, I'm content to save a seat.

Some people seem agitated by the very mention of a one. (I suspect that thinking about the quest for love as something with right or wrong answers dredges up the dizziness of freedom.) They are quick to counter that meaningful love is possible with any number of people among the eight billion in the world. It would be limiting and naive, these types will say, to think that there is only a solitary soul in the world who could be right for you. I'm not so hung up on whether the one means a single person or a class of person. My sense of the one is both-and. There might be a class of people who are potentially right for you, but once you find someone in that echelon, the relationship that the two of you build together will determine whether you're the alpha and omega for each other. Like so many things, this paradox is summed up nicely in black slang. Black folks often describe a transcendent individual as "one of them ones." Start with being and finding one of them ones. The synergy you create will turn each of you into the definitive match for the other.

The other reason people chafe when I acknowledge that I'm looking for the one is simpler, but no less intractable. Earnestly seeking a better half is unbearably wholesome.

BACK ON MY BULLY

The classic children's book *The Story of Ferdinand* was published in 1936. In it, a bull named Ferdinand defies the role assigned to his species by refusing to butt heads with other bulls. He prefers to spend his time picking flowers under the cork tree. His mother worries that this preference for noncombative behavior will isolate her son, so she encourages him to play with the other calves. Nevertheless, Ferdinand opts to spend most of his time alone. His mother eventually recognizes that he's content this way.

When Ferdinand's irritation at being stung by a bee one morning is mistaken for the bravado of a more fearsome bull, he's recruited to fight a matador. Ferdinand is physically imposing enough to scare his opponent on sight. The fight bills him as "Ferdinand the Fierce." But he proves less interested in the fight than in the flowers that the fight's female spectators adorn their hair with. The bullfight ends before it begins, much to the consternation of the matador and Ferdinand's recruiters. They return the bull to his pasture, where he retakes his perch under the cork tree with the flowers he loves.

The expectations we have for a humanoid bull and the expectations we have for black people probably overlap a lot. When I have neglected the bullring in favor of the shade of the cork tree in my own life, others have treated it like a crime against nature. A 1938 *Life* magazine article acknowledged that Ferdinand has been interpreted as a political symbol.[8] Readers have been liable to view the casual cow as a pacifist, a communist, or even an anarchist. If there's any allegorical component to the tale, the moral I'd resent most is the idea that being true to yourself usually results in being alone.

EXERCISES IN (ATTACHMENT) STYLE

From September 29 to November 25, 2024, Earth acquired what some news outlets described as a "mini-moon." The so-called mini-moon is an asteroid about thirty-three feet across in size.[1] For reference, the average city bus is about thirty-nine feet across. Earth's new neighbor was too small to detect with the naked eye or a backyard telescope.

Our OG moon formed around four billion years ago. It's been our planet's only natural satellite ever since. Earth's gravity heavily altered the mini-moon's orbit for two months, which is the flimsy basis for calling it a mini-moon as opposed to just another one of the countless asteroids that pass through the Earth's gravitational field. There was far less ado when another rock comparable in size to the mini-moon did a loop around Earth in 2022. The hullabaloo about this mini-moon, then, was somewhat arbitrary. It was like a galactic rolling stone. Strictly speaking, the mini-moon was never gravitationally bound to Earth.

Calling this fly-by-night space object the diminutive of our moon reflects low public esteem for stable, long-term monogamy. It's a lunar litmus test of the culture's reverence for love. The moon is to the mini-moon what someone who supported you through law school is to a Tinder match you had drinks with. The only thing the latter has going for them is novelty.

The OG moon is the model of faithfulness; the mini-moon, fickleness. Conferring the title of moon on the mini-moon misrepresents the gaping disparity in gravity, or rather, in gravitas.

Marvin Gaye could build a slow jam out of this celestial polyamory. We know who he'd side with, though. *I wanna be your only natural satellite, baby. A mini-moon could never love you like I do.*

Maybe childishly, I imagine that cynicism about love abounds today because we don't have a robust sense of wonder about other feats of human collaboration. Every time I'm on a plane I try to remember to say to myself, "I'm coolin' on a chair in the sky." If it works, I'll never become anesthetized to the complete majesty of slipping the surly bonds of Earth. NASA's decline might influence our level of cultural optimism about love. Crewed space flight strengthens faith in the collaborative application of human ingenuity to complex problems. When I recall that we've been to the OG moon six times, I can't help but think: Living in the same house and loving the same person for fifty years is no flight of fancy compared to that.

If I'm honest, though, space beckons to me in a way that isn't entirely sentimental. When Sinatra asks his beloved to fly him to the moon, he doesn't want to go anywhere without her. He's asking to be lifted aloft by her kiss. He'll get so high on her love that he ascends to the heavens. I am more likely to mean, drop me off there, please, and don't wait up. Space is a cold, black vacuum. It accentuates the lushness of the pale, blue dot by contrast. And I have always longed for it, lunged toward it, latched on to a light-year when offered an inch.

In college, my friend Chance and I got a kick out of referencing a scene in the movie *Superbad*. Michael Cera's character is about to leave Jonah Hill's character alone in a high school cafeteria. Hill's character blanches at the very notion.

"So what, I gotta sit here and eat dessert alone," Hill's character complains. "Like I'm fucking Steven Glansberg?" The camera pans to a shot of a lone adolescent eating a fruit cup, deep in thought. Chance would text me, "You coming to dinner or am I Glansberging it?" to assess whether he should meet me at the campus cafeteria at mealtime.

There were occasions, though, when he was glad I wasn't going to make it.

"Glansberging has to happen sometimes," he told me after I'd been sick for twenty-four hours or so. "No disrespect to you, or anybody. I gotsta brood."

Maybe the final frontier calls to me for the same reason. In the final couplet of his sonnet "When I Have Fears That I May Cease to Be," I picture Keats in zero gravity, the stars his only counsel: "of the wide world, I stand alone and think / 'til love and fame to nothingness do sink."[2] He was a capital R Romantic. Even they gotsta brood, apparently. Compulsive solitude seekers could be in good company. I guess it's that, or I'm a cold, black vacuum. I accentuate the lushness of the pale, blue dot by contrast.

The comet Hale-Bopp reached perihelion in 1997. I was ten years old, and my family had recently moved from St. Louis, Missouri, to Silver Spring, Maryland. At the time, I was obsessed with astronomy. My parents were and are generally curious people themselves, and they made sure my siblings and I assembled on the front lawn to watch the comet cross the horizon. It was a new luxury for us as a family. In our previous neighborhood back in St. Louis, you'd only hang out in the yard after nightfall if you had a death wish. I remember staring off into the distance in the cool glow of autumn twilight and trying to make sense of what I was looking at. We learned about Hale-Bopp in school. I could recite facts about its trajectory.

But what did it mean to be stuck on one of a potentially infinite number of space rocks—all of which are floating in a black expanse we barely understood—while watching a much smaller space rock streak brilliantly across the sky?

One of our new neighbors had an answer. He was the patriarch of the family next door, a man who smoked like black churches in the '60s. You could smell him before you saw him. He sidled up to my family in the yard and looked at Hale-Bopp over our shoulders.

"Judgment Day is coming," he croaked.

Reality is always at the mercy of story-making machines in our heads. Saul Bellow's *Herzog* is a testament to this. The novel acts as a trojan horse for several wide-ranging essays. The title character, Moses E. Herzog, is a history professor in the throes of a midlife crisis. He reflects on his life and his ideas in essayistic letters to his loved ones. Through them, the reader learns how preoccupied Herzog is with his own interiority, and how little of the outside world seems to penetrate. While readers might pick up on this aspect of Herzog's personality, it could come as a surprise that the same dynamic applies to themselves.

"People don't realize how much they are in the grip of ideas," Bellow says in an interview compiled in *Conversations with Saul Bellow*. "We live among ideas much more than we live in nature."[3]

Bellow's observation throws light on that time in the front yard in the late '90s. Nature was revealing itself to us in all its splendor and mystery. Instead of sitting with his awe at the phenomenon itself, my neighbor immediately moved to decode (or perhaps encode) the comet's symbolism. Hale-Bopp was not simply an erupting ball of ice and dust from the Oort cloud, the assortment of ice objects somewhere between two thousand and one hundred thousand astronomical units from our sun. It was a cosmic emissary and a harbinger of humanity's ultimate fate. For my neighbor, we were not watching a spectacle attesting to how vast and venerable the universe is. Instead, the comet was an affirmation of our centrality.

We live among ideas much more than we live in nature. The sense of detachment that pervades my relationships is downstream of my awareness that I am "nature" to other people. To some extent, they are in turn the same to me. Even if I'm close with another person, I expect that their mind's foreground is reserved for the grip of their ideas. Insofar as I am present enough in their inner life to become enmeshed with their ideas, those ideas usually won't work in my favor. Maybe this is more gracious to talk about if I invert this equation. Suppose you are Hale-Bopp, operating from a spatial and temporal vista beyond any human lifespan or life experience. Let's say I am a suburban white man in my early fifties. When we come into glancing contact, I reflexively absorb you into a mythology that was authored before the invention of the telescope. And I believe I have you all figured out. If this is the style of interface that dominates social life, a measure of detachment is in order.

On the other hand, there's much to be gained from recognizing human beings as a part of the nature we revere. Growing up around a lot of Christians, I noticed there seemed to be some relationship between religion and sensitivity to beauty. A Christian person was always going for a walk in the forest and snorkeling in their confirmation bias. *This is all so sublime and mysterious*, they'd say in so many words. *It* proves *a supreme being made it, and by extension, made me.*

People assign meaning to intense sensory experience based on whatever stories or myths or science are available for putting their experience into context. I don't share the inclination to explain natural beauty as the handiwork of a bearded man in a robe and sandals. But in a way I feel some kinship with people like that for having an intense sensory experience and needing to articulate it in the first place.

There's a missed opportunity in conceiving of "natural beauty" as something that excludes the human mind. Consciousness came from nature as well. We didn't make it in a lab. (Yet.) So, if a tree makes you marvel at an unseen architect, another person's imagination or intellect or even insanity should cause you to gape as well, because it's at least as intricate and miraculous. How can the ocean be a source of breathless amazement if an old lady isn't?

In the search for my own future old lady, the discovery of Hale-Bopp is a beacon. It's a real-life meet-cute. Alan Hale and Thomas Bopp each spotted the deep-sky object independently, the comet's motion relative to the background stars sketching out the hyphen that would link its observers.[4] The story-making machine in my own head sees this as precedent. Sometimes two strangers are moving toward each other in the dark without knowing it, conjoined forever in the laser show of the cosmos.

MORE SUGAR. LESS MESHUGGAH.

There's a literary term called *chiasmus*. It's where words, concepts, or grammatical constructions are repeated in the same or a modified form. I experience my four siblings as chiasms of each other and myself. Sometimes my brother or my sister or another sibling will be talking, and as I listen I recognize an element of myself in modified form.

I can appreciate these similarities and also understand my siblings as independent entities with their own needs, tastes, stories, propensities. We're linked but distinct, like letters in a word written in cursive. Watching the film that my sister Indigo made for her BFA thesis helped to crystallize some of my own feelings about desire. The film is called *I Only Want It If It's Sweet*. I took it in knowing my sister is the brains of the operation and came away lamenting the operation of our brains.

Indigo's voiceover narrates three vignettes labeled A, B, and C. In the first, she describes misunderstanding a Norah Jones song my mother used to play around the house. To Indigo's fourth-grade imagination, the song was about an android waiting to get plugged into a wall so that it can function. On screen, an actor poses in a chair in a room I recognize as my parents' living room. A shot of an electrical plug connecting with a socket establishes the android's energy source. The voiceover provides a correction.

"Actually that's not what it's about at all," goes my sister's voice. "It's about a lady waiting at home so she can fuck."

Vignette B is titled "Maybe Don't Beat the P***y Up." It takes place in a college-level gender studies classroom, where a student has an awakening.

"My classmate realized that maybe her wants and needs weren't intrinsic," Indigo explains to her audience. "Maybe it was something packaged for her that she just happened to pick up."

The classmate raises her hand and narrates the epiphany aloud.

"Getting choked by my boyfriend has always felt really natural and I don't know where that came from," the student announces to the class. "Or getting hit. I think I like it because that's always how it's meant to be."

I know where she's coming from. This view of sex is like a folk song; its origins are apocryphal but everyone knows it by heart. Normative sexuality is so closely associated with aggression that it's hard to pry them apart. Having soul and not being a soldier makes you unfit to serve in lust's austere and lonely offices. The only thing I like to beat up is the fretboard of my bass guitar. I'm not feigning some kind of pacifism to be woke. I am not vying for sainthood; in fact, the way even light sadism makes my stomach lurch has made me question whether I'm among the damned. Being squeamish about brutality has muddled my assessment of whether I like sex at all. I felt both dismay and relief at seeing my sister tussle with the same subject in her thesis film. One gene pool is drowning us both.

All right, look: Don't thinkshame me, Chavano. I'm just pondering here. But the word *kink* calls to mind something twisted, gnarled, knotty, taking a circuitous route from cause to effect. A dude choking a woman for their mutual sexual gratification is just the macro power structure being acted out in miniature. What's kinky about a taut, uncurved line? How is it subversive for men to derive erotic pleasure from harming women? Isn't that just performing our structural roles literally? It isn't contrary to prevailing values; it's a display of them. If everyone gets off on that—fine with me. I ain't the purity police. But don't tell me it's countercultural.

The third vignette addresses Indigo's time as a member of a high school sketch comedy troupe. She reminisces about attending a cast party where one member suggests playing spin the bottle. Another one of my siblings, Xinnie, appears on screen as a representative of teenage Indigo.

"I touched my lips for dryness, ash, and courage," Indigo narrates in the film. "Leaning over, lips parted, I tried to be something that could be wanted."

The other members of the comedy troupe take turns kissing her after spinning a plastic soda bottle. They are titillated by the experience, including its racial novelty.

"Whoa! Your lips are so big and soft," says one young woman.

"Your lips are huge compared to mine," another guy goes.

"Just kissed my first black girl!" a third person exults.

The flygirl in the buttermilk gets too close to the sun. The next shot mirrors Xinnie's point of view as the other members of the troupe close in on them. The four other actors are assembled in a line on their hands and knees. They begin to growl and grimace like animals. The camera shakes savagely as the besties get bestial.

"You thought it was sweet" is a phrase you say to someone who's been had. Someone that got hoodwinked, bamboozled, led astray. It's a snappy way of scolding a sap for their naivete. The title of Indigo's film seems to wink at this. To temper one's sexual longing with terms and conditions is regarded as quaint.

The default view of desire is unreserved fervor for being treated with id gloves; getting ogled, mauled, and manhandled with feral enthusiasm. I don't personally have one or the other on a moral pedestal. The bitter pill for me is that I find sweetness to be such a crucial ingredient that most sexual opportunities are too bland to sink my teeth into.

ON HAVING LOW JOB SATISFACTION

"The problem of woman," Simone de Beauvoir famously wrote, "has always been a problem of men."[1]

"Being a problem is a peculiar experience," W. E. B. Du Bois wrote, "even for one who has never been anything else."[2]

The overlap between these two observations forms a long, gnarly equation on the great mass-cultural blackboard, like a high-leverage scene in a physics movie. I'm like a discount Will Hunting, furrowing my brow, scribbling furiously and probing for an elegant result. I neither want to be a problem, nor act as the source of them for roughly half of the human race. The possibility of our mutual liberation probably has something to do with love, even if I haven't worked out the math yet.

The issue started to preoccupy me in sixth grade, when I traveled to the Caribbean World Series in Puerto Rico. I accompanied my youth baseball teammate Iggy and his mother Patricia, who at one point was the head coach of our team. As we drove to a stadium in San Juan one day, Patricia suddenly swore and smacked the dashboard in frustration. Iggy and I looked up, alarmed.

"I'm sorry, guys," Patricia said, shaking her head ruefully. "I just can't deal with the machismo here."

Iggy nodded sympathetically, as if machismo was a familiar scourge. I had never heard the word before, but the context was a clue. Patricia had been trying to merge onto a road and a succession of male motorists refused to make way for our car.

"I want you both to know that men don't have to behave that way." She turned to face me where I was sitting in the backseat and made eye contact. My dad had been the third-base coach on our team. He and Patricia were friendly, enough that he and my mother were comfortable sending their eleven-year-old son to Puerto Rico in Patricia's care.

"Your father isn't like that."

Then she turned to Iggy.

"And your father isn't like that."

Iggy's mom was cool enough to take us on a trip to watch several professional baseball games a day in person during the middle of a school year. It was February. I should have been cupping my chin despondently and drooling into my hand in pre-Algebra class. Instead, I was kicking it in sunny San Juan with one of my best friends, spending the day on the beach and attending baseball games in the afternoon and evening. The whole thing was Patricia's idea. If a bunch of testosterone-addled cretins were making it harder for her to facilitate this adventure, I was keen to be on her side. Pointedly naming our fathers as exceptions to the macho rule amounted to more than simply saying "not all men." In other words, I don't think she was trying to placate Iggy and me. Patricia was reminding us that we had superior role models at home, that there was no excuse for growing up and becoming complicit in her predicament. Toxic masculinity isn't predestined, she seemed to be telling us. It's the result of a series of choices, and her son and I could make different ones. The message stuck with me. It began to inform how I viewed the genesis of my own family.

When my parents got married in the early 1980s, they aspired not only to start a family but an entirely new tradition.

My father's family name was Smith. My mother's was Hillman. They shed these respective surnames in favor of Asim, a Swahili word for "protector." My four siblings and I inherited that name as well, and a new branch of the family tree took shape. As a child, when I learned about the black feminist playwright and poet Ntozake Shange, I connected her radical self-definition with my own origins. Born Paulette Williams, she jettisoned her first name on the basis that it was patriarchal, and Williams because she regarded it as a slave name. The writer adopted her new name, Ntozake, which means "she who comes with her own things," and Shange, which means "she who walks with lions," from the Zulu language.[3] This rechristening was both feminist and anti-racist. I recognized a similar impulse in my mother's decision to replace her father's name with one of her own choosing. The mothers of some of my childhood friends kept their maiden names after they were married as an expression of feminist conscience. Mom's move seemed both related and distinct. Changing her name *with* my father rang to me as a joint refutation of white supremacy and patriarchy. It was an affirmation that feminism and anti-racism were not only reconcilable but cooperative. They could combine like strands of a double helix.

Maybe this is why I think there's a philosophical and political overlap between Afrocentric self-naming and choosing your own gender pronouns. They both involve excavating something internal and bringing it decisively to the surface. The link between the two is generally overlooked. In many cases, people imagine these acts as being at odds. Today's political climate casts the nexus between being feminist and pro-black as far more embattled than my folks made it look. Afrocentric renaming was fairly commonplace in the black community thirty years ago. Now, it's primarily associated with hotepping, a usually derisive term for a conspiracy-loving, pseudo-intellectual variant of black nationalism. Hotepping is better known for its misogyny and homophobia than for any credible blueprints for black progress. The overrepresentation of hoteps creates a false opposition between being pro-black and being pro-queer.

If gender and race are social constructs, then names and pronouns are among the nuts and bolts that hold those constructs together. Afrocentric renaming is a form of prying up one of those racial floorboards. Choosing one's own pronouns can be a means of pulling a link out of the gender Jenga stack. Both of these DIY projects in affirming one's identity repurpose the culture's mortar and bricks to redeem traumatic history.

Perhaps because of and not in spite of the persecution we've dealt with on the basis of race, the black vanguard has historically recognized the contingent nature of race and gender. There's an ongoing thread in black counterculture where black people take stock of the ultimate pertinence of both race and gender, and conclude that those categories are more illusory than elemental. Start from the premise that the dominant culture misconstrues your blackness as a liability. It's not a giant leap to realize how often culture overestimates the differences between all the categories it creates.

In one of James Baldwin's last interviews, he told the writer Richard Goldstein that the best hope of a coalition between black people and gay people must be built "on the grounds of human dignity."[4]

"There's nothing in me that isn't in everyone else," Baldwin goes on. "There's nothing in everyone else that isn't in me."

In an interview in the *New York Times*, Nikki Giovanni mused on how the identities she holds might look from an interstellar perspective.[5]

"I thought if I ran into a Martian and the Martian said, 'Who are you?' what would my answer be? The *only* answer could be 'I am an Earthling.' I realized—and have continued to realize—that it would be illogical if I were to tell the Martian I'm a Black woman. That's because a Martian doesn't know what Black is, and they don't know what a woman is."

An intersection is the most popular metaphor for thinking about gender and race at the same time. One limitation of this analogy is that it can sound like race and gender only converge at particular points. You're driving along the gender road and suddenly here comes race, or vice versa. To make sense of African American life, I tend to merge gender and race the way physicists combine the three dimensions of space and the single dimension of time to create spacetime. The advent of special relativity told us that space and time are interdependent. If you're moving slowly through space, time can speed up. If you're moving quickly through space, time can slow down. You need space and time coordinates alike to describe an event. By the same token, a gender-neutral generalization about race is like a description of space that elides time. A race-neutral generalization about gender is like a description of time that overlooks space. Just as space and time are best understood in union, no one experiences either gender or race in a vacuum. One always informs the other.

Needless to say, that complexity can be hard to hold. I laughed at a *Reductress* headline that read: "Non-Binary Person Walking Alone at Night Unsure Whether to be Scared or Scary."[6] The joke seems to be that men are fearsome when walking alone at night and women are afraid. Hence a nonbinary person doesn't have a clear role in the predator/prey dichotomy. Of course, a black person of any gender walking alone at night could plausibly be read as scary. And partially *because* blackness is so often seen as a menace or threat, we have reason to be scared of others' reactions to us in turn. The joke, which typifies a prevailing style of identity-based humor, is an example of how queerness is often described and conceived of in terms of white norms. A raceless lens makes it easier to frame men and women as polar opposites. Simply considering blackness and its implications throws gender norms into flux.

There are other ways that popular notions of queerness don't seem to take blackness into account. A lot of my white queer friends will tout the importance of their queer chosen family. Assembling a community intentionally based on having similar values and interests—rather than merely genealogy—makes plenty of sense to me. But the same expansive and mutable approach to family is traditional in the African American community across all sexual orientations. We're not conferring the titles of "Auntie" and "Unc" based on DNA tests. Those honorifics are often bestowed upon people that our biological families have willfully absorbed into the fold as permanently as if they'd been born to us. This approach stems in part from enslavement, when slave owners would separate biological families by selling family members to different bidders. Enslaved people adapted to these forced separations by forging new bonds at the plantations they were sold to.

It's no surprise, then, that there are cultural conversations in the black community that suffer for lack of a queer feminist lens. Colorism informs how black people think about and perform gender. In the NBA, players will describe a timid, ineffectual drive to the basket as going to the hole "like a light-skinned dude." The more admirable way to earn a layup is to make a stout, decisive move through the lane—as a dark-skinned guy supposedly would.[7] Even in jest, this rhetoric associates pale skin with femininity and dark skin with masculinity. Black male professional athletes are criticized for partnering with light-skinned or non-black women disproportionately often.

These men choose partners against a black cultural backdrop that scorns any hint of androgyny or sexual otherness. So, it follows that black male athletes are more likely to choose women who conform with their color-coded understanding of femininity, and who consolidate the athlete's own masculinity in turn. Unfortunately for hoteps, masculinizing melanin compounds the so-called snow-bunny crisis. Any thoroughgoing refutation of colorism in the black community requires a critical reappraisal of how we understand gender.

I found being young, gifted, and black to be a lovely, precious dream only a middling percentage of the time until I met Sasha. The predicament didn't live up to its billing until I shared it with her.

Sasha and I are at a bar in Brooklyn. We're watching the New York Liberty take on the Las Vegas Aces in the 2024 WNBA Semifinals. The NY Liberty may be up 2–0, but I know the Las Vegas Aces are going to counterpunch. Just read some Eric Foner. The shape of American history tells us there's a substantial backlash any time liberty makes a few gains.

It's a culturally significant moment because women's basketball, and perhaps women's sports more broadly, is having a renaissance. My sister is meeting us at the bar to watch the game as well. Indigo is a lifelong sports non-enthusiast, but the aforementioned renaissance and the popularity of women's sports among her Brooklyn queer community has sparked a burgeoning pride in the NY Liberty.

A Trump-Vance 2024 ad comes on during a commercial break. It features a simple but effective line of attack against the Democratic contender: "Kamala is for they/them." The message is offensive and alarming in a vacuum, but in the context of a televised WNBA playoff game, it feels pointed and personal. Nearly 30 percent of the WNBA identify as LGBTQ+.[8] More than 60 percent are black.[9] Buying this time slot to accuse the nation's first black veep of queer-coded disloyalty is no less than the enemies of civil liberties taking aim at NY Liberty fans. Sasha and Indigo are appalled when they see it.

This style of dog-whistling has hit me hard before, and in a way, I'm still hollering. In 2010, former model and future rock musician Scott Brown became the first Republican elected to the US Senate from Massachusetts in nearly forty years. My parents, along with Indigo and our two younger siblings, moved to Massachusetts that same autumn. The roads in their new neighborhood teemed with Scott Brown bumper stickers. Brown's highly successful campaign slogan was "He's for us." I was certain that, new Massholes or not, my family was excluded from the slogan's latter pronoun. Black Americans have historically functioned as the "them" against which the body politic is defined. Under the shadow of Barack Obama's first presidential term, Brown's professed faithfulness to "us" was an implicit commitment to stem the tide of racial uplift. A few years later, as more and more gender nonconforming people began to use singular they/them pronouns, the Brown bumper stickers were the first thing I thought of. I had always felt more like a person than a man or a woman. But Themception didn't appeal to me; I was already black. Asking people to refer to me as "them" felt like a redundant and self-defeating promotion of a troubling subtext into text.

The bar is crowded, so at first there's only one empty seat available. I let Sasha claim it and I stand behind her. There's an older black man seated to her immediate right. He greets her and Sasha flashes her showstopping mono-dimple. I watch his eyes light up as he realizes that providence has delivered a beautiful young woman seemingly within reach. It's noisy in the bar—The Ramones are playing on the stereo, and in addition to the WNBA semifinals, there are three NFL games blaring on the various televisions. Sasha's conversation with the man beside her is difficult to overhear. I know her and how people respond to her well enough to fill in the gaps. He wants to know where she's from. She's from Houston, but she'll tell him where she lives now, which is in the neighborhood this bar is in. She asks if this guy is friends with the other black man at the end of the bar. But her phrasing makes both men uncomfortable.

"We're not *together*," the older one says. "We just know each other."

"That's all I meant by together," Sasha replies sweetly.

"It's just not the kind of thing I expect to hear, given that I'm a very masculine man," the younger guy says.

Sasha laughs.

"Oh, *very* masculine, you say?"

Naturally, the two men at the bar view this as a provocation. Each man's shoulders grow tight. Their necks protrude at an angle. A young woman is laughing at them rather than with them, and their masculinity is the joke. I know that what's actually tickling her is the younger guy's umbrage at the mere possibility that he could be read as gay. He likely pounded his chest to make sure Sasha saw him as eligible. His defensiveness backfired and diminished him.

As the conversation goes on, the man closest to me keeps glancing my direction. He is looking for a cue as to whether he is encroaching on "my territory." I'm more focused on the game actively breaking my heart—my Las Vegas Aces are getting royally flushed down the postseason commode. If Sasha needs backup, I'm happy to engage. But she seems relaxed, maybe even in her element.

Eventually the man makes eye contact with me.

"Is this your girlfriend?" he asks, seeking permission to make advances on her.

"Best friend," I say. Sasha says the same thing at almost the same time.

Here is a social contract I have clearly breached. There's no way to honor Sasha's full humanity and participate in the standard code of navigating masculine power. The older man believes he is being polite by sussing out our relationship. Patriarchy conditions this guy to see me as an agent and Sasha as a possession, as if he's a medieval vagabond asking to borrow a horse from my stable. The reality is that even if Sasha was my romantic partner, the terms of this guy's engagement with her would be entirely up to Sasha. She doesn't need me to chaperone any aspect of what's transpiring. Fealty to the homie necessitates a form of disloyalty to my gender. Because my connection to Sasha is a lot more important to me than what any barstool Don Juans might think, I have little to lose by simply remaining a bystander.

When we recount this experience later that evening, Sasha pantomimes my body language as I hovered in the background. She makes a neutral, unblinking expression. Her G'Ra impression reminds me of an android. A gendervoid android, I guess. Eat your heart out, Radiohead.

"He was waiting for you to let him know how to proceed," Sasha notes, "and I like that you gave him nothing."

This is one of the core synergies in our friendship. Gender roles are jobs and we are collaboratively quiet quitting.

RIFFS, ANDS, OR BUTS ABOUT IT

When you're a kid with lots of siblings, as I once was, you watch movies together. An ugly character comes on screen, so you turn to one of them and say, "That's you." When you're a cheeky adult with bandmates, as I am now, you stroll the corridors of the sprawling practice space that you share with countless other bands. A particularly atrocious sound rings out, so you nudge one of your mates and say, "That's your solo project."

Late to school, late to work. Every title sequence foreshadows how the credits will roll. Qué será sera G'Ra. What I will be will resemble what I've been. The future is a copypasta of the past.

This is why being a middle kid influences how I think about love. My brother Joe is four years older than I am. I'm eight years older than Indigo. Xinnie, our penultimate sibling, is two years younger than Indigo. The youngest sibling in the family is Gyasi, who came along four years after Xinnie. I figure my parents thought we were still in 1908. (We stan an Afroretroist queen and king.) Maybe only half of us would survive infancy, in which case there'd be a couple left to raise livestock. Instead, we all survived, and this family structure makes me both a big and little brother. For the first eight years of my life, I was the baby of the family. Later, when Joe was an adult and I was in my teens, I became the oldest kid in the household. The way

Joe looked after me provided a model for how I look after Indi, Xinnie, and Gyasi to this day.

Like most people, I had beef in middle school. There was someone who wanted to or did jump me seemingly every other week. I didn't hit a growth spurt until I was around fifteen, so in grades six to eight I was consistently one of the shortest and scrawniest kids in my age group. One of the more dramatic scraps I had in seventh grade was with a white kid just under six feet tall who outweighed me by about seventy pounds. I didn't have to ask my older brother to do anything. Joe formed a plan and acted on it. When Joe heard the kid was picking on me, he took the city bus from his high school to my middle school immediately after his own classes let out. He waited in the parking lot until my antagonist's bell rang. Joe didn't exchange any words with the kid. He just mean-mugged him from a distance. The message was crystal clear. I had no drama from the kid after that.

Even after my growth spurt, I never became as physically imposing as Joe. If Indigo or Xinnie had static with any of their classmates, I'd need to opt for different tactics than Joe did. But I'm shaped by his example just the same. To me, love is seeing and anticipating the needs of your loved ones and fulfilling them by whatever means you're best positioned to use. You step up when stepping up is called for. You don't count favors.

The temperate climate of our household enabled the adaptive dynamic between Joe and me. My brother's natural congeniality was nurtured in the crib. Home was where the low-resting heart rate was. My folks screamed at us from time to time, but I can't recall ever seeing them scream at each other. They were methodical, deliberate parents. Hard on us but easy on our nervous systems. Predictability reigned. Joe and I generally knew what the score was, and the mood was seldom shook by the soap opera organ. Even as our household population doubled, when three more siblings and a live-in grandmother joined the fold, noise pollution never got so out of hand that you couldn't hear yourself think. The catch being that none of this was a microcosm for the world.

Mass culture celebrates mercuriality. Equanimity lacks esteem. Admiration for the former and contempt for the latter hinders love because stable relationships require temperance. A healthy romance takes patience, restraint, flexibility, and forgiveness. Unlike an immature love, which swings perilously from dizzying highs to miserable lows and back again, the pleasure of mature love stems from its steadiness. If most of us aren't cultivating that sense of balance in the other spheres of life, how equipped are we to do so in our relationships?

Songwriting is an area of my life where balance eludes me. Hopelessly infatuated with words, I often cram too many into a song. Non-lexical vocables, or wordless vocals, are a safeguard. They fill space without overloading the listener. Shoo bop shoo wah. Na na na. They give songs space to breathe. At least once a day I find myself wishing I could use them in conversation. In an anxiety-saturated social landscape, silences make many people nervous. Pauses in conversation leave us alone with our own minds. Those gaps invite questions. On average, our stamina for indeterminacy is quite low. What's the meaning of the dead air? Did we say the wrong thing? Are we being judged? The popular aversion to silence is hard for me to accommodate. I like to absorb what I'm being told and I like to choose my words carefully. Often, I am underwhelmed by the other party's capacity to listen, and reluctant to flap my gums just for my health.

I could soothe my interlocutors—and abdicate the burden of speech in one fell swoop—with some well-placed whoa ohs. Like a way of simulating hold music in person. All circuits are busy right now, but I value your call. The colloquial use of musical nonsense syllables could retrain our dialogical muscles. It could help to wean us off our dependency on knee-jerk reactions. Tolerance for ambiguity, comfort with the solitude of our own minds, and reflection before we react can make us all more lovable and more loving. Let's try it for the next twenty-five pages or so. Here's to being the change, eh? If music be the food of love, shamone.

GABBA GABBA HEY

"We've not been trained. We've not been conditioned to understand you," the comic Mo'Nique told host Shannon Sharpe on a 2024 episode of the *Club Shay Shay* podcast, diagnosing what she sees as the disconnect between black women and black men.[1] "We've been trained to fight against you. We've been trained to go against you.

"We've watched our mommas, our grandmommas, our aunties speak ill of a black man," she went on. "So now when a black man comes and he's good, you're waiting for the bad. Because grandmomma told you black men weren't shit. Momma told you black men weren't shit. Your auntie said black men ain't shit."

The bad PR problem that Mo'Nique alludes to is a real phenomenon. The prevalence of this love-aversive conditioning is part of the reason that black folks applaud healthy black love so heartily when we see it. Describing this training, however, can become a self-perpetuating cycle. We're seldom regaled with tales of black childhoods that affirmed and nurtured the possibility of idyllic love. On this front, my grandmothers and my mother were practically a ministry of propaganda.

My paternal grandparents were married for seventy years. When I think about the time I spent with them when I was very young, what stands out to me now is how well they worked as a team and how often they spent time apart. Those two facts only now strike me as related. My grandmother never drove. She affectionately referred to her husband as her chauffeur. My grandfather never shopped. Grandaddy would drive the three of us to department stores all afternoon, and then he would park and wait patiently in the station wagon while Grandma prowled for bargains. There was a mutual dependence between them, but also a considerable amount of breathing room. In the two-story house they shared once their six children had grown up, the main floor was Grandma's terrain and the downstairs area belonged to Grandaddy. The main floor was decorated with Grandma's wide array of plants and books, a voluminous collection of family pictures consistent with what you'd expect of a woman with six kids and twelve grandchildren, and a life-size cutout of Michael Jordan lining up a free throw.

Downstairs, my grandfather kept sports equipment, handyman tools, books, ancient newspapers, and an old police scanner he'd listen to in order to keep a bead on what was happening in the neighborhood. I suppose Grandaddy's zone could've been called a man cave, but it didn't have the resentful energy I associate with the term. I never felt like I was posting up in the He-Man Woman-Haters Club when I wandered down there to spend time with him. Grandaddy had one bedroom to himself on the main floor, but he generally didn't sleep in it. Since Grandma went to bed earlier than he did, Grandaddy often hung out in the other bedroom at night so as not to disturb her. In the morning on weekends, they'd emerge from the master bedroom together upon waking, so I assumed Grandaddy joined his wife once his own fatigue set in. The relationship seemed thoughtfully choreographed and palpably organic at the same time. I started to think about it analytically in my teens.

Maybe Grandma and Grandaddy never seemed to be at each other's throats because they were never breathing down each other's necks. Their example—along with my mother and father's, and my maternal grandmother and grandfather's—makes lasting, enthusiastic monogamy feel like a family business I have dragged my feet on taking over.

When I describe this conundrum to friends my age, my grandparents' relationship becomes more like the Egyptian pyramids. To these modern Hinge aficionados, even though Grandma and Grandaddy's love affair took place only two generations ago, it's an engineering marvel so fantastic it might as well have been built by aliens.

LA, LA, LA, LA, LA, LA. LA, LA, LA, LA, LA, LA.

I admit that it's perverse to see Jim Crow as Cupid's jilted handmaiden. But hear me out.

My college girlfriend and I were both named after poets. We rhymed almost immediately upon meeting. We were enjambed, to my great relish, within three months of knowing each other. This was one of our more prosaic moments.

The poet's namesake and I are walking back from lunch in Harlem in late 2014. We happen upon a small, bubble-shaped structure on the street. It looks a bit like a shed you might find in the back of a suburban home, except it's asymmetrical and crooked. You'd have to stoop to get through the entrance, and there might not be a ton of room to stand up in once inside. A sign on the exterior tells us that it's an avant-garde theater space. Someone puts on performance art inside the structure. The stage appears to be dark for the moment.

"This is totally some white people shit," the poet's namesake sneers.

I let her know that I disagree. I don't push back as hard as I would like to, though.

"No way," goes the poet's namesake, standing her ground. "Can you imagine any black person being into this?"

This was a familiar posturing. The poet's namesake probably thought street theater sounded wack. A few years earlier, there was a popular, satirical blog called *Stuff White People Like*, and assigning various universal interests to particular races was seen as canny cultural critique. My girlfriend's disdain for this DIY theater space, and her insistence on framing it as something intrinsically white, is a function of the Mean Girlification of black culture. In one scene of the seminal 2004 coming-of-age flick, *Mean Girls* protagonist Cady Heron produces a diagram of her high school's cafeteria tables. Each table in the school's lunchroom is labeled with an archetype. Band Geeks and Girls Who Eat Their Feelings occupy tables near the front of the room. Jocks, Cheerleaders, and Preps stake out their territory near the middle. Racial minorities are largely limited to three groups: Cool Asians, Asian Nerds, and Unfriendly Black Hotties. While the other high school cliques are constituted by what they do, these groups are defined by what they are—racial others. There are two types of Asian people, but their salient quality is that they're Asian. Some of the school's black students roll with the Jocks, and Cady's hierarchy acknowledges the remaining black students as fetching and aloof, but their group's key criterion is their hue. My girlfriend, and many people like her, absorbed this cheeky conflation of *who* someone is (their tastes, interests, activities, and relationships) with *what* someone is (their race, gender, sexual orientation, and social class) without examining it. As she saw it, making fun of experimental theater bolstered her authenticity as a black person. By her reasoning, what you are should comprehensively shape and determine who you are.

This point of view isn't unusual. Even well-meaning progressives can forget that blackness is its own cafeteria entirely. Black people—being, you know, people—have personalities that overlap with every single archetype on Cady Heron's diagram.

A case in point: My mother has been passionately engaged with theater making for most of my life. She cofounded a troupe consisting exclusively of other black women called Pamoja in the early '90s. A good stretch of my childhood was spent waiting backstage as she led rehearsals, built and designed sets, and coordinated press for the troupe's performances. You could characterize a lot of the work Mom and Pamoja did as experimental. The fun part is that even as my girlfriend issued an edict about what is and isn't black, she was also unwittingly violating a hallowed, stereotypically black precept. Since black experimental theater enthusiasts didn't exist in my girlfriend's morphology, she didn't realize she was talking about my momma.

This problem is a byproduct of school desegregation. A study designed and conducted in the 1940s by psychologists Kenneth and Mamie Clark influenced the outcome of *Brown v. Board of Education*, the famous 1954 legal case that led to the integration of American public schools. The two psychologists used four dolls, identical except in color, to evaluate the mental impact of racial segregation on black children.[2] Participants were asked to identify the race of the dolls and to indicate which doll they preferred. Most of the children went for the white doll. NAACP lawyers used the doll test to argue that racial segregation damaged black children's self-esteem. Sounds right. But ending segregation didn't restabilize black self-esteem. Since then, we increasingly measure ourselves based on our level of contrast to whiteness.

Ironically, a composite society makes purism more attractive. The absence of a formal barrier to interracial contact turns it into an all-purpose scapegoat. Anything you don't like about other black people can be blamed on their perceived proximity to whiteness. Under a separate-but-equal mandate, you might disparage black people who make experimental theater, but you've got to accept it as a native presence in the culture. In the post–Jim Crow era, though, saying your opps are the oppressor is the most efficient way to inflate a petty gripe into a moral crusade. It's like pulling a fire alarm at school because you have a math test that day.

My father is twenty-four years older than I am. He was two years old when de jure segregation ended with the Civil Rights Act of 1964. Though the legislation did not include the phrase "with all deliberate speed," it still applied. Baba grew up in St. Louis, where school desegregation didn't happen in a substantive way until 1977. Had my father not been enrolled in a racially integrated gifted program from fifth through twelfth grades, he would have experienced his entire childhood without any significant interaction with white people, just as three of his older siblings did. Segregation residue was more pronounced in my father's youth. Affirmative action had yet to be defanged, which meant there was a larger and more socially connected black contingent in a lot of majority white spaces, including the campus where he met my mother. A quarter-century doesn't seem like enough time for black people's self-concepts to undergo such a drastic shift. But when Baba met the Black Momba during her freshman year, he wasn't judging her by Cady Heron's standards.

Physical cosmologists put their observations into context using what they call a Copernican principle. It states that observations from Earth reflect an average position in the universe.[3] We circle an average star in an average galaxy in an average supercluster. This means that the things we see from that location and time are not special. I generally use the Copernican principle as a personal solipsism antidote. If something is happening inside me, it's probably happening to others, whether or not our commonality is ever confirmed.

In his essay "Jean-Michel Basquiat, Flyboy in the Buttermilk," Greg Tate writes: "My maternal grandfather used to say, Son, no matter where you go in this world and no matter what you find, somewhere up in there you will find a Negro."[4] I love the convergence between the Copernican principle and intrepid black self-awareness being passed down like an heirloom. Homespun wisdom and insight from on high can intersect. And why not? An earthy vantage point and a lofty one are both average positions in the universe.

The poet's namesake could have literally found me somewhere up in that DIY theater space. It was my kind of spot. What nettled her on sight struck me as pretty cool. Even if I didn't know anyone like my mother, or had not been exposed to any black experimental art, I would assume that if I was into it, some other black people are, too. Racism is, of course, at odds with the Copernican principle. It supposes that differences in skin, hair, and bone exceptionalize some observers and standardize others. But even those who fancy themselves anti-racist, as the poet's namesake certainly did, rehearse racism's assumptions within their critiques of whiteness. We're like this. They're like that. If *we* get close to *that* we're being like *them*, and that's debasing ourselves. I sympathize, but those italics are not mine.

The Copernican view of the Milky Way galaxy could trickle down to Milky Way candy bars. Black folks are sometimes called "chocolate." Not to be the friend that's too woke, but we might just as well describe chocolate as flesh-colored. Flesh that resembles a Milky Way bar is within the normal spectrum of human appearance. Calling dark skin "chocolate" positions blackness as exceptional rather than standard. The default way of framing the world is anthropomorphism—attributing human characteristics to nonhuman entities. To reverse that equation just because the humans in question are black is to needlessly decenter ourselves.

That afternoon in Harlem, I was haunted by visions of our future flesh-colored children. I wondered how they'd fare if and when they gravitated to something not dreamed of in my girlfriend's narrow philosophy. What would it do to them to have a mother who thought their natural impulses were extrinsic to the Motherland? Choosing to eventually co-parent with the poet's namesake felt like appointing the Roman Inquisition to raise Galileo.

SHA BOOGIE BOP

The whole idea of diverse education—the sense that universities should include historically underrepresented people not so much because it's right and just but because their presence will enrich the experience of their historically overrepresented counterparts—is a stratagem designed to placate bigots and cowards. That said, it's pretty dope to be outside at dusk with a fellow student who comes from someplace without fireflies.

It has happened to me twice. Both times I felt born again. Watching someone else absorb the existence of lightning bugs was electrifying by proxy.

A companion who takes in your home turf with soft eyes restores your own sense of wonder and novelty. Connecting people who have separate frames of reference, even if you have to shoehorn them together, mitigates jadedness.

Relationship scientists John and Julie Gottman argue that paying attention predicts relationship success. A relationship is composed, in large part, of bids for attention. When one partner makes a bid, the other partner may turn toward their loved one by tuning in. They can also reject the overture by choosing not to pay attention and in effect turning away from their loved one. The Gottmans' research found that couples who remained married for more than six years turned toward each other 85 percent of the time.[5] In marriages that dissolved, the spouses accepted each other's bids for attention only roughly one-third of the time. Diversity can provide incentive to heed such bids. I've been completely blasé about fireflies for the vast majority of my life. When schoolmates from China and Egypt, respectively, lit up at the sight of these everyday insects, the glow proved contagious. My schoolmates' excitement not only heightened my engagement with them as individuals but with my environment overall. "Difference" can strengthen rather than compromise connection.

When it comes to phenomena less innocuous than fireflies, having a friend with a fresh gaze can help you to diagnose ills that much more quickly. My friend Oda is from Norway, but she's completed various stages of her education in different corners of the globe. We met in undergrad when we were both attending a small Quaker liberal arts school in Indiana. Recently, she returned to the US as a visiting philosopher through a Fulbright fellowship at two different American universities. One was based in Atlanta and the other in New York City. Being in different regions in consecutive semesters informed her commentary. When we caught up on FaceTime, her reflections on her trip to the States helped me to see my own experience in a new light. A Scandinavian observer and a black American one can form a unique dialectic. I'm a stranger in my own homeland, tolerated through gritted teeth in a house I helped to build. Oda is a white foreigner, which means she can pass for a settler until she opens her mouth. We are both insiders and outsiders at the same time, but we're not inside or outside in any of the same ways. By comparing impressions, we create a tapestry of proximity and distance, affection and contempt, doubt and credulity. This combination is high in entertainment value whether or not it coalesces into something like truth.

Oda told me that the backdrop of mass incarceration casts a shadow over her entire experience in America. She was stricken by the knowledge that it is legally permissible for the state to end her life.

"I don't expect I'd ever do anything that would lead to getting the death penalty," she told me. "But at home it's not even possible. The longest prison sentence you can get is twenty-one years."

She observed that American police have never been unkind to her, which she attributes to the one-two punch of her whiteness and generally law-abiding nature. But even the way American cops move carries a menacing undertone. Oda saw a stark contrast between American police and Norwegian police. In her country, cops greet you as affably as a hotel clerk or a restaurant hostess might. Part of the reason Norwegian police are less threatening is that they're unarmed, but they're also not on edge like American police seem to be. To her, American cops are all coldness and coiled muscles, poised to strike at the slightest provocation—or even the illusion of one. I'm not posing this as some revelation; wariness of police is as endemic to the black community as cocoa butter. Still, hearing this confirmation from someone with a different lens reminded me of how many draconian American norms I take completely for granted. Like police seeing their beats as theaters of war.

Of course, the police aren't the only ones prone to unnecessary roughness. The brusqueness of American speech and manner was the first thing that stood out to Oda during her

Fulbright semesters. She ventured that the material conditions play a role. In Norway, there are structural protections for people who lose their jobs, get sick, or make life-destabilizing mistakes. These safeguards encourage goodwill between and among Norwegians. There is less incentive to believe that someone who has fallen on hard times deserves their plight. No such luck in the USA. To live in a society with militarized police, a peerlessly tenacious carceral system, rampant gun violence, and a gossamer-thin social safety net is to undergo a daily insensitivity training. We develop calluses on our hearts, and because we see this hardening as so crucial to making it, we forget they aren't the lithe organs they ought to be.

"When we think of an extreme place, we tend to imagine a country like North Korea as an example," Oda pointed out. "But the American version of capitalism is the most extreme form in history, making the United States an extreme place."

We're unlikely to connect this extremity with the fact that our country leads the world in divorce. But what are the odds that it doesn't contribute? Unchecked rugged individualism creates a population ill-equipped to try a little tenderness.

KOO KOO KACHOO

It's a Saturday in November, the kind it's getting absurd to describe as unseasonably warm, given that seasons as we know them seem increasingly inapplicable. Keesha, a family friend whom I think of as a bonus sibling, has invited me to a bus tour of St. Louis. I'm along for the ride. Keesha and I are seated near the back of the bus. The tour is advertised as an exploration of public policy that has shaped the city. A director of programming from the local history museum is our tour guide. As we rumble down St. Louis streets, he rattles off an impressive array of facts and anecdotes about the city's design. Within about ten minutes, it's clear that his commentary has an overarching theme. The impetus to preserve racial segregation, and in effect reinforce the line separating the city's haves from its have-nots, has motivated St. Louis's structure and development. The most sterling example is what our guide describes as the Delmar Divide. Delmar is a major street in St. Louis. The perception is that the north side of Delmar is the poor end and the south side is rich. High-end grocery stores like Whole Foods and Straub's populate the prosperous end of Delmar. White Castle, Aldi, and check-cashing establishments predominate on the other side. A determined class crusader might frame the fault line as more economic than racial, but it's clearly a combination of the two. Our tour guide tells us that the neighborhood north of Delmar is over 90 percent black and its southern counterpart is around 30 percent black. He describes this disparity as a remnant of "restrictive covenants." The city real estate board and pro-segregation housing associations forced white landlords into agreements that forbade the resale of their homes to people of color. These agreements were binding for periods up to fifty years.

There's a Bernie Sanders–looking dude seated directly in front of me. Between Bernie and the window is another white senior citizen, and the latter has had enough of the race talk. In a conspiratorial whisper, he says to Bernie, "So this is all about blacks. That's all this is."

After the tour there is an open discussion as tour attendees dig into a catered lunch. A white woman with glasses who looks to be around sixty-five makes conversation with Keesha. I sit quietly nearby. Glasses is excited about a community gardening project that's just underway in North City. The trouble is, there aren't a lot of people in the community who have experience with gardening. Specifically, Glasses finds it challenging to use the Weedwacker herself. To no avail, she's tried recruiting people to help through area schools.

Suddenly, Glasses raises her voice. I realize that this is an attempt to draw me into the conversation.

"We just need, like, good men to do the work," Glasses tells Keesha while looking at me out of the corner of her eye. "It would be great if we could rent out good men."

She flashes her teeth at me in what I figure she believes is a smile. It's more like a leer. Moments ago, we were both aboard a bus tour that excavated decades of racial animus simmering just below the topsoil. Knowledge of those timeworn tensions has had zero neutralizing effect. Instead, those eldritch energies now percolate between us unchecked. We've bypassed a Freudian slip for a Freudian bellyflop. This person is asking to rent me. Like a video from Blockbuster. Like a tuxedo on prom night. Like a rare text through interlibrary loan. The undisguised racism smarts enough to trigger my own elitism.

"Did you really just say that?" Keesha deadpans. "Did you really ask to rent him?"

"I tend to do more cognitive than physical labor," I tell Glasses without looking at her.

How ponderous that community gardening is viewed as an intuitive remedy for mending the Delmar Divide. It can so easily replicate the dynamics of sharecropping. It screams misplaced priorities louder than a mandrake. As a species, we're more equipped to tend to plant life than nurture healthy relationships with each other. What would be the social equivalent of a green thumb—the style of earthiness that helps the people around you to grow in all the ways they urgently need to? It's a hard row to hoe, but I'd like to start breaking ground. We'll need more than good men to do the work.

A-WOP-BOP-A-LOO-BOP-A-WOP-BAM-BOOM!

I don't know the exact moment when my frontal lobe achieved full maturation, but whenever it was, the odds are good that I was standing in the kitchen of an imitation Chinese food restaurant chain at the mall. The frontal lobe finishes developing in your mid-twenties. I hustled at this place on and off from ages seventeen through twenty-four, working my way up from busboy to server. The intermediate step between the two posts was working as a food runner. This role involved organizing the appetizer and entrée windows. Food runners arranged each table's orders on trays and ferried those trays through the dining room to hand deliver the steaming, greasy food to its intended recipients. During particularly busy shifts, the entrée window would have an expo, a go-between linking the head chef and his cooks to the food runners. The expo dove into the helter-skelter of entrées that piled up in the window during the rush period. He organized the entrée tickets as they emerged from the machine. Then, he'd tick off each dish the kitchen staff plopped down in the window as the head chef oversaw the ticket's completion. If the kitchen staff didn't complete a given order correctly, the expo was responsible for notifying the head chef and making sure the mix-up was resolved. This allowed the food runners to focus exclusively on delivering food. I had some success as an expo. The key, as I saw it, was to communicate respectfully and remain composed. A part of me enjoyed the challenge of navigating dinner rushes without having a fit. I was a naturally understated person. I thought that I'd found a task where being less reactionary than average was an asset. The restaurant was a hotbed of hotheads. Screaming matches between the various strata in the restaurant hierarchy were commonplace.

Eventually, the manager who supervised food runners pulled me aside. He told me I'd be assigned fewer expo shifts going forward. The manager acknowledged my competence at overseeing the entrée window. The problem, however, was that the back-of-house staff wasn't fond of working with me.

"Of course they don't respect you," the manager said gently. "You never yell at them, cuss them out, or even raise your voice, really."

It hit me all at once. Being expo was a task in which the social and practical objectives were completely at odds. I had proven that staying loose allowed me to run a tighter ship. None of that mattered, however, if the macho kitchen guys saw me as soft. A dose of volatility would better endear me to my coworkers than doing my job well.

The manager's feedback is consistent with a broader cultural reverence for intemperance. The first two times I read *Mrs. Dalloway*, my sympathies lay with Septimus Warren Smith, the shellshocked World War II veteran who serves as a kind of double for protagonist Clarissa Dalloway.[6] Septimus is treated by the eminent psychiatrist Sir William Bradshaw. Dr. Bradshaw determines that it isn't madness ailing Septimus, but rather, "a lack of proportion." As a younger person I saw this diagnosis as patronizing—Septimus's problem wasn't that he participated in slaughter and witnessed the slaughter of his friends, but rather that he was making it a bigger deal than it was. I saw Dr. Bradshaw as cold, dismissive, and arrogant, an exemplar of the obtuseness plaguing my own time and place. I now recognize the urgency of seeing our woes at scale. When it comes to making big deals out of things, Americans reflexively dramatize the same way we fall for the upsell of a McDonald's value meal: We tend to supersize it.

My first semester teaching full-time, the writing department that I worked in agreed to hold anti-racist pedagogy workshops at every other faculty meeting.

"I'm sure you're all doing great anti-racist work in all of your classes," our department chair told us, charitably, over Zoom. "This will be a chance to share it with your colleagues."

An older professor balked almost instantly. He made clear that he supported everyone's use of anti-racist pedagogy. But he drew the line at relaying what was happening in his classroom to the entire department.

"Being expected to share the anti-racist work that we're doing in class could result in professors being policed," he moaned.

This meeting occurred a few months after police shot and killed twenty-six-year-old medical worker Breonna Taylor in her bedroom. Our department's push to emphasize anti-racist pedagogy was a response to that killing and the summer 2020 uprising catalyzed by the murder of George Floyd, whom police officer Derek Chauvin fatally asphyxiated on video. In this context, my colleague's choice of metaphor—comparing mild oversight from his colleagues to "policing"—was both unsurprising and wildly out of proportion. It's reasonable that police would be on the professor's mind in the conversation at hand even if no one had mentioned cops explicitly. At the same time, invoking police in a writing department meeting misrepresented the stakes. Some of the other professors in the department rushed to mollify the one who complained. Others, offended by the inflammatory comparison, grew angry and began to chide him. Both responses ultimately prevented a sober assessment of the argument's merits and faults.

Would this professor's department mates stand on his neck until he died? Could sharing anti-racist lesson plans escalate into a no-knock invasion of his house during which he was shot to death while he slept? What actual harm might the older professor suffer from this version of "policing"? At the very worst, he *might* be publicly embarrassed. Even that was unlikely, given that the department was overwhelmingly white and generally forgiving of racist miscues.

My colleague's skittishness about the anti-racist pedagogy workshop was completely overblown relative to the plausible outcomes. As I watched the melee unfold on the Zoom call, I wished Dr. Bradshaw from *Mrs. Dalloway* would make a house call. Most of us get way more reps at thinking and behaving rashly than allowing cooler heads to prevail. On so many television shows, the characters fly off the handle at the slightest provocation. They take each others' words and actions personally no matter the context. The protagonist of your favorite show is about as likely to de-escalate a tense situation as a police officer is. Forget being meditative or conciliatory; reactionary tendencies drive entertainment value. With the exception of a heartwarming denouement or two, audiences generally aren't tuning in to see actors calmly sorting out their differences, or extending generosity and patience to their competitors and opponents. A steady diet of antagonism-driven media makes people think that having outsized emotional responses to things is the recipe for having an interesting life. We begin to associate discord with sizzle and tranquility with tedium. There's so much impetus to be impetuous.

WHOA-OH-OH-OH

It's fair if the public has grown tired of writers—people who make and manipulate narratives for a living—warning everyone about the dangers of story addiction. But there is a story we need to fall out of love with if we're ever going to get better at loving people. I'm talking about the pluck-to-peril ratio. In many of our culture's most popular tales, the main character must overcome an obstacle, and the obstacle becomes increasingly perilous as the story unfolds. What endears us to the main character is their pluck. They earn our allegiance through some combination of industriousness, ingenuity, and intrepidity under trying circumstances. The same quality is what allows them to ultimately overcome or mount vigorous defense against the peril. When a story has too much peril and the character doesn't have enough pluck, we tend to lose interest. When the character is too plucky but doesn't face an adequately perilous situation, that's not very engaging either. The ideal proportion between pluck and peril is very close to one to one, but not quite! It's chef's kiss when a character comes heartbreakingly close to surmounting the peril but tragically fails. We get fist-pumping satisfaction when the peril very nearly wipes out the plucky hero, but the latter ekes out a victory by channeling reserves of inner strength they didn't know they had. These stories don't only live in the realm of imagination. The pluck-to-peril ratio influences how we think about real life as well.

NBA Hall of Famer and tireless ad pitchman Shaquille O'Neal has a crowd-pleasing tale about his stepfather's approach to toughening up his stepson. As a rookie, O'Neal played a subpar game at Madison Square Garden. When the game ended, his stepfather, Sgt. Phillip Harrison, asked why the young NBA star had underperformed.[7] O'Neal admitted that the pressure of playing on a big stage had gotten to him. Harrison's response was to take O'Neal to meet a homeless family at 5 a.m. the following morning. He pointed out that O'Neal's battle with nerves was nothing compared to the family's struggle to survive.

"You spoiled motherfucker, making all this money, talking about pressure?" Harrison admonished. "This is pressure: when you don't know where your next meal is coming from."

That day, O'Neal used his resources and connections to help the man secure steady work. He helped the family get an apartment and paid for it himself. The lesson changed O'Neal's perspective.

It's a heartfelt story. I can understand why it moves people. For starters, the story appeals to the popular jealousy of professional athletes. They play what is disingenuously called a "children's game" for a living, and because me and my buddies can simulate a drastically inferior iteration of that game in the park on Sundays, professional athletes are somehow undeserving of the immense fame and wealth that some of them gain in exchange. This reading overlooks the fact that Shaq was paid the way most participants in American capitalism are paid: a fraction of the value he created for someone richer than him. You're not overpaid if you have a skill that fans pay through the nose to ooh and ahh at. Believing athletes are undeserving also downplays how hard they have to train and prepare to compete with the most physically gifted and determined people in the world. The Big Diesel was twenty years old in his rookie season. In this particular game, he was facing off against Patrick Ewing, a living legend and physical marvel on par with Shaq who had the benefit of ten years of experience on his side. The matchup took place in a historic arena colloquially known as the mecca of basketball. Feeling some anxiety under those circumstances hardly makes someone weak. I don't know about you, but most of the people I know get nervous if they reach the Starbucks counter before they've figured out which latte they want to order.

Shaq's anecdote exemplifies how and why it's so commonplace to scold someone for having basic human emotions. O'Neal was facing less peril, in his stepfather's eyes, than the man who was struggling to feed and house his family. The parent-to-child message was, your feelings are invalid unless the obstacle you're facing is incomparable and unprecedented.

An individual's subjective experience of hardship is usually proportional to their personal frame of reference, not to the total possible extent of suffering in the world. I don't like carrying my bass guitar on the subway. I am also aware that some musicians carry cellos on the train. Since I don't play cello, and there is no scenario where I might plausibly have to carry one around, I am content to periodically kvetch about the cargo I do tote.

You can shame people out of expressing the self-pity they feel, but not without debilitating long-term consequences. Not every iota of self-pity is a pity party; sometimes it's like a pity petit déjeuner. We owe the latter a measure of tolerance. High regard for the pluck-to-peril ratio encourages people to suppress rather than work through negative emotions. What if Sgt. Harrison had made the Big Diesel feel heard before reminding him—as he probably already knew—that his woes paled in comparison to those of the indigent? What if Shaq's stepfather had reassured the star center without sneering at his vulnerability? The pluck-to-peril ratio is not only a formula for structuring the stories that resonate most; it's also a standard we use to apportion compassion.

There's a connection between this Shaq story and a talking point from his podcast that became fodder for a sequence on *The View*.

"Open up to a woman?" Shaq said incredulously to his cohost on *The Big Podcast with Shaq* in early 2024.[8] "Never. No. . . . Once you do, whenever something goes down, they're going to throw it back in your face."

This clearly misguided relationship advice drew criticism in a way that Sgt. Harrison's lesson about "real pressure" did not. Shaq's phrasing on the podcast is giving misogynist. It makes sense to presume his resistance to opening up with people is particular to women. Sgt. Harrison's lesson about pressure, however, might have encouraged Shaq to believe that honest self-disclosure is too risky to venture in general. In Shaq's athletic prime, one of his many nicknames was Superman, a fearless comic book hero nearly immune to harm. Shaq remained territorial about this nickname even after his retirement. He fumed publicly when his successor, Orlando Magic franchise player Dwight Howard, competed in the 2008 All Star Weekend dunk contest with the famous *S* insignia on his chest. Shaq's commitment to the illusion of being too heroic to be hurt runs deep. As the story goes, his stepfather threw his admission of weakness in his stepson's face as a reflex. Shaq likely carried Sgt. Harrison's training into his romantic relationships. I suspect that the seven-footer's size played a role in his stepfather's impatience with his stepson's anxiety. In sports and elsewhere, it's customary to joke that someone is simply "too big" to experience self-doubt, fear, or discomfort. There is a draconian expectation that people can suppress emotion in proportion to their stature. It's harder to see goliaths as plucky. We expect, somehow, that they tower over even nonphysical obstacles.

The panel on *The View* predictably took a different one than Shaq.

"Partners need to speak to each other. They need to communicate," *View* cohost Sunny Hostin said.[9] "And what better communicators are there than women?"

The fear of confirming negative stereotypes about your social group is called stereotype threat. I like to call the equally dangerous corollary stereotype *treat*: when generalizations about your group provide an intoxicating hit of ego gratification that precludes seeing your own behavior clearly. Women are subject to generally all of the same cultural messages about pluck and peril that men are. In some ways, they have even more incentive to invest in them; a woman whose behavior is seen as weak incurs demerits for her entire gender, while a man's failure is his alone. The perception that women are naturally more sensitive, understanding, and empathic than men, and that men in turn are more rational, objective, and lucid than women, is like grade inflation. Whichever side of it you're on, it can create the illusion that you have less to learn than we all do.

Sgt. Harrison may have originally punched Shaq's ticket to the lonely hearts club, but his thinking wasn't uniquely male. Strongman exploits on the court earned Shaq the distinction as the most dominant hooper in the history of his sport, but even bruisers nurse bruises.

Commitment to the pluck-to-peril ratio is why catchphrases like *white privilege* and *fragile masculinity* are so easily stripped of their social justice import and reduced to schoolyard taunts. Those terms are meant to indict structures. Their primary selling point, though, is that they offer a noble pretext for calling someone weak. When people are taught to measure themselves based on the strength of their opposition, trivializing their hardships strikes at the core of their self-worth.

I'm not suggesting that we'd all be better off whimpering and collapsing into heaps at the first sign of adversity. Resilience and stoicism obviously have their place. But for all our love of checks and balances, American culture's emphasis on fortitude is quite lopsided. Being allowed the space to express and process hurt deepens your own capacity to have compassion for others. Stiff-arming anybody who doesn't keep a stiff upper lip makes the world less hospitable to love.

OOOH-BOP-BOP-BOP-BOP

A country this obsessed with driving should use cars to spread team spirit. When I'm in charge, all car horns will be tuned to thirds, fifths, and sevenths of each other. That way, whenever people road-rage they also barbershop harmonize. Traffic will actually jam. Every stop at a red light will offer the possibility of romantic serenade. Let's fight declining birth rates with soaring harmonies. We'll call it esprit de cars. But I suppose even I should know this is naive. Being in an ensemble isn't always a leveler. Maybe it never is.

I have an enduring fascination with the British boy band One Direction. Their name has such a collaborative, fraternal ring to it, as in: We're all moving and pulling in one direction, to our collective benefit. And to an extent the name is reflective of the operation. But even they had a discernible hierarchy. It wasn't a flat organizational structure. We're all pulling in a single direction and everyone gets a piece of the pie, but they're differently sized pieces, and we aren't all pulling the same amount of weight. The hierarchy within 1D isn't based on anything objective. It's barely merit related, but it exists just the same. Nice guy Niall Horan's solos are spare. He usually has a few lines per song where he's featured, and those lines are rarely in the chorus. Louis Tomlinson, the member who boasts the most songwriting credits to his name, is roughly even with Horan in the vocal hierarchy. Tomlinson's solos sneak up on you. His moments are usually either in the second verse or in the bridge of One Direction songs. Tomlinson exudes a casual affability that balances the diva vibes emanating from the upper-tier members of the band.

The late Liam Payne was known to fans as Mr. First Verse. He's often the tone-setter in the beginning of One Direction songs, and he carried himself as if he was the definitive frontman. His voice is fairly nondescript, though, and when he took over the more difficult vocal parts when Zayn Malik left the group in 2015, the talent deficit was conspicuous. Zayn had carried the group vocally, executing the most technical runs and dazzling high notes. But success in pop music is rarely reducible to having the best chops. Zayn managed to pull off the nifty magic trick of serving as the band's second banana and being too cool for the whole thing at the same time. His reserved, brooding style made him susceptible to being upstaged by Harry Styles, who has since become the biggest post–One Direction solo star. In live performances Harry is often perched at stage center. Harry wasn't quite the premier singer in the band—that distinction belongs to Zayn—but he was clearly the most charismatic. On the band's biggest singles, Harry's isolated vocals usually enunciate the titular lyric, which fits. He was the obvious choice for making sure a song sticks the landing. It was also Harry who thought up the name One Direction. He claims it didn't mean anything and that he only chose it because it sounded good. I doubt that I'm the only Directioner to close read it as a mission statement. I see the deceptive equality of One Direction as representative of how the concept of equality works in general. We expect people to know how to treat each other reciprocally, but they have few if any precedents to show them how that's done. Even the contexts or activities that announce themselves as mutual and cooperative have an undeniable stratification lurking somewhere in there. The phrase *double standard* is even a bit misleading, because standards are multiple way more often than not.

Zayn and Harry are my favorite 1D members, but I identify with Louis most, at least aspirationally. His archetype is probably the most useful to the world: a glue guy guiding the game plan behind the scenes while claiming only a measured share of the limelight. A romantic coupling is, to me, not wildly distinct from a two-person boy band. We're going to present ourselves as equal on the surface, but some disparities in competence, vanity, and agenda will inevitably lead to asymmetries. If we manage to weather those without mangling the choreography, well, that's what makes us beautiful.

SHOOP SHOOP SHOO BE DOOP

I wish the following was a Jussie Smollet Joint. Unfortunately, this actually happened.

At a mid-2024 band practice, our drummer Scott recounted a racist incident from his childhood. He was on something like a quiz bowl team in middle school. The team practiced in groups of three. Scott, who is Asian, ended up in a group with two black guys. When the white quiz bowl coach saw this configuration, he snickered.

"You know what your team should be called? The Ethnic *Sirs*," quipped the coach.

When Scott told me this story, we were set to play Arlene's Grocery, one of our favorite Manhattan venues, the following night. Since two of the bands' other members were out of town, we'd be performing as a trio consisting of myself on vocals and bass, Scott on drums, and Sir on guitar. Hence why that particular incident felt apropos. The following night onstage, I conveyed the gist of Scott's story as a segue to our original song "Model Minority," a diss track about the infamous anti-affirmative action litigant Abigail Fisher.

"We're called Baby Got Back Talk," I roared, windmilling strums on my bass guitar. "But tonight, we'll be known as the Ethnic Sirs. This next song is in that quiz bowl coach's dishonor."

A middling weeknight crowd cheered dutifully. Stage banter has incantatory power. If I had known what lay in wait for us that night, I might have thought twice about stoking anti-black status anxiety over a PA system.

After the gig, I was chilling with the head girl, my girlfriend at the time, at a burger place nearby. In the Australian school system, one girl and one boy student are chosen for a leadership role in which they model the qualities other students are meant to emulate. The head girl had held that post in her high school days. Now, in her early thirties, she still carries herself with the long-striding, straight-backed self-possession that got her elected. My bandmates and a couple of our friends were at the counter ordering food, while the head girl and I posted up near the back of the restaurant. A short, brown man in a baseball cap with bloodshot eyes was glaring at the head girl. He was racially ambiguous, but not white. I could see that there was some kind of discomfort or static between them, but I wasn't sure what. The head girl made eye contact with me.

"We need to get out of here," she said, wincing. "Now."

I nodded. She headed toward the exit while I walked to the cash register to gather our crew and relocate.

In the time it took me to round up our people, the angry guy in the baseball cap followed the head girl out of the restaurant.

The two of them exchanged terse and inaudible words on the other side of the glass store front. I rushed outside and stepped to dude.

"Yo," I said, "is there a problem?"

The man looked at the head girl.

"I don't have a problem with you," he explained. Then he looked at me, his eyes flashing. "My issue is you."

"Me?" I echoed, my blind spot for MAGAs with melanin getting the best of me. "What for?"

"I have a problem with you niggers being with them," the man spat. He looked from me, to the head girl, to my bandmate Sir and his wife. Sir is black and his wife is white. The sight of Sir and I, two nerdy-looking black punk rockers, with tall blonds on our arms made this guy have less fun. Call it Great Replacement Praxis. For her part, Sir's wife audibly gasped at the sound of a hard *r*. She let go a few choice words of her own and charged the guy. With a running start, she put both hands on his chest and shoved. The man stumbled but regained his footing. He cursed at Sir's wife, but his focus seemed to be elsewhere.

The incensed incel glanced longingly at the head girl.

"I would never hurt her," he gushed, like he was swearing a sacred oath. He turned back to me. "But I'll fucking kill you."

Welp. Here was peril. What kind of pluck would I muster? My bass was in a cloth case on my back. I considered taking it off and wielding it as a weapon. Suppose I thrashed this dude, though. The police were infinitely less likely to believe my story than to take this nutter's side. If seeing me with Stereotypical Barbie made him feel like he wasn't Kenough, New York's finest wouldn't take kindly to it, either. My foe was diminutive. I'm average sized myself, but I had considerable height and reach advantages over dude. Not to mention black people are scary. Presumably even nerdy ones. It was suspicious that he felt so confident taking me on. Did he have a more deadly weapon of his own?

Before I could decide how to respond, the head girl stepped forcefully between my attacker and me. She towered over this guy by six inches or more. She spread her arms behind her, using her considerable wingspan to shield me. She refused to move.

Fragile masculinity was the unstoppable force. White privilege was the immovable object. There were three women in a parked car to our left. Hearing the commotion, one of them extended her arm out of her window, recording us on her phone.

"Just what I need," I muttered. "A viral video of a white woman saving my life."

I could feel the head girl's abdomen vibrating as she barricaded me from harm's way. Her face wasn't visible since she had her back to me, but I knew she was cracking up. Somehow, in the middle of an attempted hate crime, we were suppressing mutual giggles. My gal's gallantry meant she was acing the pluck-to-peril ratio. As for me, a woman was protecting me from getting my ass kicked. If we want to be charitable, we could say she was holding me back from defending myself and likely being arrested or worse. To my pluck-to-peril ratio credit, I *was* laughing in the face of danger, okay?

The gridlock distracted our foe long enough for Scott, a six-foot-two and muscular man whose role in our band is hitting things with sticks, to bear hug him from behind. Sir backed Scott up, and the two of them calmly talked the guy down while pushing him down the street in a direction opposite from the head girl and me. I was still worried the man had a gun. As my detractor receded farther and farther, the head girl kept her body glued to mine. We grappled and shoved, like NBA bigs battling for post position. I understood her caution, but I didn't want to let Sir and Scott out of my sight. What were the Ethnic Sirs without solidarity? If the triggered racist was strapped, though, he thankfully never waved his gun. He disappeared down the avenue, shouting every epithet he could think of over his shoulder. When the threat had been neutralized, my bandmates and our crew reconvened and hugged it out. We never did determine whether the would-be hate criminal had followed us from the show, or if the dustup was just a coincidence.

There's a thin line between giving due credit and turning any white person with anti-racist mettle into John Brown. But I was moved that the head girl saw and anticipated a loved one's need. She fulfilled it with the means she was best positioned to use. She stepped up where stepping up was called for. The relationship didn't last, for reasons including but not limited to race. I'm shaped by her example just the same.

Before she passed, my maternal grandmother told relatives that she hoped the head girl would join our family. The two of them never met. My grandmother knew that when Indigo had been struck by a car in New York while I was at work in St. Louis, I had asked the head girl to meet Indi at the hospital to look after and advocate for my sister in my stead. Which she did with aplomb. That occasion was enough to convince my grandmother of the head girl's suitability. Indigo thankfully remains as spry as ever. My relationship with the head girl flatlined. I don't want to get too Loving Day about this. But maybe my grandmother was thinking on different timescales than my own.

GLUTTONOUS PUNISHMENT

Some studies warn that eating processed foods—like for instance, the vegan equivalents of bacon cheeseburgers—neutralizes the nutritional benefits of a plant-based diet.[1] A similar principle applies to patronizing black-owned restaurants like Slutty Vegan, which touts a message of empowerment while addressing customers as sluts. You seek out the black-owned restaurant to eat your cultural vegetables, but the result is less wholesome than advertised. Peasant's palate that I have, I think the grub at Slutty Vegan is tasty. I get distracted by the food for thought.

It isn't entirely unique to us, but it's wild how fervently black people believe that it's revolutionary to embrace your degradation. Walk into this joint and the employees shout things like "Welcome, sluts! We can take your slutty-ass order if you get in this line first." I like absurdity and perverse humor as much as the next person. But I don't need any help being disrespected or put down. Paying someone to talk to me like I'm worthless is redundant to the totality of my black experience.

It seems like this should be a common reaction. But some black culture consistently glamorizes subjugation, and the Slutty Vegan gimmick is an extension of that. Our commitment to corporal punishment is an example. Many of us are deeply invested in the idea that we must punish our kids harshly before the white man can. Racism and tough love necessitated by racism converge to create the impression that even if the underlying motives differ, there is bipartisan agreement, so to speak, that your blackness means that you should be treated less gently than others. It's fashionable to call each other nigga (and bitch). These practices are forms of doubling down on the things that harm us, but we conceive of the doubling down as an antidote.

You could make the case that referring to ourselves in unflattering terms deprives our critics of ammunition. Audre Lorde writes that "nothing I accept about myself can be used against me to diminish me."[2] On its face, opening a verbal abuse–themed vegan restaurant is an application of that wisdom. Except I think that Lorde is talking about accepting things that are *true* about yourself. The nigger is a myth, an invention that serves its creators. The idea that black women are lascivious or unscrupulous relative to all people is also a fabrication. Both of these lies were created to naturalize inequality, and at least initially, to insulate enslavement from critique. Accepting a lie at face value and then enshrining it as gospel is not doing what Lorde (and others) are talking about. Unless, of course, you believe the fictions of white supremacy are facts.

It's hard not to see the existence of a slur-to-term-of-endearment pipeline as a symptom of a deep-seated allergy to earnestness. Why work so hard to defrost offensive terms when warmer words are in arm's reach? Reclaiming a slur offers the safety of ironic distance. Expressing affection in unambiguous terms is riskier. A historically loathed people can experience invective as a love language. Our version of Pavlovian conditioning has made the stick into a carrot. And a heavily processed, GMO-ridden one at that.

PEDAGOGY OF THE COMPRESSED

The late, great record producer Mark Rubel once told me that there's a knob you can use in the studio to make recordings "sound more good." He joked that sound engineering is generally complex, but this knob offered a painfully simple cheat code. The cheat code was compression. If you slap a compressor on a song, it will intuitively "sound more good" to even the least trained ear. Compression flattens the dynamic range of a recording so that there is less disparity between its loudest and quietest sounds. You could liken compression to the temperance necessary to sustain mature love. Fewer jagged soundwaves make for a more polished listen, just like an even-keeled relationship dynamic makes a smoother partnership. In black people's cases, though, we're subject to a compressor that condenses the full spectrum of emotions and sensations we experience and communicate. In turn, we compress ourselves out of habit. When your ear becomes accustomed to hearing the compressed version of a performance, the raw version sounds unrefined.

One night after a show in Queens, New York, several different people came up to me and asked if I'd learned the bass in church. More than one person mentioned that they had never heard a punk bassist with "gospel chops." Relative to the average American, I spent little of my youth in church. I definitely never played a lick of bass in the lord's house. It would've been perplexing. But I've been black a long time.

It's bananas that Du Bois was trying to convince everyone that black people have souls—and we're basically still litigating that—but the idea that we're inherently "soulful" is consensus. The comments about my bass playing remind me of how rock critics described former Hootie and the Blowfish frontman Darius Rucker's vocals in the '90s. Much of the group's press highlighted how "soulful" their lead singer was. The persistent connection between blackness and soulfulness makes me wonder how varied and expansive our repertoires are perceived to be, even among other black people. The word *soulful* connotes worldliness, acquaintance with struggle, weary melancholy. The term has a weighty solemnity, as if every time a black person emits a musical sound from their body, it's saddled with four hundred years of subjugation and sorrow. By contrast, white rockers, especially in the punk and indie subgenres, are repeatedly described as *twee.*

As a musician and as a person, I often feel more twee than soulful. (My sister Indigo's short film, *I Only Want It If It's Sweet*, speaks to a related tension. The word *twee*, British in origin, comes from a representation of a child's pronunciation of sweet.) Whimsy and levity shadow my every move. I don't see my tweeness as proximal to whiteness, or as something that represents an aspiration to be anything but black. That said, being black makes tweeness less palatable to the people around me. Access to tweeness has stakes. If being twee is a form of unreserved tenderness and earnestness, not having it on the menu shortchanges the possibility of satisfying connection.

Jazz titan Miles Davis was once asked if black musicians are genetically superior to white ones.[1] Davis acknowledged that there was a difference between the two, but not in ability.

"Do black musicians hurt more?" the white interviewer pressed.

"It's not that cliché," Davis said.

"It's not that easy to say that because you came out of slavery you play on the beat," the interviewer allowed.

In response, Davis recalled a conversation he had with one of his instructors at Julliard. The instructor suggested that the blues comes from the sound of black people being despondent at night. Davis told the interviewer that he rejected this explanation.

"My father is rich. My momma is good-looking. And I can play the blues," Davis countered. "I've never suffered and I don't intend to suffer."

There's little about Davis's discography that one would call twee. But he was unwilling to see black musicianship flattened into the maudlin bleating of monochrome martyrs. We have range. Traumatic history always threatens to compress it.

The inverse of Davis's argument is also true. You can suffer and still operate in shades beyond a kind of blue. Showing your true colors can in fact lead to suffering. Wearing too serene a smile, for instance, is frowned upon. The last time I saw my paternal grandmother Joyce alive, she warned me to be careful of my whereabouts in St. Louis. She worried that hood dudes would be suspicious, if not outright contemptuous, of me on sight.

"You're kind of jive, G," my grandma said, laughing. "I mean, I like that you're jive. But everyone can tell, and that can be dangerous."

Her point was clear. Them boys will be boys if your boy is too buoyant.

Lacking the leeway to be jive in safety, I searched for supplements in the free box on the campus of a Quaker college. Maybe

I hoped to siphon off the freedom overflow that someone else wasn't using. Inside, I stumbled upon a brightly colored propeller beanie. It was homemade. Someone had punctured the top of a baseball hat and stuck a toy airplane axle and propeller through it. Between the axle and the propeller, there was a tiny unicorn ornament. When I wore the hat, the unicorn perched at the crown of my head like a faithful pet. The propeller would twirl slightly in the wind. How fanciful. How strange. I was amazed its creator would abandon it to the free box.

I may not be street smart but I'm certainly not street remedial. It was obvious that the sight of me rocking the propeller beanie at the big age of twenty-two would rub many onlookers the wrong way. And precisely for that reason, I couldn't resist. Earlier that same year, I'd auditioned to become a cast member on MTV's *The Real World*. At the end of the group audition, all of us hopefuls were asked to choose one adjective to sum up our whole swag. I chose quixotic. At the time I was too quixotic to realize that picking that word all but guaranteed that I wouldn't be cast. My free-box find symbolized exactly this clash: my quixotism vs. the real world. Every time that propeller spun in the breeze, I was getting my lick back. *Twee at last, twee at last!* Or so I thought. The propeller beanie turned up in the trash can at my parents' house.

"It looks adorable on you," the Black Momba said apologetically. Apology more in the sense of self-defense than contrition. "But I can't have you out here looking like that."

What's salvaged from the free box is just as soon condemned to the dustbin of history. One person's trash is another person's treasure is a mother's trash again.

I'm complicit in cranking the compression knob on black folks. One of my favorite salutations is, "All right, now—be smooth." In telling someone this, I am fastening the straps on the straitjacket of elegance. There are three audio-engineering terms that can be used to explain the limited grace extended to black people's emotions. Clipping is the point at which a signal overwhelms an audio system. If the level of your audio exceeds this point, you will not increase the output level. Instead, you will end up with distortion. The average signal level at which an audio system is designed to operate is called nominal level. Headroom is the safe zone between nominal level and the point when your signal starts to clip. If your audio system has a lot of headroom, it means there is space for a signal to surpass the nominal level without becoming distorted. If your system has minimal headroom, a signal can barely go above nominal level before it becomes distorted. Heavy is the headroom that won't sustain a propeller beanie crown.

When my college buddy Nix and I first became friends, I noticed that whenever we were clowning on the phone, Nix would only laugh for a few seconds at a time. At first I wondered if they were self-conscious about the timbre of their laugh, as some people are. The truth was more tragic. Nix told me that they contained their laughter out of reflex. Laughing too loud or too long is read as ghetto, Nix pointed out. Nix's limited mirth allotment was a protective measure. Truncating their laughter was an attempt to stay within the nominal level. If they exceeded it, they'd clip; the audio system through which black people are received would distort the signal. Nix's laughter would be read as crass, vulgar, or buffoonish. Even if there was more headroom in our particular rapport, Nix was in the habit of operating as if the world would grant them no headroom at all.

Learning more about Nix's modulation happened to converge with some pointed commentary about my own. At the time, Sasha and I were taking a class together on magazine writing. While I thought I was friendly enough with Virginia, the professor who taught it, Viriginia and Sasha acted like they had mingled blood under the monkey bars. They hung out outside of class, and when they did, Virginia prodded Sasha for gossip. Virginia had noticed that Sasha and I were tight. She was surprised that Sasha had been able to get close to me.

"Oh my god, that guy has such a wall up," Virginia claimed. "He's so handsome though. He has such an angry, handsome face."

Afterward, Sasha gave me the highlights of her hang sesh with Virginia. We laughed about the white professor's choice of adjectives. The conjunction of angry and handsome sounded the fetishization bells. Her hasty supposition that I was somehow emotionally unavailable seemed like a (jungle?) feverish projection. It might be more flattering to be called handsome if it wasn't so vividly enmeshed with perceived brutishness.

"It does seem like there's something about my face that makes people think I'm this sinister, unhappy dude," I told Sasha.

"Something about your face is right," Sasha snorted. "*It's the melanin.*"

Any consideration of how my fearsome reputation complicates the pursuit of love has to begin with Sasha's canny reminder that it's the melanin, stupid. Stereotype threat shapes all social terrain, and the singles scene is no exception. But that's barely the half of it. Though it's easy to forget in these rigidly identitarian times, personal qualities that don't show up on a census also influence our social experiences. In that respect there is something else about my face. People have commented on my stoic and unreadable demeanor for most of my life. At work, in school, on dates, and everywhere in between, I've consistently been called things like "affectless" and "poker-faced." I view this characteristic as value neutral, and equally attributable to nature and nurture alike. My mother tells me I inherited it from my father. My paternal grandfather's grill wasn't especially expressive either. At the same time, I know that an ambiguous resting face is something one is more apt to cultivate because of the pervasive responses to melanin. I might not be so unflappable if there weren't so many people and things trying to flap me. Maintaining a placid exterior is useful for navigating racism. Provided that my veneer is more stolid than sweet, keeping that cover also fulfills the directives of patriarchy. I'm not always so sure what's motivating my emotional self-regulation—the desire to confound the Man or the pressure to "take it" like one. In either case, customary stoicism can hamstring intimacy. As a black person interested in women, I have two powerful transhistorical incentives not to indulge or communicate my emotions. Women in turn have substantial reason not to trust it when I do.

Virginia, my professor, was spot on in the manner of a math student whose wonky computation somehow lands on the correct answer. What she called "a wall" was my habitual attempt to stay at nominal level. My signal was clipping despite my best efforts, though, since I was being read as an angry person. The lack of headroom has gone to my head and shows up on my face.

In relationships, everyone wants to be Reagan at the Brandenburg Gate. We might not be Great Communicators ourselves. But still we yearn to scream, *Mr. Gorbachev, tear down that wall!* It's easy to be impatient with another person's reluctance to open up. But there are usually legitimate reasons for their caution. Mapping the world's propensity to misunderstand us using nominal level and clipping metaphors could help us carve out more headroom in the heart space. Pinpointing where and how we feel most limited equips our loved ones to help make us more free. Signals and distortion are apt frames for interpersonal connection. It doesn't hurt to be reminded that your subjectivity is generally opaque to everyone but you, and that you rely on signaling to offset this. Racism, misogyny, and transphobia are often described as systemic phenomena. Accurate as that may be, it's sometimes too abstract for granular understanding. Seeing the effects of those isms in terms of an audio "system" grounds them with sensory detail. Which is not to say that only big-picture social ills shape the headroom in our relationships. A variety of factors are at play.

Leeriness of clipping can also influence us to withhold useful critique from our loved ones. Flimsy egos reduce headroom. In an economic system where so many are depressed, anxious, or some combination of the two, constructive feedback is often seamlessly absorbed into a given person's negative self-talk.

When I had dinner with a close writer friend after I secured my first book deal, she was miffed that she had learned the good news from a social media post. The writer had sold her own first book several months before, and we had kept a running dialogue about the process. There's not much of a gap between how this person writes and how she talks. She is an electric conversationalist who speaks in pull quotes. As writers with overlapping skills and interests, we had a friendship that could also be called a collaboration.

"Why didn't you tell me your book proposal was on the market?" the writer asked me. She wasn't angry, but perhaps hurt.

"Sometimes when we hang out it's hard for me to get a word in edgewise," I explained. "I'm not always sure that you have an appetite for all the goings-on in my life."

It's not that my friend was greedy, or that she selfishly bogarted the airtime every time we linked up. It was more that she was always liable to work up a lather talking through her latest brilliant insight or observation, and I was perfectly comfortable as a rapt audience. When she gathered enough momentum on one of her riffs, she became a bop soloist commanding the bandstand. I was like an awestruck Beat poet, nodding vigorously and shouting "Go!" at her.

"Are you saying that I don't listen to you?" the writer shot back, her voice quavering. She grew suddenly teary. "Because that's exactly what [my ex] said after we broke up."

The signal had clipped. I instantly backtracked at the mention of her former boyfriend. The pair had a torrid but tumultuous multiyear relationship, and my friend was still recovering. It was clear that any supposed continuity between my comments and the ex's post-breakup recriminations would foreclose the possibility of a substantive discussion. I didn't have the context to know exactly what the ex meant when he lobbed that barb at my friend, but his grievance and mine are probably related. There wasn't enough headroom to explore the possible overlap. My friend's wounds were too fresh for her to absorb any unflattering self-knowledge in that moment. I offered some consoling words about the breakup and let the original topic at hand wither on the vine. There was blame on both sides for this lost opportunity for growth. My writer friend was guilty of projecting her anxieties about her former relationship onto her friendship with me. I had shied away from admitting how our dynamic made it hard for me to self-disclose in a satisfying way. I couldn't risk it. George Orwell wasn't personally Orwellian. Machiavelli wasn't himself Machiavellian. Yet their names are minted into adjectives for things they merely diagnosed, rather than actually did. Even when we acknowledge that a messenger is not responsible for the reality their message describes, we ultimately tack it on their jacket one way or another. "He who spelt it, dealt it" is a faulty syllogism, but it has considerable traction. The brief tension reinforced the underwhelming nominal levels of our rapport, and the friendship waned as a result.

Occasions when I have brazenly bypassed nominal levels—consequences be damned—sometimes replay in my mind like a sitcom clip show, where flashpoints from earlier seasons tessellate into a larger narrative. If all of the times that I have clipped on purpose were edited together, there'd be an obvious choice for the culminating scene. In the moment before I picked up my computer chair and launched it at my bedroom window, I visualized myself doing it. It was the early winter of 2013. A stray bolt of melancholy had hit me with the precision of a drone strike. I had been prone to bouts of staggering hopelessness as far back as I could remember. The latest one shook me like a dashboard hula girl. I knew that throwing the chair would alienate the poet's namesake, who looked on. It was likely that she'd read it as somehow related to her. It wasn't, aside from the fact that having a live-in audience to my undoing limited exactly how undone I was willing to become. Sobbing like a starlet in an Oscar bait close-up would have been more cathartic. The middling substitute I ultimately settled for was a strategic choice. The clichés about angry men leaving holes in plaster walls echoed in my head. Still, a fit of rage would be forgiven more quickly than a crying jag would be forgotten. I knew that after the window had smashed, I would have to collect the shards of the relationship. There would be an hour-long reconciliation process. I would have to reassure my person that I loved and needed her, even though only the former was true.

As a child, when I particularly frustrated my mother, she'd recount the hours she'd spent in labor with me. A doctor cracked that the baby was going to have one hell of a set of lungs on him, given how much noise his mother made getting him here. The Black Momba mostly wasn't hollering because of her agony at that moment. Instead, she saw being in labor as primetime for the primal screams she repressed most of her life. Crib to coffin, there's reason to expect that raising my voice half a dB will warp me into O. J. Simpson in the eyes of everyone in earshot. In almost every case I will subdue myself to prevent this, largely so as not to hasten my coffin's necessity. As I watched the computer chair sail through the air and break the window, I was aware that my tantrum wouldn't fix anything. Sometimes a thing must shatter when a person can't. On the first day of my life, my mother taught me there are few reprieves from restraint. One must seize a plum opportunity to plumb one's own depths. To surrender the signal to the noise. To define a headroom of one's own.

WOULD YOU STILL LOVE ME IF I WAS A [BOOK] WORM?

The writer Phillip Lopate once observed that Anton Chekhov's body of work offers the consolation of "Yeah, that's the way it is."[1] Rather than promising his readers transcendence or redemption, Chekhov reflected the dismal quality of their own lives back to them. The gift lay in confirming their reality. This approach may have resonated with Chekhov's Russian countrymen, but it's a harder sell to Americans. The theorist Lauren Berlant was on to something when they said our lives are organized by a cruel optimism, where the things we expect from life are actually obstacles to our own flourishing.

"People are trained to think that what they are doing ought to matter," Berlant told the *Big Brains* podcast in 2019.[2] "That they [themselves] ought to matter, and that if they show up to life in a certain way, they'll be appreciated for the ways they show up in life, that life will have loyalty to them, their job will have loyalty to them, or their intimates will have loyalty to them, or their dog will."

This national reverence for the just-world fallacy sets everybody in our culture up for disappointment, but a more grounded horizon of expectation hasn't caught on. Confirming an American's reality can land more like naysaying than comfort. As modes of consolation go, I'm a big fan of "Charge it to the game." The phrase probably entered African American vernacular as some reference to the drug trade or being a player in the sexual marketplace. "Ball up top"—a reference to starting a new sequence of play in a basketball game—and "Fuck it, we ball"—which became a meme based on a tweet by rapper Young Thug—are rhetorically similar to "Charge it to the game." In my imagination, charging it to the game has merged with a '90s ad campaign for Mastercard. "The game" is a credit card I fish out of my wallet several times a day. I use it to absorb the attrition of navigating an indifferent universe.

SEXUAL GESTALTISM—200 CREDITS

At the dinner table one evening, my mom tells my father that she's noticed I have a type. Not a physical type, she clarifies. She thinks I consistently seek out a similar package of skills, interests, and sensitivities. Some number of women I have either dated or had crushes on have spent time in comparative literature doctoral programs. Mom announces this to Baba as if she has discovered I'm a chubby chaser, a furry, or a monthly subscriber to Blacks on Blondes dot com. I don't understand how this is a revelation or notable in any way. As far as I can tell, there are around forty-three people in the United States who read books. If you date women within a certain age group who read for fun, more than a few of them are going to be academics. I like people who are keen to examine the world and just as importantly, to take care of it. People with those qualities are often bookworms.

Later, true to form, I'm discussing a book with a friend. I mention an essay in which a writer in a happy relationship with her boyfriend describes and decodes her dread about becoming his bride. The writer sees straight marriage as a Faustian bargain; a woman is allowed to be selfish, greedy, and status-obsessed during the wedding prep and on the big day itself. In exchange, she'll be completely subsumed by the man's long-term interests and gratification thereafter. I mention that I'm familiar with this exact style of apprehension. The kind of people I have been involved with tend to have complicated feelings about marriage. They are wary of being instrumentalized as a man's helpmeet with no agenda, significance, or mark on the world of their own. They see even minor capitulation to a male partner as a slippery slope. This can blur the distinction between kowtowing to *a man* and showing consideration for someone one cares about. Grappling with these issues in several successive relationships has heightened my own unease. At my most irreverent, I describe checking the marriage and children boxes as "going nuclear," meaning that starting a family is like aiming an atomic weapon at my and my partner's fragile reserves of joie de vivre. (You have to say it with a Dubya Bush accent, though—so that it's more like *nuke-yuh-ler*—to capture the down-home provinciality of the move.) I want this to be a joke, but maybe my id means it. I tell my friend this tension is a predictable hazard of being drawn to badass women.

My friend asks me about the "aesthetics" of badass women, as if I'm alluding to a particular look. She suggests it's the kind of thing I might be fetishizing. I tell her that by badass I mean a sensibility. I try to describe the kind of person who is sharply aware of her social and political condition. Someone who questions and resists it. I'm not inattentive to get ups. I do have a hard time disaggregating them from get downs. I rarely feel like someone is a cutie if I don't first recognize them as acute. It's not the first time I've had the sense that naming these preferences doesn't compute for others. A description of my type is presumed to be a typo. I'm prompted to refine my search. *Did you mean: "ass and titties"?*

I have something like a romantic patient zero, a figure in the past who possibly set this whole mess in motion. All of my romantic stories might actually be interpolations of that first one, just edited and condensed for obscurity. In sixth grade, I heard through the pre-adolescent rumor mill that a cute girl in my homeroom had a crush on me. It was not completely clear to me what I was supposed to do with that information. I was flattered. But where could we really go from here? I hadn't even grown hair under my arms yet. We were two of maybe twenty total black people in our grade at the magnet program where we went to school. I wondered if she had landed on me as a crush by picking names out of a hat. Then one day I was reading the Sunday comics. I noticed that the girl had submitted a hint to an advice column called Hints from Heloise. Heloise herself had chosen and published it, apparently. I was completely impressed. I sought out the girl at lunchtime and congratulated her on the publication. We picked up momentum from there. Eventually I asked her to be my girlfriend and we "dated" for a bit. I wrote her some poems that she read as carefully and thoughtfully as our extensive, magnet-school English homework. For Valentine's Day, I bought her a very saccharine heart necklace I picked out in Puerto Rico. And then she dumped me and I listened to Mariah Carey a lot to get over it. Through a friend, she returned the heart necklace to me to put the finest point possible on her disenchantment.

I now recognize the entire drama as an odd childish rehearsal for the future. I can see how the Hints from Heloise thing made me admire this person more. It wasn't the prestige per se; it was the ingenuity, the drive I figured it took for a sixth-grade girl to dream up her hint, send it in, and get picked. And when I got to know her, she was pretty much the personality I would have anticipated based on that precocious publication record.

I adored her for it. She was smart, tough, a bit domineering, and she had an excellent sense of humor. It embarrassed her to cry about anything, for any reason. When she felt uncertain or vulnerable about something, we could only unearth it together through careful, painstaking conversation. We ran in different middle school social circles and weren't really allowed to go to each other's houses. As a result, most of this conversation—and most of the relationship overall—took place on the phone or AOL Instant Messenger. I can still remember the alloy of ardor and dread that snaked through my body when her screen name lit up on my Buddy List. For her part, I don't actually know whether she liked me for any reasons having to do with me. She thought I was pretty but that might have been all. A few years later she started dating girls (in addition to and not instead of boys). There's a fairly straightforward progression from approaching my first love interest on the basis of "damn, girl; I like your Hint. What up?" and the type my mother was profiling at the dinner table. Only now do I begin to wonder if that first nudge I got from Heloise was not a hint but a misdirection.

The Saturday after Valentine's Day I'm on a date with someone promising. Sasha set us up. While I'm chatting with my date over a mediocre veggie sandwich, I picture Sasha having met this woman elsewhere, sizing her up and concluding "Hmm, G'Ra would certainly like this person." I'm both relieved and mildly amazed as I realize Sasha was right: She can read the font of my type like seemingly no one else can. Sasha's expert matchmaking reflects a kind of love I am moved and grateful to have already, even if the ultimate goal of the gesture is intended to tee up a surpassing version of the same thing. Prior to meeting Sasha's nominee myself, I have read my date's writing and watched some of her public talks. She is a black woman mega-babe with a mind to match.

It's dangerous to flatten every experience you have into a reenactment of what came before. Failing to notice how the present echoes the past can be equally costly. Watching my date nibble on an unremarkable salad and listening to her explain how she grew up, I feel my heart flexing and surging into an existing groove, like a seasoned ballet dancer tugged by an offstage puppeteer into holding an arabesque. My date and I have spoken exactly once on the phone before this occasion. We've only been hanging out in person for a couple of hours. On my end at least, the potential is obvious. There is a structure of feeling I can readily build around this person, a well-practiced position I can assume. But just because I can doesn't mean I ought to.

I think about the pre–social media mailers that were sent out to my childhood home, the ones meant to spread the word about missing children. Each "Have You Seen Me?" mailer featured a picture of the missing child at the age they were when they disappeared. Next to that photo, there was a computer-generated "age-progression" that simulated how the child might look with the elapsed time. I wrack my brains, search my memory like those mailers asked the locals to do. Have I seen her? Is the woman sitting across from me an age-progressed iteration of bookworms who'd burrowed into my heart before? Or am I only spooked by ghosts of Valentine's Days past?

UNRAVELING SOCIAL FABRIC—700 GAME CREDITS

One downside of consistently attracting and partnering with this broad category of person is that when paired, we make a combo that is more duplicative than interlocking. Professionally, we end up pushing twin boulders up the capitalist hill, rather than distributing the burden of one boulder between two powerful parties.

I had hoped that upward mobility would have a phase like reaching thirty thousand feet on a commercial flight. A comfortable professional plateau would become cruising altitude. At which point I could put my rise on autopilot and cruise around casually for a partner. By the time I reached my mid-thirties, I was already twice as old as my mom was when she became a parent. This was largely by design. My mother is seventeen years older than my oldest brother. Her mother was nineteen years older than she is. I was raised to understand that it was my responsibility to build on my parents' ascension from poverty to middle-class status. Having a family too early could hamper my ability to improve my station. And yet before I could even take a victory lap for fulfilling those goals, I had already fallen behind on another imperative: to provide grandchildren while my folks are young enough to enjoy them. Cruising altitude never came. Comparable black women professionals don't typically have the luxury of autopilot either.

The woman Sasha set me up with is a couple of years older than I am. She is more senior in her academic rank. Her ascent has reached thirty thousand feet, but she isn't free to move about the cabin; she makes clear in our conversation that she is still hustling. Sasha and the woman she set me up with have a number of mutual friends. Those friends say that the woman dates somewhat regularly, but the men she dates keep "playing in her face." It's a familiar synopsis of an eligible person's love life: It's not going well because everything is everyone else's fault. It's doubtless that her suitors are imperfect and bring garden-variety male foolishness to the equation. It would be impressive, however, to learn that she'd assessed whether her own actions, tastes, choices, habits, had a single thing to do with her singleness. If nothing else, structural factors might play a role. This person is one of our generation's most educated and accomplished black folks in her field. I could understand if the rest of us felt, to her, like the Untalented Nine-Tenths. Why rush to form a team if you're going to have to carry it on your back?

In academia, when someone earns a job offer and negotiates a job at the same school for their romantic partner, we describe the incoming hire as having a "trailing spouse." The phrase calls a rickshaw to mind. The incoming hire sprints to campus at full speed, yanking the vehicle's twin handles behind them as the trailing spouse lounges complacently in the carriage. This configuration may not lend itself to symbiosis. The feminist in me is determined not to saddle any woman with picking up my slack. The slave-descended part of me is wary of sacralizing hard work. I don't want to lag behind anyone like a ball and chain, but I don't want shackles of my own either.

For black people on the come up, specifically, I prefer a framework like what NASA calls ISRU, or in situ resource utilization.[3] The reasoning is simple: Deep space exploration should maximize space-based resources. It's a method of using what's available at mission destinations, instead of ferrying all needed supplies from the point of departure. Carrying supplies from square one will only weigh you down. If you are boldly going where few black people have gone before, choosing from the pool of folks on the same journey is ISRU. Negotiating job offers for you and your partner is ISRU as well, because you're sustaining mission personnel (your copilot) using the mission destination (the college or university where you're hired). In terms of profession and life stage, I'm in a similar situation as the woman Sasha set me up with. Sharing resources to conserve energy for joint survival could be expedient.

The zeitgeist isn't exactly teeming with intel on how couples can best synergize. Lauren Berlant argues that Americans are living without national sentimentality for the first time since the nineteenth century. What Berlant describes as "the gradual diminution of the Great Society and New Deal model of social accountability" has eroded faith in the American dream. There is less of a sense of public good to rally around, and the everybody-for-themself ethos is no favor to love. For instance, there's agreement among coastal progressive types that chivalry is antiquated and distasteful. The same applies to the traditionally gendered division of labor. Flouting these norms for anti-sexist reasons usually means doubling down on individualism. An enlightened man doesn't expect his female partner to spearhead their household's domestic labor just because she's a woman. He contributes to that labor himself. Philosophically, I'm with it. Practically, though, this does diminish the additive value of being married. As a single person, I cook and clean for myself. The kind of women I tend to date are typically doing the same. We don't have the same incentive to join forces as more traditional couples. Cooking and cleaning for two people is double the amount of work each of us is tasked with now. Getting married or cohabitating doesn't provide the opportunity to outsource any of our responsibilities. It only offers us company while we fulfill them. It better be some company then, right?

In my experience, dating a woman in her twenties or thirties necessarily involves significant emotional and psychological stewardship. They exist in what we could call a sour spot. I single out that age group because that bracket seems especially unsupported—they are chafed by economic instability, workplace and street-level sexism, and pressure from extended family, while navigating the development of a career. This is not to say that women are uniquely high-maintenance. Only that the level of support that young women need (or at least would like) and mostly seem to not have is a challenge largely unsung. This dynamic has studded my romantic experience in a way I don't really hear straight people ever talk about.

The sour spot is compounded by the American insistence on moving outside the family home immediately upon turning eighteen. There's a support gap in our culture where people are not directly backed by their parents and siblings anymore but also haven't had time, money, or opportunity to start their own families. As a result they're just twisting in the wind in certain ways, balancing endless responsibilities and neuroses more or less alone. When I talk to single dudes who date women, a lot of things come up but I can't say this is among them. It could be that men are very often struggling in life themselves and looking for a helpmeet, which precludes them from even thinking about how women need helpmeets in turn sometimes. Or these men are focused on being "a provider," which is usually meant in a purely economic capacity. Otherwise the dude is mainly thinking about how to keep things light enough with a given woman that she won't ask too much of him in terms of commitment, time, monogamy, or emotional engagement. His ability to keep playing the field is contingent on minimizing his obligation to her. Emotional labor is coded as something women thanklessly and disproportionately perform for men. The observation I'm making is not a complaint about having to do emotional labor. (As labor goes, I'm better suited for the feelings-based variety than most alternatives.) I'm inventorying the degree to which it is called for. And highlighting the structural reasons why the need is so great during a particular phase of adulthood, and more so for driven, intellectual women. They show up in life in a high-octane, highly hopeful way. They expect life and jobs and their dogs to be loyal to them. There are only so many times I can tell them to charge their disappointment to the game.

GAMELESSNESS—200 CREDITS

As much as I max out my game card, I am not much of a game spitter. I don't put on airs to entice someone I like. I'm not bragging, Chavano; this isn't necessarily wise. There are pros and cons to not running a long con. My MO is, Well, Someone Will Be Into It. It's not for the faint of heart. Being a lifelong devotee of seemingly unpalatable music, I've learned that even art that flouts conventional standards of quality tends to find the audience that will appreciate it, however tiny that audience may be. From that I extrapolated that I didn't necessarily need a crisp hairline or chiseled cheekbones to attract admirers. Some people would inevitably like me for me. There are always people who like things that lack nearly *all* ostensible appeal. The benefit of this outlook is that I never busted my hump trying to be prom king. There are a range of kinds of desire. I am liberated by the knowledge that I don't have to comply with the most ballyhooed criteria. The primary drawback, however, is perhaps best encapsulated by folk punk troubadour Jeffrey Lewis's song "Cult Boyfriend." In it, Lewis playfully identifies himself with the song's title. He tells the listener that though Lewis is not a mainstream heartthrob, what his female fans lack in numbers they more than compensate for in enthusiasm. This would be all well and good, except the oscillation between anonymity and adulation is dizzying.

That exact toggle has been central to my experience with love. To a niche demographic, a cult boyfriend can seem like a chimerical figure, a surreal answer to prayers. Deservedly or not, I have inspired this reaction from a number of friends and love interests alike. Being exalted usually portends a swift and merciless demotion. When someone views you as a dream person, your humanity gets slept on. You're destined to tarnish that perception when your better angels falter even briefly. It's a challenge to be received as levelly human, as neither godsend nor gorgon.

Cult boyfriend status comes with a madcap fearlessness. Rejection is a monster who has lurched from the closet so often that it's lost some mystique. To this I owe the temerity to pursue someone as dazzling as the woman Sasha set me up with. Badass women are prone to the godsend/gorgon conundrum, too. I have fresh hope that we could relate to each other on this basis.

The other major pitfall of anyone being Into It is a problem she's probably dealt with herself. When someone genuinely admires the way you show up in life, that very awe can make them doubt the value of how they show up in theirs. It leads to a tactic best described as feinting with damned praise. Division by addition. Elevating you to create distance from themselves.

"I think you're so extraordinary that I want to be in the best position possible for this relationship to work."

"I just felt like you were so brilliant and wonderful and I was nervous that you'd realize I was not those things."

"I've always wanted a man who can challenge me intellectually like you do, but I'm not sure I can keep up."

The above comments are from three different people who either broke up with or ghosted me soon after making them. Even being a godsend can make you a kind of gorgon.

PLANE AND THEATER TICKETS—400 CREDITS

The woman Sasha set me up with agrees to go on a second date with me. The day before the date, a Saturday when we are slated to have dinner and attend a French absurdist play called *Malaise dans la Civilization*, she texts me to cancel and apologize. She has a writing deadline this weekend and can't spare a few hours away from her desk. I tell her that I understand and that I appreciate the communication. I can't tell whether bailing on the date at the last minute is meant to be a roundabout rejection of my advances overall. So I press for clarity: Is she interested in going out with me a second time in general? If she's dropping a hint to leave her be, I want to make sure I'm picking up what she's putting down.

"Totally interested in going out again," she texts, after a lengthy pause. "The thing that's tricky for me is the distance." She goes on to explain that she was recently in a long-distance relationship for many years. At her current stage, flexibility and spontaneity in making plans is important to her. Since I'm flying in and out of New York City, where she lives, from St. Louis, where I teach, it's difficult to have that fluidity with me. These are sensible reasons to hesitate. But I had asked her out, bought the tickets, and made the plan more than three weeks before. If my city of residence was an obstacle, why wait until I've flown to your city to tell me that? And why make me ask about our prospects—instead of just telling me when you canceled at the last minute? Being a fellow writer, I empathize with the pressure of a Sunday deadline. Still, I was skeptical that she couldn't take a break from writing to have dinner together. If this was an attempt to let me down easy, she certainly didn't try very hard. I'd looked forward to the date for nearly a month. I was reluctant to see my optimism as cruel, but it was tempting.

It was more thematically appropriate to watch the show alone after getting curved like spacetime than it would've been to watch it on a date. The play's cocreator, Alix Dufresne, believes it represents the depth of human obtuseness. *Malaise* "is a bit of a metaphor about being—the French word is *inconscient*, which is not careful or not conscious about each other and ourselves, which is what capitalism brought us to," Dufresne told *Stir* magazine.[4] "The state of the planet, the state we're in, because we're running around bumping into each other being totally not conscious of each other and ourselves in the world." Sitting alone in the dark as Dufresne's characters stumbled; erred; failed; blurred the boundary separating the play from the audience, I stared wistfully at the empty seat next to me and thought, *Yeah, well, tell me about it, Dufresne. Inconscience is playing in my face.*

A modicum of Chekhovian consolation—priceless.

POWER SHADOW AND ACT

Are you there, motion-activated hand soap dispenser? It's me, a black-ass hand.

This mental dialogue recurs when I'm at the airport, trying to freshen up in the high-tech bathroom. It could be that the soap dispenser is moody to everyone. Or maybe it behaves more or less cooperatively according to a color gradient. Each time it happens, I think about AI researcher and activist Joy Buolamwini. During her graduate studies at MIT, Buolamwini was working on a facial recognition program when she realized it couldn't detect her skin tone. The program only realized she was there when she wore a white mask. To characterize this phenomenon, Buolamwini coined the term *the coded gaze*, which she defined as "the power to shape technology and whose preferences and priorities are baked in."[1] In my standoff with the motion-activated hand soap dispenser, I can't help but wonder whether the coded gaze is operative, even though the detection process concerns hands and not faces. Buolamwini's research found that the algorithm she was using, as well as many similar algorithms, performed best at picking up "pale males." The technology was significantly less successful at recognizing darker-skinned or non-dude faces. This discrepancy is a result of skewed face datasets that do not represent the global majority, which Buolamwini describes as power shadows.

"The past dwells in our data, right?" says Buolamwini.[2] "And so does the present in terms of who holds power."

So, power shadows loom as a possible explanation when I struggle to activate the soap dispenser. But they also get my gears turning about my maker. I talk to the soap in a manner that recalls the young protagonist from Judy Blume's middle-grade classic, *Are You There, God? It's Me, Margaret.* A power shadow occurs when a creation reflects the biases and limitations of its creator. Facial-recognition algorithms were crafted for the mugs of white men. This effectively gave computers a schema for a human face that excludes most of humanity. From this, one might reasonably surmise that our intelligent designer is anti-black, among other things that hamper a capacious sense of humanity. Just look at the power shadows that fall on us. Whatever algorithms guide human behavior, we lack cogent criteria for recognizing each other as well. Naturally, this compromises our self-knowledge in turn. I see these factory settings as less than conducive to love. Meeting and magnifying each other's light is no mean feat when one is seldom seen to begin with.

Hollywood is known for shaping face values. It's often criticized for propagating unrealistic beauty standards. Most people don't look like A-list ingenues, the thinking goes, so holding them up as physical ideals dooms the common person to disappointment and self-loathing. Our ability to love—ourselves and each other—is harmed just as much by exaggerating our inclination to be kind and generous as it is by judging our bodies according to imposed standards. In late 2023, actress Emily Blunt drew widespread criticism when a clip of Blunt making fatphobic remarks resurfaced online. The clip took place during a 2012 appearance on *The Jonathan Ross Show.* Blunt makes a gratuitous comment about a restaurant server's weight. She jokes that the Chili's employee probably ate for free at her job. The usual social media pile-on ensued. Blunt was forced to apologize for something she'd said nearly a dozen years earlier.

"I've always considered myself someone who wouldn't dream of upsetting anyone," the actress said in a statement, "so whatever possessed me to say anything like this in that moment is unrecognizable to me or anything I stand for."[3]

If it's true that celebrities are role models—that people in other walks of life are measuring themselves against the jawlines, haircuts and waist sizes of the culture's most visible and celebrated figures—then they shape what we expect of ourselves behaviorally and ethically, too. I definitely dream of upsetting anyone. Sometimes I dream of upsetting *everyone.* To keep those antisocial impulses in check, I have to cop to them first. I doubt Blunt is uniquely self-deluded. Her hyperbolic account of her own benevolence reflects the pieties of our time. Demanding unwavering virtue from famous people warps our expectations of ourselves. It prevents any credible inventory of the foibles endemic to being human.

The most telling word in Blunt's apology is "unrecognizable." She casts her gaffe as so contrary to her values that she can't reconcile it with who she is. Her algorithm can't face it. But of course a thin, conventionally attractive person whose career success is closely tied to her appearance could develop a superiority complex on that very basis. Blunt's framing typifies what I call the guardian angle: a too-precious view of the self that deflects accountability and inhibits growth. In this particular case, Blunt was accountable in the sense that she apologized under duress. A more honest reflection on the mistake, however, might recognize the obvious relationship between the fat joke and what Blunt stands for.

I'm not picking on the *A Quiet Place* star. There's nothing egregious about her error or her fumbling attempt to own it. We all have a guardian angle. To become more loving and more lovable, it's one we need to subtend. Maturity means accepting that misdeeds can and generally do derive from our true selves. Even when we vow to correct them going forward, we will nonetheless stumble from time to time. This form of self-awareness is so rarely modeled in American public life that basic humility is a transgressive act. To practice care, commitment, respect and trust, you have to think critically about yourself, your loved one, and the world that has marked you both. You have to learn your own rough edges to sand them down.

In his autobiography, Benjamin Franklin delineates a plan for attaining moral perfection. He set out to "live without committing any fault at any time" and devised a method for achieving it.[4] Organizing his quest according to thirteen virtues, Franklin practiced one virtue per week and diligently recorded his progress. Tellingly, his initial list included only a dozen virtues, but a Quaker friend informed him that Franklin was seen by others as arrogant. Franklin added "humility" in response to the feedback.

"On the whole, tho' I never arrived at the Perfection I had been so ambitious of obtaining, but fell short of it," Franklin admitted. "Yet as I was, by the Endeavor, a better and happier Man than I otherwise should have been if I had not attempted it." Like Emily Blunt, he dreamed of never upsetting anyone. He also woke up. So many crackpot notions of the Founding Fathers retain extensive contemporary cachet. (Second Amendment, I'm looking at you, big dogg.) Yet we totally ignore when Franklin was putting us up on true game. Incorrigibility is a feature, not a bug. Mature love accepts it as such.

I used to wonder why writers always describe people as "flawed." As if without that word, we'd think somebody is an ethereal beam of light. That it's normal to describe someone as flawed—like it's notable or distinct to be imperfect—suggests that a delusional view of personal goodness is commonplace. This leads to miscalibrated expectations in love. We open our arms to new love wider than our eyes. We end up blindsided by both our and our partner's ample shortcomings, as well as the forgiveness, flexibility, and generosity needed to navigate them.

Living in an identitarian age always makes me wonder: What is the baseline against which "marginalized communities" define themselves? What, precisely, lies within the middle cell of a Venn diagram linking the haves and have-nots? Our collective capacity for love suffers for lack of consensus on what's common to all humans. This blinkered understanding of what we all share is likely a reason that impostor syndrome afflicts so many. If you don't know what the genuine article is, you're more likely to worry that you're a crude imitation.

I encounter the phrase *secular humanism* most often when a religious person wants to distinguish their faith-based outlook from that of the country's mainstream. But I'm not sure humanism is a mainstream value. Seeing each other as human doesn't come to us very easily. Most people think of humanism as something of a center-left sham, a pretext for Nike releasing a Pride month–themed sneaker or something.

Toothy humanism is love's true accomplice. Toothy meaning it has both bite and humor. A species-wide esprit de corps you wear with Voltaire's grin. The French Enlightenment writer's signature smirk was a symbol of his puckish intelligence. His grin represents laughter that's close to tears; a tragicomic view of the human condition that doubts hierarchies and champions freedom. When I look another human being in the eyes, I have the visceral sensation that we are both subsets of something much larger. I can also tell that, more likely than not, the other person thinks I'm a monkey. Toothy humanism minds this infernal absurdity and gets on with it. It's the snickering recognition that the ties that bind us all together are as potent as our childish attempts to deny them. That feeling when your species is a problematic fave but you're never leaving the fandom.

When we struggle to see each other, love that leaps without looking is inevitable. What can we do to get out from under the power shadow? I went searching for a penumbra at an event at the University City Public Library called Meaningful Conversations: The Spirituality of Depolarization. The gathering took place in late 2024. It was an implicit response to the Trump administration's looming second act.

A man with a nametag labeled Andy shared a possible remedy to polarization. He thought food could do it. Andy had a dispute with a guy at his job. Then, one day Andy wandered into the cafeteria at work and was struck by a sight he called profound: his opp eating lunch. It hadn't occurred to Andy that he would ever see the man he disagreed with doing something "so vulnerable." Andy felt a sudden swell of compassion for his would-be enemy. His story reminded me of a colleague I'd had years ago who refused to ever eat in front of her undergraduate students for fear that they'd lose respect for someone engaging in such a mundane activity. She told me that if her students watched their teacher feed herself, her magisterial aura would dry up on the spot. I thought that was ridiculous when I heard it. Yet here was Andy, belatedly vindicating her. What I take from both of those observations is that people struggle to see others as lateral with themselves, even though we mostly assume our humanity is self-evident. When you think about the transposition that adages like "Do unto others as you would like done unto you" ask of the individual, you might imagine that the journey from their perspective to another person's is like crossing a busy street, but it's probably more like downward-facing dog: an exacting gymnastic task that takes practice to learn and discipline to sustain. The finesse required to achieve that transposition might one day become light work. For now, though, our relationships are served best when we accept it as a skill to cultivate jointly.

The understanding that an object continues to exist whether or not it can be detected by our senses is called object permanence. Swiss psychologist Jean Piaget theorized that it develops within two years of birth. Piaget saw it as a signature achievement of an infant's growth because the physical world is nearly incomprehensible without it. If Andy and my colleague are to be believed, a highly circumscribed view of subjects might be endemic to the social world. We can, apparently, meet a walking, talking, carbon-based life-form and not readily assume that they eat if we haven't witnessed it. I call this subject transience, the likelihood that the standard-issue dimensions of your mortal experience are not taken for granted by the people around you unless they are witnessed. Humankind is in a sensorimotor stage. In the long arc of the universe's history, we're only in our Terrible Twos. Just as a child in the first of Piaget's four stages begins to discover themselves and their environment, our sense of who we are as a species is still nascent. Some of our struggles in love stem from this limitation. If we don't know that other people need to eat unless we see them do it, we're unlikely to grasp—let alone attend to—all the other ways they need nourishment.

Kimya Dawson, the anti-folk singer-songwriter best known as a former member of early 2000s indie darlings the Moldy Peaches, has an incisive solo song related to this called "Same Shit/Complicated." I think of it as a love song. It's about recognizing other people's complexity because you know that anyone hoping to understand you will need to extend the same grace. In the course of making the case that people are invariably complicated, the song's lyrics proclaim, among other nuanced things, that nice police officers exist. In context, I don't read the song as defending police from critiques of state violence. I think Dawson is saying that even cops have humanity, and people are more and other than the sum of their worst misdeeds. The Kimya Dawson Reddit suggests that Dawson no longer performs the song in the 2020s. Dawson even changed the lyric on Spotify, allegedly because leftists read them the riot act for humanizing police. Blue Lives Matter trolls have used Dawson's lyric as a gotcha. To my mind Dawson, who self-identifies as "a Black mom" in the song, got it right the first time. Out of love, Dawson was trying to gently usher us from the sensorimotor stage into a savvier, worldlier view of ourselves and others. As youngsters in the first phase of cognitive development are wont to do, Dawson's audience responded by kicking and screaming. The backlash to a clear-eyed protest song speaks to a deep, bipartisan commitment to these painfully facile good person vs. bad person binaries. Ironically, only a cop-like view of Dawson's artistry would determine that their measured analysis of individual police officers is counterrevolutionary. Strident opposition to the song proves Dawson's point. The complexity Dawson attributes to all people plays out in both directions: A mild suggestion that cops can be nice makes folks who imagine themselves as nice people start acting . . . exactly like cops. We all have a police officer in us. The nightstick, whether rhetorical or literal, is going to come out with the most ferocity when we think we have a righteous basis for the use of force. Being extremely carceral at the cultural level trickles down interpersonally. Even people who claim to be, for instance, prison abolitionists, can be loath to accept that every person is on a continuum with themselves. A truncated view of the human family narrows the heart's downy wingspan.

"Same Shit/Complicated" offers an addendum to the conventional wisdom that says never meet your heroes. From Dawson's point of view, we might just as well hesitate to meet our villains, as they too will subvert expectations in destabilizing fashion. The song points out that flesh and blood encounters make people more difficult to flatten into odious caricatures. An aphoristic reminder that people—heroes and villains alike—tend to be admirable in some ways and contemptible in others is long overdue. If we can learn to expect this of others, we might be able to accept it as true of ourselves. As things currently stand, though, "having humanity" is a floating signifier. Finding a way to give it a soft landing would be doing love a solid.

For all our confusion about each other's humanity, modern people spend a fair amount of time proving theirs to computers by solving captchas. Captcha is an acronym that stands for Completely Automated Public Turing Test to tell Computers and Humans Apart. You could be forgiven, then, for thinking that the ability to count the correct number of stoplights in a blurry JPEG is our common link. But Shakespeare gave us a better one to work with. Hamlet said, "I could be bounded within a nutshell and count myself a king of infinite space." As he writes in *Brief Answers to the Big Questions*, the late theoretical physicist Stephen Hawking was fond of this quote.[5] Hawking, who suffered from a motor neuron disease that gradually paralyzed him over decades, was confined to a wheelchair, but he used his formidable imagination to travel the galaxy. Hamlet's quote likewise applies to the black experience. From enslavement to Jim Crow to mass incarceration, we've endured containment in a succession of nutshells. We've relied on our inner chambers for sustenance and tactical response. Black folks' and Stephen Hawking's unique circumstances notwithstanding, the scenario that Hamlet sets out applies to all of humankind. I mentioned the possibility of a social green thumb earlier. If you want to keep a houseplant alive, the care instructions are fairly clear. What best practices apply to nurturing a person? The *Hamlet* line provides a clue.

Everybody is both a serf and sovereign. We rule over our subjectivities with few checks or balances. It's there, in our inner worlds, where we are kings of infinite space. Meanwhile, in the world beyond ourselves, we're limited in size and scope. We depend on our corporeal forms. The nutshell, then, represents our mortal bodies and our paltry significance in the enormity of the universe. Inside, you're the most important entity in the history of time. You're the marquee name with no possible understudy. This is why people have incredibly clichéd experiences and feelings but readily conclude that they're the only ones having them. Outside, you're one of eight billion roughly similar bags of cells and waste with an expiration date. The inside is the enclosing medium through which the outside is experienced. You're at once indispensable and trivial. But the former feels closer to home than the latter, and you regard your triviality with a measure of disbelief. Of course you forget to take the trash out sometimes, even though your partner reminded you. Of course you take up space in the middle of the sidewalk, even though other pedestrians are clearly trying to slalom past. Of course you think that the best pop music, the coolest fashion, the lowest crime, and the happiest families coincided with your particular childhood. Of course you contradict yourself. Of course you confuse your thoughts with what you've said out loud. Of course you are, despite your best efforts, subjective with yourself and objective with others. A human being is always juggling bondage and boundlessness. To love one well is to embrace the infinity and the nutshell alike. And who needs patient indulgence more than the dual occupant of a fiefdom and a prison?

When Marvel's *Black Panther* film dropped, I was teaching freshman composition. All of the graduate teaching fellows held their office hours in a room on campus called the Writing Center. While you were coaching your young charges on their essays, you could overhear what your counterparts were saying and doing with their own students.

One of the other comp instructors enjoyed the new black superhero movie. She also wanted to let you know that she had outsmarted the premise.

"If Wakanda is supposed to be a futuristic paradise," my colleague mused, "why do they have ritual combat?"

The movie's rendering of Wakanda, an idyllic, technologically superior African nation, answers a question I ponder often. Let's say capitalism falls tonight. Are the barbaric, exploitative, hierarchical impulses that we sublimate into capitalism going to go away? I don't believe the economic system is the cause of those drives. Instead, the primacy of those drives in the human psyche is part of what makes capitalism palatable. Economic competition is a form of ritual combat. In Wakanda, the nation's abundant supply of vibranium, the most powerful substance in the Marvel Cinematic Universe, offers material prosperity for all. Relieved of the struggle to survive, Wakandans still can't hold hands and sing kumbaya all the time. They're human. In their utopia, controlled doses of literal combat replace the figurative kind as a safety valve for antisocial behavior.

Real-life civilization can't exist without repression. Our genetic code is imprinted with the same level of aggression as our cave-dwelling ancestors. Now that there aren't any roving woolly mammoths to take down, that aggression has, in some ways at least, outlasted its evolutionary usefulness. The science accords with my anecdotal experience. People, including myself, seem eager to lash out. In the absence of a rational outlet for our aggression, we'll gleefully concoct an irrational one. A formal ceremony where snarling foes stand in a river and lunge at each other with spears hardly seems anachronistic.

If I'm getting to know someone romantically, one of the most revealing things they could tell me about is their relationship to aggression. If the person has reflected on how, when, and why they are most prone to aggression, there is at least a slim possibility that they're capable of holding themselves accountable for eventually mistreating me. They're also more likely to be understanding when I am inevitably less than kind to them.

Forget love languages. The best icebreaker would be confessing your go-to ice *builder*. When your demons grab the yoke, what kinds of things do they make you do? The three primary modes of aggression, as I see them, are passive, oblivious, and aggressive. I favor the latter, but they can all catch me slipping. While we all cycle through each of them, each modality's hold on us varies in degree, depending on our personalities and life experiences.

Passive aggression is expedient in decorous settings. You can use the fact that it's passive to deny that it's aggression. Oblivious aggression offers its own plausible deniability. Oh, did my wantonly offensive comment about you hurt your feelings? I didn't even realize I was doing anything. The trouble is, many of us are sincerely self-oblivious, and our sputtering disavowals of ill intent are both honest and irrelevant. The oblivious aggressor dons the cloak and dagger, but it's a see-through cloak. Aggressive aggression puts all the cards on the table and then flips it over. Prices and participation may vary. Collect them all!

When I worked for social justice organizations, much of my time was spent glad-handing my counterparts at other orgs. This involved not only learning their names and pronouns but listening to what they saw as all of their structural hardships.

You can likely blame this trend on selective readings of the *Combahee River Collective Statement*. The crusaders I worked with believed that itemizing their "marginalizations" proved their moral credibility. (They were also, subtly, flexing their pluck-to-peril ratios.) Introductions would be way more interesting if we went around in a circle and listed all the ways that we're vectors of harm, rather than leading with our claims to victimhood. No one has any trouble remembering when and where they're getting raw deals in life. Few seem aware of how often they're authoring them for others in turn.

In the summer of 2016, I met someone whose ice builder mirrored mine. She was my boss. Ms. James (not her real name) was a black nationalist. *Black Panther* hadn't come out yet. If it had, Ms. James was the kind of person who would readily identify with Erik Killmonger. The ruthless mercenary character stages a coup to take over Wakanda and wield its formidable resources to challenge the oppression of African-descended people across the globe. Ms. James ran a summer program for black and brown economically disadvantaged youth. She hired me to teach in it. We generally got along fine until she launched into a monologue about how previous generations of black folks had been "meek." My boss saw this meekness, or reluctance to meet white supremacy's force with force, as the primary reason that anti-black oppression persisted in the twenty-first century. She wanted the students we worked with to develop more backbone than their ancestors. Our instruction needed to help them do so.

The hubris of this analysis stunned me. What my boss saw as meekness, I saw as sound strategy. Black Americans have never had the numbers to counter racist violence with vengeance. In our case, minority status is not merely political but numerical. I credited our ancestors with surviving their barbarous conditions and keeping their souls intact in the process. If anything, our students needed to understand themselves as heirs to that heroic legacy, as opposed to viewing it as something they needed to compensate for. The capacity to forgive, to embody the humanity that is withheld from you, is a sign of immense strength. What if we *didn't* enshrine organized violence as the summit of human potential? If a better world is possible, emulating black people's "meekness" is likely humankind's best chance to manifest it.

I distilled these counterpoints and conveyed them to Ms. James. Since she was disrespecting the ancestors in front of the staff, I challenged her argument in front of the staff, too. She went back at me. I parried. From my guardian angle, my rebuttal was calm, composed, and respectful. But when a colleague recounted the showdown the next morning, she summed it up by saying, "That was the day I found out G'Ra is a gangsta." If the ancestors were as meek as Ms. James argued they were, I apparently hadn't been channeling them as well as I hoped.

The following day, I braced myself for retaliation from Ms. James. Honestly, I expected her to play the victim. I assumed oblivious aggression was her flavor. She'd view her claim that earlier generations of black folks weren't tough enough as completely jejune, and thus she'd see my vigorous pushback as unprovoked. Instead, Ms. James greeted me just as kindly and collegially as if we'd never clashed at all. If she was sore about the argument, or felt that I'd undermined her leadership in any way, she gave no outward indications. Ms. James and I actually seemed to banter more than normal. At that job, I generally operated like a wraith. I fulfilled my duties without exposing much of myself, deflecting the spotlight if it landed on me and mostly only speaking when spoken to. On this day, though, Ms. James and I found ourselves working side by side and making chitchat fairly often. An unfamiliar sensation spread over me.

It took me until the end of the workday to sort out what it was: I was feeling closer to her.

The goodwill was puzzling. Neither of us budged out of our ideological corners. Ms. James reiterated her earlier stance as casually as if we'd never discussed it. She hadn't forgotten our argument and she wasn't convinced, just unfazed. I realized that spirited debate was so ordinary to Ms. James that she took none of it personally. Inveterate dissenter as I happened to be at that point in my life, I figured talking back had built-in drawbacks. Any time I stood up for myself carried the risk of being shamed as an intellectual bully. This occasion broke from that pattern. We'd both gone gloves-off aggressive-aggressive. Like positive and negative numbers of equal magnitude, we canceled out.

I was shook. Deep down, I knew that the fear of being guilted for being an intellectual bully was a deterrent that I relied on. It kept me in line. A dynamic in which I was free to speak my mind *and* retain peace of mind was a threat to my equanimity. Ms. James wanted all the smoke. Interacting with her provided incentive to be my most combative self with no incentive to subdue me. When two people have the same ice builder—and by ice builder I mean a reflexive means of alienating others—there's a possibility that they essentially form a polar bear club. Their repartee acts as a ceremonial plunge into frigid depths. The two parties measure themselves by how well they suffer the shivers, and call it invigoration. A pact based on mutually assured, low-grade hypothermia is not the variety of connection that interests me, but it is nonetheless a powerful one. I kept my distance from my boss after that, for fear that the arctic vortex between us threatened to suck me in permanently.

When the summer ended and I began to put the job behind me, I confessed this professional tension to another black woman I'd worked with. I didn't want to be baited into getting in the ring with someone who boasted a vibranium jaw, I told her. I preferred to avoid the ring entirely. This aspiration mainly concerned the workplace, but I suppose the romantic parallels were too obvious to overlook. My coworker scoffed.

"You're going to have to date white girls then," she said.

I thought of Joy Buolanwimi, staring into a facial recognition algorithm and scratching her head about why it couldn't see her. The machines have a narrow view of who is human and what is endemic to being human. Which means that despite being designed for the purpose of recognizing people, they can't detect the majority of extant human faces. The machines reflect the power arrangement of the society in which they're produced. We could interpret that to mean that white men, particularly, who create the algorithms in their own image, have a narrow understanding of who is human and what is endemic to being human. But if the power elite slant the algorithms, they also influence thinking throughout society about what is definitional to personhood—including the extent to which racial and gender minorities recognize themselves. My coworker, jokingly or not, implied that my boss's zeal for sparring was typical of black women. The aggression that I see as characteristic of the species, she saw as especially pronounced among black women, and less present in white ones. I had to wonder if this reading resulted from a pixelated self-concept.

Whether my coworker was laughing or wincing, I couldn't tell you. Her features were in shadow.

PRESENT COMPANY ACCEPTED

I seem to befriend as many type A literalists as type X free spirits. This makes a 6 p.m. dinner plan a conundrum. I'm either twiddling my thumbs alone for thirty minutes or getting chewed out for rolling up ninety seconds late. I would like to think of time as the great equalizer. As mysterious as the fundamental medium of experience happens to be, everyone is navigating it in some way or another. But clearly how we mark and interpret time varies widely from person to person.

In my early twenties, my community college geography class got into a discussion about time. I mentioned my frustration that our culture fetishizes youth. The false sense that youth is the greatest currency seemed to make the entire population throb with anxiety. What security could there be in believing that an always-declining, unrenewable substance is the most valuable commodity?

My geography professor raised an eyebrow. His hair was white and wispy as a cirrus cloud.

"I'm surprised to hear you say that, G'Ra. You're speaking against your own interests."

Apparently, there were people who believed they would never get old. Then, as now, I often pondered how much sand was in the top half of my hourglass. I noted that even that amount of sand was temporary. To properly chart a course for what I wanted to achieve and experience before the majority of my sand had dwindled, I needed to be mindful of the downward drift. My professor's response reminded me of how people treated male feminists, white anti-racists, and well-heeled Marxists. Those parallels seemed glaringly inappropriate. A man, if he manages not to die early, will not inevitably become a woman. A white person can live a long healthy life assured they will never be black. But young people are just old people–elects, rolling their eyes at the lame duck incumbents until their own terms start. I thought we were all waiting our turn for the knitting needles and rocking chairs.

Joni Mitchell sang that you don't know what you've got 'til it's gone. Schopenhauer said it's mostly loss that teaches us the worth of things. The universe has only one foregone conclusion. Why not let that knowledge teach us the worth of things now? Everyone is more lovable when they die. A death-denying culture reserves its warmest embrace for its coldest bones. All sins are more forgivable, all flaws more winsome, all divisions more reparable when our expiration dates are firmly front of mind. What could make us better collective shepherds of the future and stewards of one another than befriending our transience? The best way to give the Reaper hell is to give him dap. Foreshadowing every stage of life (including death) for young people the way *What to Expect When You're Expecting* is a primer for pregnant folks would transform society. *What to Do When You're Doomed* should be curriculum from K–12 all the way up through higher ed. The core lesson: Time will happen to you unless you're unlucky. Every stage of the life cycle has dignity, beauty, and value.

A sober view of time won't come easily to a civilization like ours. We're generally wary of knowledge and fearful of introspection. Banning books, criminalizing anti-racist education, legislating a Don't Say Gay Act—all those things are driven, in part, by resistance to reckoning with the past, or by plugging our ears and stamping our feet against the future. DNA tests represent a curious exception to the rule. We might not have a great appetite for history overall, but digging into our genealogical pasts is all the rage. Most people probably have a living family member who has a deeply illuminating life story or history that is never uncovered or talked about while they're alive. But we spit in these vials to chase down ghosts even though those ghosts are more likely than not the loose counterparts of our grunting, taciturn, TV-dinner fathers. I understand that the ghosts seem more romantic and inviting. Some sepia-toned haint is always way more interesting than anyone who wiped your ass for you. What a treasure it would be, though, to be relished before you're a relic.

Pop culture doesn't offer many forceful critiques of the idealization of youth, either. An awful made-for-TV movie called *A Wife's Nightmare* has burrowed in my brain just because it bucks the trend.[1] The movie's protagonist, Liz, is a working mother and wife. Her husband has become besotted with a young woman who claims to be his illegitimate daughter. When Liz confesses her jealousy of the younger woman, Angie, a friend that Liz describes as "my Oprah," puts things in perspective.

"What is it about this girl that's got you so twisted up?" Angie asks as she and Liz stretch after a run.

"Well, she's nineteen, for starters," Liz replies.

"So what? Look at you," Angie shoots back. "You've built a career, a family, a home. Anyone can be nineteen."

I'm with Angie. The crinkles around our eyes are earned stripes. But we probably shouldn't have to learn to love our whole lifetimes from Lifetime original movies.

As an educator, artist, and art appreciator, I'm always thinking about the link between how art is received and the stage of life at which it is encountered. A lot of who I am seems to come down to the right prose at the right time. In a related scene from *Luther* season one, John Luther's ex-wife, Zoe, and mad genius/serial killer Alice Morgan discuss the origins of the hard-boiled detective's philosophy.

Zoe says that Luther's police work is driven by a core belief: that "one life is all we have, life and love. Whoever takes life steals everything."

Alice asks Zoe if she agrees.

"I don't know," Zoe replies. "I think that if he'd read a different book by a different writer at just the right time in his life, he'd have been a different man."

It's striking to me that Zoe Luther sees the timing of her ex-husband's reading diet as the key to who he is. In other words, the man's worldview and politics don't come from nature or nurture, but from *literature*. (Is that what ACAB really stands for—All Cops Are Bookworms?)

I figure most people have a children's book that they read at some critical stage of early social and emotional development. That book has lastingly shaped how they operate, including how they think about life and love. Some of my more successful first dates have involved discussing this subject. What's written in the stars was perhaps first written in the well-thumbed pages of a book on your childhood nightstand. There's a lot to be gained from drilling down to the bookworms at our cores.

From about ages five through seven, I was obsessed with a children's book that I remember as *Brave the Dragon*. It stars an anthropomorphic dragon named Brave. He is drawn as if he's a youthful dragon, and he hangs out with young children who are not dragons. In the illustrations, there are a group of human children having fun at what looks like recess, and Brave is there using the swings, going down the slide and playing kickball, too. He has wings, looks frightening, and can presumably breathe fire, but the kids are unfazed. The turn in the book occurs when the hectoring townspeople decide that Brave is a scourge. He hasn't done anything harmful to his human friends, but the adults see him as a ticking time bomb. They capture Brave and bind him in the town's square. The children vouch for Brave's character, but their testimony is less compelling to the townsfolk than their natural prejudice.

I'm sure someone saves the day and Brave is freed to rejoin his human friends on the playground. But I can't remember the denouement at all. My paternal grandmother probably read this book to me no less than one hundred times in my youth. I recruited my older brother Joe into the *Brave the Dragon* cult as well, and we read it together just as often. I doubt I could articulate what fascinated me about the story at that time, but I know what imprint it left. The townspeople's bias against Brave is a simple allegory for racism. Though I was already highly conscious of being black at that age, and thinking about racism on some level as a result, that's not a complete explanation for my interest in *Brave the Dragon.* I suspect that it shaped my entire orientation toward the world. Brave's story offers some takeaways that clearly influence how I move today.

Even if you are perfectly harmless and beloved by the people who know you well, your appearance and the preconceived notions that strangers have about your appearance can overshadow the track record of your behavior. A sublime afternoon on the yard with the gang can easily give way to a tearful night in chains. Human beings may struggle to organize, say, a surprise birthday party, but they can single out and collaboratively antagonize a perceived foe with frightening effectiveness. Tolerant, open-minded children grow up to be hectoring townspeople. Anticipate these dynamics as you navigate the world. Buckle up. You must be Brave.

I have not tracked down a copy of *Brave the Dragon* to compare its reality with my memory of it. The central takeaways might well be a function of my own private Mandela effect. If I have misremembered it, I find that no less revealing. When it comes to deciphering that mysterious chamber inside our chests, our uncritical fabulations are reliable clues.

I was properly exposed to the marshmallow test in a college human development class. But it feels like something I've always known about in a sparsely detailed or even mythicized pop cultural way. Valuing delayed gratification is integral to the upward mobility script, and perhaps doubly so for black folks. In the original version of the test, small children are offered a single marshmallow and told they can eat it immediately. The children are also told that if they agree to hold off on eating the marshmallow for a length of time, they can eat two marshmallows instead. Researchers used the results to substantiate a link between the ability to wait for a treat in childhood and a number of positive life outcomes like better stress tolerance, higher SAT scores, and superior self-esteem.

In my twenties, the operative logic of the marshmallow test haunted my dating life. I could meet someone who felt romantically suitable and entertain the possibility that this would be the last person I'd ever date. Making a long-term commitment at that age felt like eating the first marshmallow. It was a safe move. Sweet, stable, risk averse. I knew, however, that my life experience was limited, and that as I gained more seasoning, my selection criteria were likely to evolve. Maturity could improve my discernment. That might mean that waiting longer to partner could result in a doubly rewarding relationship. I thought I might buy myself more love by spending more time. Having been raised by a pair of ascendant black folks, delayed gratification was already encoded in my psyche as something associated with striving, sobriety, and self-control. Resisting the temptation to partner early proved less taxing than I imagined. I started to worry that maybe I just don't like marshmallows that much.

MARSHMALLOW ONE

In the spring of 2018, I remember lying in bed with my grad school girlfriend, the Queen of Swords, when I called the "time + self-denial = (2)gratification" formula into question. I describe her as the Queen of Swords, or QoS, because when we were in the talking phase, she fictionalized our first link in a tarot-themed short story, where that card was her authorial surrogate and the King of Cups represented me. QoS finished grad school the year before I did, and I was a couple weeks shy of completing my MFA as well. We were cuddling, half-watching a histrionic Netflix series and sharing an order of takeout fettuccine alfredo in QoS's apartment in Harlem. I was living on less than $30,000 a year in New York City. QoS's economic situation was similar. Yet my hunch was I was facing the end of a phase that would in retrospect become the good old days. It was the first time in my life that I'd consciously pondered the question, What could I really do that would make my life better than it is right now? Would being richer and watching this same show on a bigger screen and eating roughly the same fettuccine from a more lavish restaurant on a more comfortable bed actually enhance this moment?

QoS and I had each applied to separate lists of doctoral programs. She accepted an offer on the West Coast, while I had provisionally agreed to move to the Midwest. People tell you to listen to your heart but mine often mumbles. It didn't make sense to me to stay together long distance unless we were going the distance. In tarot, the King of Cups card represents a balance between reason and emotion. The card is a reminder to cultivate deep knowledge and awareness of self. While I understood why QoS had chosen the King of Cups as a symbol for me when we first met, at the highest-leverage moment of our relationship, I worried I wasn't living up to my billing. I was still under the sway of some notion that delay multiplies delight. It felt somehow less courageous to hang on to the Queen of Swords than to let her shuffle the deck.

TWO MARSHMALLOWS?

The 2020s began with the US potentially on the brink of nuclear war with Iran. But when I took the daughter of a family friend out to see a play on the Lower East Side, the world felt rich, vast, sparkly, luscious in a way that it hadn't in a long time. I appreciated the irony that my stars were aligning just as the dogs of war seemed to be going off leash. The family friend's daughter was someone I'd heard about for years but somehow never met. I had a sense of her personality, though, from hearing stories, and we followed each other on socials. Her mother and my father had worked in the same office for a decade, during which they developed a friendship. My mother spoke glowingly of her mother's "spiritual pedigree." Even though her mother was Buddhist and not Christian, like my mother, the Black Momba was impressed.

The family friend's daughter and I had both grown up in the suburbs of Washington, DC. When she moved to New York City she reached out to me at the suggestion of her mother, who knew I'd been an Apple dweller for the previous six years. We each tuned into the alluring mix of familiarity and novelty between us. It was literally true that we'd been waiting to meet each other nearly our whole lives. The fairy tale potential was apparent to us both, and connecting face to face only heightened that sense of promise.

We had a few incandescent hangouts in January and February of that year, and soon after exchanged text messages at a level of volume and intensity that felt powerfully intimate. Wariness of COVID and observance of social-distancing guidelines began gaining traction between our first and second dates. The first shutdown happened in mid-March. I didn't want to leave things completely elliptical between us, even though we couldn't safely kick it in person.

G'Ra: Hey so I was thinking

In some ways it feels painfully tone deaf to even mention this, but I guess quarantine throws a wrench in everything. The immediate future is murky in so many ways that I figure our intentions, at least, might as well be clear.

G'Ra: I had a super rad time with you both times that we went out, and I think you're fabulous. I would love to keep getting to know you and see where things go, global pandemic permitting. You are the sort of person I'd just as well court old school style like some Victorian novel, someone worth letters and longing in the absence of proximity.

G'Ra: I'd like to know how you're feeling. If you're not interested in me that way, I'm happy to take a step back. In any event I thought I'd make my case—for clarity.

The family friend's daughter lamented the poor timing.

"I just don't feel in a place to develop things romantically right now," she wrote back. "For many reasons, but especially with everything going on."

A few weeks into quarantine, something must have shifted. Without explanation, she began sending me videos of herself dancing to pop songs in her living room. I wasn't sure how to interpret the seeming change of heart. Being crazy in love and stir crazy in quarantine were difficult to distinguish. Via Zoom and phone calls, our rapport escalated again. We made plans to see each other again in the early summer.

The first time we met up after the pandemic struck, I was conspicuously aware that we couldn't touch. She'd been in the streets for the massive anti-racist uprising precipitated by the senseless deaths of Breonna Taylor and George Floyd. Since it would be a few days before she would get her COVID test results back, we agreed on a hands-free hang until we could be sure she wasn't infected. At this time, I was unreservedly ablaze with sentiment. I burned for some way to convey emotional proximity while social distancing. After some contemplation I landed on the idea of handing her a box of watermelon Sour Patch Kids when we met at the subway. The gesture had a couple of layers of subtext. First, she'd told me that she loved actual watermelon, for both its taste and its aesthetics. The electric pink, green, and yellow hues of the box's graphic design mirrored the luster that she brought to my life. More importantly, I intended the sour and sweet candy to represent the rush of seeing her in the flesh—mingled with the agony of keeping my hands to myself. She seemed bewildered by the gift at first, even after I'd explained what I meant by it. A few weeks later, when we were both assured of being clear of COVID, I was setting the table at her place while she made breakfast and found myself rummaging through the cabinets of her kitchen. I was touched to see she'd retained the empty candy box. I hoped it would function as a totem, permeating her apartment with the nascent goodwill and affection that had motivated the gift.

Though the pandemic was obviously an adverse circumstance, it aided the love affair because it bought me time. Until New York City managed to flatten the curve, I was relieved of the pressure to trace any with my fingers. We got to know each other more carefully and I gradually got comfortable. Later that summer, fireworks went off almost every night for months where she lived in Brooklyn and near my place in Harlem. The family friend's daughter was a civil rights lawyer. In bed, we swapped theories about whether the noisy spectacle was some kind of Trump administration psyop, and in between the fireside chats, we made fireworks of our own.

A few times a week, I took a long, potentially risky subway ride from Harlem to her Park Slope apartment. She usually shared her place with three other people, but in the early summer of 2020, all three of her roommates had fled the city. They continued to pay rent in case the pandemic subsided. The roommates left most of their belongings behind, which gave the apartment the eerie aura of an apocalyptic outpost. I carefully removed my outer layers in her foyer each time I arrived. We would greet each other in the foyer without contact. I turned on the faucet in her kitchen and let the water run. Our gazes lingered as I scrubbed my hands in her sink as if both our lives depended on it, counting to 60 in accord with the CDC's COVID-prevention guidelines as the warm water rushed over my fingers. The tension thickened in proportion to the steam rising from the sink. Mortal peril made hygiene tantric. Touch became the lushest luxury.

A family friend's daughter: I keep thinking about the concept of magic and how I actually don't think it's portrayed enough in movies. Magic just isn't in vogue anymore.

G'Ra: Maybe we're the avant-garde bringing it back.

In a letter to Czech writer and translator Milena Jesenská, Franz Kafka wrote: "Perhaps we don't love unreasonably because we think we have time, or have to reckon with time. But what if we don't have time? Or what if time, as we know it, is irrelevant? Ah, if only the world were ending tomorrow. We could help each other very much."[2]

That summer in the largely abandoned apartment, the world seemed to have ended or perhaps might end tomorrow. The specter of mass death energized life. There was no vaccine yet, so the two of us were like a tiny tribe of uncontacted peoples, insulated from the broader world. We formed our own micro culture. There was an elaborate inside joke about the word *bildungsroman*. "Casket-only heartbreak" emerged as a shorthand for being together indefinitely. When I couldn't make the trek to Park Slope, I sent her voice notes reading poems aloud to her. While much of society had skidded to a standstill, I felt even more aware of the sand dwindling from the upper half of my personal hourglass. The pandemic was likely to eat up the duration of my mid-thirties and beyond. If this was the two-marshmallow scenario, loving unreasonably made some sense. We shared hopes, dreams, respiratory droplets. And at the same time, some part of me was certain that if I fully relaxed my guard around her, I would be captured, bound, and put on trial in the town square. Such is the trouble with the neurosis we all bring to love. A groundless worry gains credence when the sour nothings our loved ones whisper under their breath embolden our inner fabulist.

Although the years-long buildup to our convergence initially seemed to be an asset, I came to understand that we may have fared better if I had met this person earlier.

"I've almost concluded I could never be happy in any relationship," she told me once in passing.

She'd heard her share of hoofbeats, and no matter what I did to prove I was a zebra, she could only see a horse. Her deep skepticism about my intentions never abated. She gave me a supposedly tongue-in-cheek nickname: Nemy. It was short for nemesis. Every time I tried persuading her that our glass was half full, she was more inclined to lift the glass and splash it in my face with all the conviction of a plucky action heroine thwarting a dangerous admirer. She was so certain that my affection was insincere that I started to question it myself.

G'Ra: So often I'm in disbelief that I'm stuck on this planet but I'm glad I got to meet you.

A family friend's daughter: Why disbelief? You'd rather skip out and leave me here!

G'Ra: Nope. I'm building a three-seat rocket ship, trust.

A family friend's daughter: Three?

G'Ra: In case you don't want to have [redacted] Jr. on your lap the whole time.

Earlier that year, after a few disappointing dates with other people, I'd taken a friend's advice and combated my listlessness by making a list: I laid out all of the traits I was looking for in a partner. Once I started dating the family friend's daughter, I was charmed to realize how much she lined up with a list I'd made before we ever met.

"No, no, don't show it to me!"

"I'm showing you because—"

"No, I really don't want to see it! It's going to make me feel bad."

"If I believed that, I genuinely wouldn't ask you to look."

She grabbed my phone from my hand, lips pursed with exasperation.

The list read:

- Good politics
- Robust, mutually gratifying sex life
- Practical day to day lives complement one another (independence, okay being around each other's friends, like to hang out and do recreational things in compatible way)
- Intellectual companionship
- Simpatico humor
- Style (not necessarily fashion sense)
- Has a coherent life plan and goals separate from me, but that I fit into in a not catastrophically disruptive way

When she met my gaze again, she looked unimpressed.

"Well, that doesn't seem very hard to find," she said flatly.

Her most recent ex-boyfriend, someone she'd been with on and off for many years, seemed to be the primary cause of her declining faith in love. Once, when she'd returned from a bus trip late at night, he refused to pick her up from the station. Her phone died and she was stranded in a poorly lit part of town. She was forced to walk several miles home in the dark. At first, she viewed the incident as the relationship's extinction-level event. The couple had dealt with problems before, but she feared that this was the point of no return. Her ex was close to her parents, so she spoke to her mother about the relationship to collect her thoughts. Her mother didn't bat an eye at the boyfriend's dereliction of duty. She told her daughter that her husband—her daughter's father—had been unwilling to pick her up from a similar location late at night thirty years before. And that he'd left his then-girlfriend to walk home alone in the snow. The mother didn't relay this anecdote to one-up her daughter, nor was she commiserating. She made the case that these relationship nadirs were surmountable rather than disqualifying.

I knew when I heard this story that our chances together were cooked. There was no way I would be able to compete with that. Turbulent romance was practically a family heirloom. Her family's undead past lurched in lockstep with the present. When she measured me against the love prototype she'd been brought up with, my earnestness was a liability rather than a strength. In one of the final late-night voice notes I sent her, I'm reading John Keats's sonnet "When I have Fears That I May Cease to Be." In the ninth line, Keats addresses a "fair creature of an hour." I knew as I recited it that our own hour was in its fifty-ninth minute. The magical carriage would soon turn into a pumpkin, or even already had. The remainder of my .16 cosmic seconds would be spent alone or with someone else.

We began to bicker and exchange recriminatory texts until the thread wilted entirely. A few months later her ex-boyfriend reappeared alongside her in the vacation photos her family shared online. The IRL edition of the marshmallow test had bested me, thwarting Cupid with my own cupidity. That's what I get for thinking it was sweet.

BOLTZMANN BOY N THE VOID

You might not always get two marshmallows, but supremely improbable things can happen if you wait long enough. That's one of the implications of the Boltzmann brain hypothesis. Named for the physicist Ludwig Boltzmann, the thought experiment suggests that a human brain could form spontaneously in the void, and that such a brain might contain the memory of having existed in the universe. Some cosmologists suppose that statistically, human brains are considerably more likely to form from random fluctuations than from the biological route. Which would mean that a dispassionate look at the numbers points to the conclusion that you are probably wrong about your identity, your memories of the past, and your place in the world. This is because you are not a human raised on Earth, but actually a Boltzmann brain hovering in the frigid, sterile, vacuum of unending spacetime.

Over a long enough period of time, particles could collide to spontaneously form any structure of any degree of complexity. While it might feel like your interior world is an accumulation of experience you've accrued as a living observer, it's ultimately a complex pattern of neuronal impulses based on electromagnetism in your brain. A proxy of your personality, beliefs, and memories could pop into the ether even if you never properly existed. Rare fluctuations—like the formation of your exact collection of neurons configured in precisely the correct way—become not only plausible but guaranteed en route to infinity.

The Boltzmann brain hypothesis is uncomfortably analogous to the African American experience. We're continually told that we're without history, without culture, even without family. Our attempts to tell our stories and put our own lives into context are often disbelieved. We don't fully belong to any of the three continents that have shaped our trajectories and which we have shaped in turn. Inside we feel like we're part of the human race. Outside we're treated like some cosmic anomaly.

This similarity between the black interior and a Boltzmann brain is consequential when it comes to love. My brain contains the impression that happy, stable relationships are not only possible but worth it. I've been a living observer of an inspiring love lineage. The way my father loves my mother, the way my grandmothers loved my grandfathers and vice versa, all seems tangibly real. And if it's real, then it's replicable. The collision with the family friend's daughter made me wonder if the hope in my heart was the illusion of a Boltzmann brain.

The Boltzmann brain hypothesis is generally viewed as an indication that the prevailing theory of the evolution of our universe is flawed. Scientists use the idea as a diagnostic tool. If a cosmological model predicts that we are all more likely to be Boltzmann brains than organic observers, then the model is probably wrong, even if definitive disproof has yet to materialize. As Caltech theoretical physicist Sean Carroll puts it, "BB-dominated models are self-undermining or cognitively unstable—we cannot simultaneously believe that such a model is correct and believe that we have good reasons for that belief."[3]

That's the vision of the universe I'm rocking with. A stolen person on stolen land can steal a heart or two before I steal away into the dead of night.

A couple of years ago, Sasha's then-thirteen-year-old daughter starred in a Baby Got Back Talk music video. Thirteen is a common age at which punk rock awakenings occur. While we were shooting, Sasha, her daughter, and my bandmate Rhi got into a conversation about what makes someone old. Sasha's daughter opined that her friends' parents were all "over forty" and essentially "spiritually dead." She declared age twenty-seven the event horizon for youth. But whether or not you're officially old depends on "when you give up." Rhi, in their early thirties, and Sasha, in her mid-thirties, were horrified. Sasha's daughter gestured at me.

"Look at him. He's never going to give up."

She clarified that her mother, my bandmate, and myself weren't spiritually dead. This distinguished us from most of the adults that Sasha's daughter knew. While Rhi and Sasha took some comfort in this, they both seemed alarmed that a seventh grader saw us as past our primes.

Sasha's daughter is on the cusp of Generation Z and Generation Alpha, but she identified more with the former. She argued there were clear generational differences between Gen Z, Millennials, and the young children she knew that belonged to Gen Alpha. Even at thirteen, she used some timeworn clichés to organize her sense of people younger and older than her. Zoomers were more grounded and realistic than out-of-touch Millennials. Gen Alpha, from Sasha's daughter's observation, were loose cannons. Raised on iPads and stunted by the years of formal schooling they lost during the pandemic, these youngsters were frighteningly feral.

I felt a mix of admiration and amusement. The fact that Sasha's daughter was already diagnosing spiritual death assured me that the kids are all right, as they usually are. At the same time, it was funny to hear her rehearse the standard generational fault lines. (Here she was, a relative baby, anchoring a music video for an Unc punk band called Baby Got Back Talk, and talking back about it. Time is a flat circle pit.) Seeing older people as clueless and younger people as threatening made her sound Millennial to me. Who sound like Gen X. Who sound like boomers. She was having a junior moment. You don't really hear people call things a junior moment. Partially because there's such reluctance to acknowledge that juniority is momentary.

Our species is young. The universe is much older. To once again borrow Carl Sagan's framing, if you mapped the history of the universe onto a football field, humans have been on Earth for the length of your hand. From this vantage point, the idea that people born in 1962 are so different from those born in 1987 and in turn so different from people born in 2011 feels unbearably shortsighted. To somebody born in 3050 we are all a silent black-and-white film; a daguerreotype; a telegraph; or worse! By worse I mean, we might be better compared to something highly modern right now that will become antiquated way sooner than 3050. Quantum computers, for example, aren't widely available at my time of writing. If this book remains in print, quantum computers might be practically Stone Age to someone reading in 3050. My contemporaries and I rarely think of, for example, the difference between someone born in 1710 and someone born in 1734. Both of them existed before electric lamps. Whatever the differences in their respective frames of reference, the 1710 person and the 1734 person have a great deal more in common with each other than with us.

My theory is that on some level, everybody senses their staggering triviality relative to the cosmological unfolding. Making a big deal out of generations is one of the ways we enlarge ourselves and inflate our eye-blink lifespans into significance. The same things that flatter our existential vanity compromise our ability to see ourselves in one another. Three of the demographics I'm around most insist on their own nonstandard time. There's colored people time. There's queer time. And there's punk time. All of these variants mean "fifteen to twenty minutes late." How identity specific can lateness be if all of these groups tend to tarry?

In a way, colored people, queer people, and punks agree with physicists. There is no such thing as a simultaneous instant of time across all observers. Physicists call it the relativity of simultaneity. In 1989, the physicist Roger Penrose posited the Andromeda paradox, a thought experiment that shows how according to special relativity, observers moving at different relative speeds have different sets of events that they regard as the present.[4] Motion affects the experience of time. If you and I are in relative motion, you see a set of events happening at once. I see the same events as happening one before the other. This is the universe guiding us on the finer points of closeness.

Our smallness and our togetherness are what create the illusion of now. A singular now doesn't exist on a larger scale, which I take as a vital reminder. We usually think of wanting to create a future with another person as the ultimate romantic entreaty. But it's no less heartfelt to coalesce enough to give each other a present. The best way to share a moment in the fluid enigma of time is to lean into the metronomic influence of another person's heartbeat, pull them closer and synchronize your motion.

ACKNOWLEDGMENTS

My immense thanks to my sage and steady editor Maya Fernandez and the fabulous team at Beacon. It's a tremendous honor to be involved with such a legendary press. The care and consideration that you've shown my work means everything.

I'm grateful for the Center for the Literary Arts at Washington University in St. Louis and the great privilege of participating in their Creative Practice Workshop, where I incubated this manuscript with invaluable insight and encouragement from my colleagues, Professors Danielle Dutton, Nancy Berg, Julia Walker, and Todd Decker. Thanks also to WashU Professors Kathleen Finneran, Edward McPherson, Heather McPherson, Marshall Klimasewiski, Carl Phillips, Bill Maxwell, and Zach Ezer for their friendship and moral support.

Big props to my bandmates Rhiana Nisnevich, Jake Lazaroff, Sir Lee, Nakul Agrawal, Scott Raymond, Mikiel Peratino, Matty Regan, and Opus Grabmeier for their inspiration and solidarity, and for being generally ideal companions for traveling around playing original rock and roll songs in sweaty places.

The ideas in this book were refined through years of dialogue with these dear ones and key interlocutors:

Sasha Bonét, Jonathan Wiens, Nix Mendy, Naomi Gordon-Loebl, Makeesha Coleman, Emily Stein, Chris Craver, Oda Davanger, Myles Allen, Thomas Ordaya, Maya Cooper, Andrew

Weiss, Madeline Cameron Wardleworth, Kareena Gianani, Carlton Mabrey, Kristin Damo, Pat Cronin, Orla Tinsley, Nat Meneses, Pony Gabriel, Frederick Ashworth, and Nico Rios.

I continue, as always, to rely on the love and belief of the Asim Team. Thank you Mom, Baba, Joe, Indigo, Xinnie, and Gyasi.

NOTES

INTRODUCTION

1. Samuel P. Huntington, *The Clash of Civilizations and the Remaking of the World Order* (Simon and Schuster, 1996).
2. Carl Sagan, in *The Dragons of Eden* (Random House, 1977), displayed in the exhibition *Story of Time and Life at City College of San Francisco*, https://fog.ccsf.edu/~kwiese/TimeLife/content/CosmicCalendar.html.
3. Alfred Kinsey, *Sexual Behavior in the Human Male* (Indiana University Press, 1948).
4. Madelyn Snodgrass, "The Importance of Christianity to Black Americans," Public Research Religion Institute, February 27, 2023, https://www.prri.org/spotlight/the-importance-of-christianity-to-black-americans/.
5. StarTalk, "Why Rockets Don't Fly Straight Up," YouTube, 8:28, November 21, 2023, https://youtu.be/woCJ4saWatg?si=cb621GLkz7y8xCyF.

CONDUCT DETRIMENTAL TO THE MEME

1. Kirsten N. Morehouse, Benedek Kurdi, Ece Hakim, and Mahzarin R. Banaji, "When a Stereotype Dumbfounds: Probing the Nature of the Surgeon = Male Belief," *Current Research in Ecological and Social Psychology* 3 (2022): 100044.
2. Paul C. Taylor, "What If the Problem of Racism Has No Solution?" *Washington Post*, April 17, 2020, https://www.washingtonpost.com/outlook/what-if-the-problem-of-racism-has-no-solution/2020/04/16/b5f43360-6183-11ea-845d-e35b0234b136_story.html.
3. Jared Sexton, "Afro-Pessimism: The Unclear Word," *Rhizomes: Cultural Studies in Emerging Knowledge* 29 (2016), http://www.rhizomes.net/issue29/pdf/sexton.pdf.
4. "Race, the Floating Signifier," transcript of talk featuring Stuart Hall, Media Education Foundation, 1997, https://www.scribd.com/document/95993818/Stuart-Hall-Race-the-Floating-Signifier-Transcript-407-1997, accessed May 12, 2025.
5. "Race, the Floating Signifier."

6. Emily Style, "Curriculum as Window and Mirror," *Seed*, first published in *Listening for All Voices*, Oak Knoll School monograph, Summit, NJ, 1988, https://www.nationalseedproject.org/Key-SEED-Texts/curriculum-as-window-and-mirror, accessed May 12, 2025.
7. Edmund Burke, "Of the Sublime Part I, Section VII," in Jeanette A. Laredo, *A Guide to the Gothic* (Denton, TX: University of North Texas Libraries, 2019), https://pressbooks.pub/guidetogothic/chapter/edmund-burke-from-on-the-sublime-and-beautiful-1757/, accessed May 12, 2025.
8. Burke, "Of the Sublime Part I, Section VII."
9. Cheryl I. Harris, "Whiteness as Property," *Harvard Law Review* 106, no. 8 (June 1993): 1719, https://harvardlawreview.org/print/no-volume/whiteness-as-property/.
10. Harris, "Whiteness as Property."
11. *Atlanta*, season 2, episode 7, "Champagne Papi," "That Look Scene," written by Ibra Ake, Jamal Olori, and Taofik Kolade, directed by Amy Seimetz, aired April 12, 2018, on FX, YouTube, :25, https://youtu.be/BG5KUrO3sPE?si=DCvR8_TNyVtA6LAz.
12. Dorothy Roberts, *Killing the Black Body: Race, Reproduction, and the Meaning of Liberty* (New York: Vintage, 1998).
13. Rhaina Cohen, "What If Friendship, Not Marriage, Was at the Center of Life?" *The Atlantic*, October 20, 2020, https://www.theatlantic.com/family/archive/2020/10/people-who-prioritize-friendship-over-romance/616779/.
14. James Baldwin and Audre Lorde, "Revolutionary Hope: A Conversation Between James Baldwin and Audre Lorde," *Essence*, December 1984, https://garadinervi-repertori.blog/post/618941624479858689/revolutionary-hope-a-conversation-between-james.
15. Mandy Len Catron, "To Fall in Love with Anyone, Do This," *New York Times*, January 9, 2015, https://www.nytimes.com/2015/01/11/style/modern-love-to-fall-in-love-with-anyone-do-this.htm.

LONGING FOR THE CROOKED CROWN

1. Taylor Dafoe, "The Plastic Crown Worn by Notorious BIG for a Photo Taken Days Before His Death Sold for $60,000 at Sotheby's First Hip-Hop Sale," *Artnet*, September 16, 2020, https://news.artnet.com/market/notorious-big-crown-sothebys-hip-hop-1908629.
2. Zora Neale Hurston, *Barracoon: The Story of the Last "Black Cargo"* (New York: Amistad, 2018).

MOTION CAPTURE

1. Emily Gulla, "A Brief History of the Word Spinster and How It's Still Used Today," *Cosmopolitan*, February 14, 2020, https://www.cosmopolitan.com/uk/love-sex/relationships/a30868873/spinster/.

2. Virginia Woolf, "How Should One Read a Book?" *Yale Review*, October 1926, https://yalereview.org/article/virginia-woolf-essay-how-should-read-book.
3. Jennie Han, "Critical Thinking, Judgment and Empathy," *Amor Mundi*, April 1, 2013, https://hac.bard.edu/amor-mundi/critical-thinking-judgment-and-empathy-2013-04-01.
4. Damian Jones, "Snoop Dogg Confirms Jay-Z Wrote Dr. Dre's 'Still D.R.E.' in Full," *NME*, July 31, 2020, https://www.nme.com/news/music/snoop-dogg-reckons-jay-z-was-responsible-for-writing-dr-dres-still-d-r-e-in-full-2719412.
5. Bruna Nessif, "Dr. Dre's Ex, Michel'le & Dee Barnes, Speak Out on Abusive Past Not Being Shown in *Straight Outta Compton*," *E! News*, August 15, 2019, https://www.eonline.com/news/688074/dr-dre-s-exes-michel-le-and-dee-barnes-speak-out-on-abusive-past-not-being-shown-in-straight-outta-compton.
6. Jodie Lyons, "Interview—Coffee, Punk, and Life with Bill Stevenson, Descendents," *Ragged Press*, February 14, 2017, https://raggedpress.wordpress.com/2017/02/14/interview-coffee-punk-and-life-with-bill-stevenson-descendents/.
7. Ned Vizzini, *Teen Angst? Naaah . . . : A Quasi-Autobiography* (New York: Random House, 2000).
8. Kevin Sweeney, "What to Know About the Men's Basketball Transfer Portal," *Sports Illustrated*, March 26, 2025, https://www.si.com/college-basketball/what-to-know-about-the-mens-basketball-transfer-portal.
9. Becky Little, "How G.I. Joe Jump-Started the Action Figure Craze," History.com, October 11, 2022, https://www.history.com/articles/action-figures-g-i-joe-star-wars.
10. Susan Gonzalez, "Director Spike Lee Slams 'Same Old' Black Stereotypes in Today's Films," *Yale Bulletin and Calendar*, March 2, 2001, http://archives.news.yale.edu/v29.n21/story3.html.

SHTICK SHIFT

1. Prince, "The Most Beautiful Girl in the World," YouTube video, :04, posted by Prince, February 17, 2022, https://youtu.be/FuXbKLiW1UI?si=wSaZkt8DmgJ-IoAW.
2. Frantz Fanon, *Black Skin, White Masks*, trans. Charles Lam Markmann (London: Pluto Press, 1986), 250.

TRICKLE-DOWN EXCEPTIONALISM

1. Jesse Washington, "Where Did the Love Go? In Today's Black Pop Music, Love Songs Are Harder to Find," *Andscape*, February 14, 2020, https://andscape.com/features/where-did-the-love-go-in-todays-black-pop-music-love-songs-are-harder-to-find/.

SIX DEGREES OF DEROGATION

1. Cathy Park Hong, *Minor Feelings: An Asian American Reckoning* (New York: One World, 2020), 55.
2. Adolph Reed Jr., "Du Bois and the 'Wages of Whiteness': What He Meant, What He Didn't, and, Besides, It Shouldn't Matter for Our Politics Anyway," nonsite.org, June 29, 2017, https://nonsite.org/du-bois-and-the-wages-of-whiteness/.
3. Natasha S. Alford, "Michael B. Jordan Is Not Corny & Neither Are Black Boys with Big Dreams," *The Grio*, March 2, 2023, https://thegrio.com/2023/03/02/michael-b-jordan-is-not-corny-neither-are-black-boys-with-big-dreams/.
4. Joshua Espinoza, "Lore'l Addresses Viral Michael B. Jordan Red Carpet Interview: 'It Gave Will Smith Thing,'" *Complex*, March 1, 2023, https://www.complex.com/pop-culture/a/joshua-espinoza/lorel-denies-bullying-corny-michael-b-jordan-compares-will-smith-thing.
5. Kevin Fredericks (@KevOnStage), "Black People Will Roast You for Anything," Instagram video, February 26, 2024, https://www.instagram.com/reel/C3ocWVbpCAC/.
6. Andrew Bustamante, "10% of Americans Are Psychopaths," YouTube, May 24, 2024, https://youtu.be/gizg584IjaE?si=-doXp27VrCNiDhF5.
7. Jonathan Wiens, wedding party thank-you note, May 2021.
8. "Ferdinand the Bull, Who Loves Flowers, Is Now a Grownups' Hero," *Life*, February 21, 1938, 46–47, https://books.google.de/books?id=tEoEAAAAMBAJ&lpg=PA46&pg=PA46#v=twopage&q&f=false.

EXERCISES IN (ATTACHMENT) STYLE

1. Michael Levitt, "A New 'Mini-Moon' Comes to Earth This Fall," NPR, September 21, 2024, https://www.npr.org/2024/09/21/nx-s1-5121914/mini-moon-earth-asteroid.
2. John Keats, "When I have Fears That I May Cease to Be," Poetry Foundation, https://www.poetryfoundation.org/poems/44488/when-i-have-fears-that-i-may-cease-to-be, accessed November 5, 2025.
3. Gloria L. Cronin and Ben Siegel, eds., *Conversations with Saul Bellow* (Jackson: University Press of Mississippi, 1995).
4. Daisy Dobrijevic and Elizabeth Howell, "Comet Hale-Bopp: Facts About the Bright and Tragic Comet," Space.com, February 9, 2022, https://www.space.com/19931-hale-bopp.html.

ON HAVING LOW JOB SATISFACTION

1. Simone de Beauvoir, *The Second Sex*, 1949, trans. Constance Borde and Sheila Malovany-Chevallier (New York: Vintage Books, 2010), 8.

2. W. E. B. Du Bois, "Strivings of the Negro People," *The Atlantic Monthly*, August 1, 1897, https://www.theatlantic.com/magazine/archive/1897/08/strivings-of-the-negro-people/305446/.
3. Kenneth Miles, "Trenton's Finest: Ntozake Shange," *Trenton Journal*, March 31, 2022, https://trentonjournal.com/trenton-s-finest-ntozake-shange/.
4. James Baldwin, *James Baldwin: The Last Interview: And Other Conversations* (Brooklyn, NY: Melville House, 2014), 70.
5. David Marchese, "Nikki Giovanni Has Made Peace with Her Hate," *New York Times*, December 26, 2021, https://www.nytimes.com/interactive/2021/12/27/magazine/nikki-giovanni-interview.html.
6. Freddie Shanel, "Non-Binary Person Walking Alone at Night Unsure Whether to Be Scared or Scary," *Reductress*, May 17, 2023, https://reductress.com/post/non-binary-person-walking-alone-at-night-unsure-whether-to-be-scared-or-scary/.
7. The Grio Staff, "Kobe Bryant to Teammate Jordan Clarkson: 'Stop Playing Like a Light-Skinned Dude,'" *The Grio*, January 4, 2016, https://thegrio.com/2016/01/04/kobe-bryant-to-teammate-jordan-clarkson-stop-playing-like-a-light-skinned-dude/.
8. Andrew J. Stillman, "Meet All 37 of the Queer Women in This Season's WNBA," *Yahoo! Sports*, April 15, 2024, https://sports.yahoo.com/meet-37-queer-women-seasons-121642283.html.
9. Richard Lapchick, "WNBA Receives Top Grades for Racial and Gender Hiring," ESPN, December 14, 2022, https://www.espn.com/wnba/story/_/id/35246462/wnba-receives-top-grades-racial-gender-hiring.

RIFFS, ANDS, OR BUTS ABOUT IT

1. Club Shay Shay, "Mo'Nique on Ciara's Prayer & Black Women-Black Men Relationships," YouTube video, :25, February 13, 2024, https://youtu.be/-rKY5xQcr2I?si=lH7L-OJCRFqLSBxY.
2. Kristel Tjandra, "Science, Civil Rights, and the Doll Test," *Peaceful Science*, February 12, 2021, https://peacefulscience.org/articles/science-civil-rights-and-the-doll-test/.
3. Marcelo Gleiser, "What Does the Copernican Principle Say About Life in the Universe?" *Big Think*, September 22, 2021, https://bigthink.com/13-8/copernican-principle/.
4. Greg Tate, "Jean-Michel Basquiat, Flyboy in the Buttermilk," *Village Voice*, November 14, 1989, https://www.villagevoice.com/jean-michel-basquiat-lonesome-flyboy-in-the-80s-art-boom-buttermilk/.
5. Sierra Stein, "Attention Bids and How They Save Relationships," Clarity Clinic, https://claritynwi.com/attention-bids-and-how-they-save-relationships/, accessed November 5, 2025.

6. Virginia Woolf, *Mrs. Dalloway* (New York: Harcourt, Brace & Company, 1925; repr., Penguin Books, 2021).
7. Jeannine Mancini, "NBA Star Shaq Learned 'True Meaning of Pressure' After His Dad Took Him to a Homeless Family—He Paid $36,000 to Get Them off the Streets," *Yahoo! Finance*, January 13, 2025, https://finance.yahoo.com/news/nba-star-shaq-learned-true-170018958.html.
8. *Breakfast Club Power* 105.1FM, "Shaq Says Men Should Never Open Up to Women," YouTube, :18, January 30, 2024, https://youtu.be/BpJGxyuXdRU?si=zDZwqDBkgXIYK5u7.
9. *The View*, "Shaq: Men Shouldn't Vent to Women," YouTube, :55, February 2, 2025, https://archive.org/details/youtube-KkVM_sMGFUI.

GLUTTONOUS PUNISHMENT

1. Christine Ro, "Should We Be Worried About Vegan Ultra-Processed Foods?" BBC, October 12, 2024, https://www.bbc.com/future/article/20241011-what-explains-increasing-anxiety-about-ultra-processed-plant-based-foods.
2. Audre Lorde, *Sister Outsider: Essays and Speeches* (Berkeley, CA: Crossing Press, 2007), 146–47.

PEDAGOGY OF THE COMPRESSED

1. . Josh Morrison, "Miles at His Best," YouTube, :24, April 5, 2011, https://youtu.be/-8jeVWbPN1o?si=Oir8SYSy5sdO7ZPP.

WOULD YOU STILL LOVE ME IF I WAS A [BOOK] WORM?

1. Lania Knight, "An Interview with Creative Nonfiction Writer Phillip Lopate," *Poets & Writers*, May 16, 2008, https://www.pw.org/content/interview_creative_nonfiction_writer_phillip_lopate.
2. *Big Brains* podcast, "Why Chasing the Good Life Is Holding Us Back, with Lauren Berlant," University of Chicago, November 4, 2019, https://news.uchicago.edu/podcasts/big-brains/why-chasing-good-life-holding-us-back-lauren-berlant.
3. Leonard David, "Mining the Moon, the Gateway to Mars," Space.com, November 10, 2004 https://www.space.com/525-mining-moon-gateway-mars.html.
4. Adrian Mack, "In Genre-Busting Malaise dans la civilization, Four Oblivious Characters Dismantle Expectations and Unleash Chaos," *Stir*, March 4, 2024, https://www.createastir.ca/articles/malaise-dans-la-civilisation-theatre-la-seizieme-pi-theatre.

POWER SHADOW AND ACT

1. Tonya Mosley, "'If You Have a Face, You Have a Place in the Conversation About AI,' Expert Says," NPR, November 28, 2023,

https://www.npr.org/2023/11/28/1215529902unmasking-ai-facial-recognition-technology-joy-buolamwini.

2. Ishita Vaid, "AI Researcher Joy Buolamwini Discusses Bias in Facial Recognition Technologies at Duke Event," *Duke Chronicle*, February 19, 2025, https://www.dukechronicle.com/article/2025/02/duke-university-joy-buolamwini-artificial-intelligence-researcher-discussed-biases-in-facial-recognition-technologies-the-coded-gaze.
3. Emlyn Travis, "Emily Blunt Is Sorry for 2012 Video of Her Calling Chili's Server 'Enormous': 'I'm Appalled,'" *Entertainment Weekly*, October 21, 2023, https://ew.com/celebrity/emily-blunt-apologizes-calling-server-enormous-video/.
4. David G. Allan, "Ben Franklin's '13 Virtues' Path to Personal Perfection," CNN, March 1, 2018, https://www.cnn.com/2018/03/01/health/13-virtues-wisdom-project/index.html.
5. Stephen Hawking, *Brief Answers to the Big Questions* (New York: Penguin Random House, 2018), 41.

PRESENT COMPANY ACCEPTED

1. *A Wife's Nightmare*, dir. Vic Sarin and Vijay Sarin, Brainstorm Media, 2014, Amazon Prime Video, 44:55–45:08, https://www.amazon.com/Wifes-Nightmare-Jennifer-Beals/dp/B00U4P6QUO.
2. Franz Kafka, *Letters to Milena* (New York: Schocken, 2015).
3. Sean M. Carroll, "Why Boltzmann Brains Are Bad," Walter Burke Institute for Theoretical Physics, California Institute of Technology, February 6, 2017, 3 https://arxiv.org/pdf/1702.00850.
4. Sabine Hossenfelder, "The Andromeda Paradox Even Confuses Physicists," YouTube, April 27, 2025, https://youtu.be/i7Rx6ePSFdk?si=7kQocf3fTB8vOtRb.